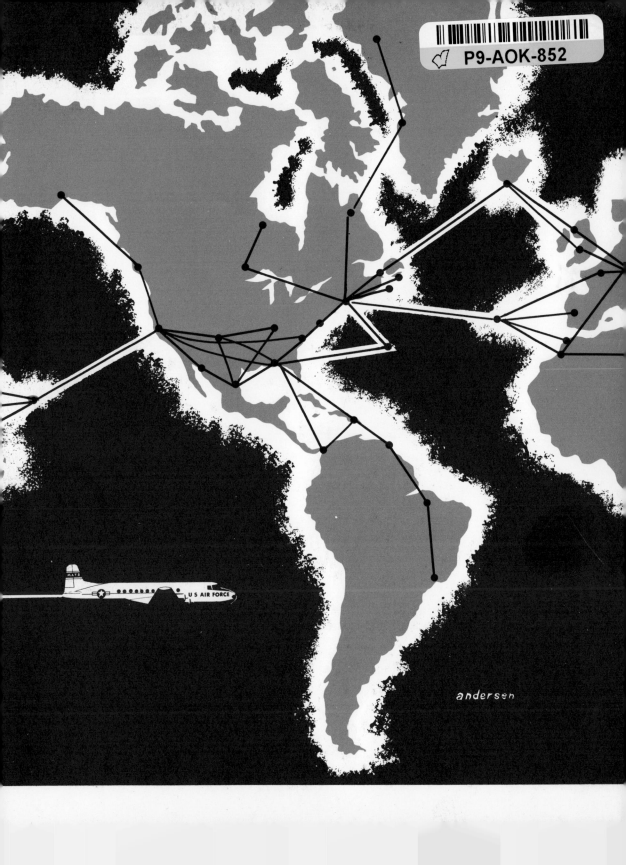

andersen

LIFELINE IN THE SKY

LIFELINE
IN THE SKY

The Story of the U.S.
Military Air Transport Service

Written and Illustrated

By

CLAYTON KNIGHT

WILLIAM MORROW and COMPANY
New York   1957

The statements made in prefaces are usually inexplicable before and redundant after the book is read. But in the case of the account that follows, it seems wise to say here that the Military Air Transport Service is flexible and subject to shifts and changes. Officers and men are moved around a great deal and emphasis on various features of the line changes with the surging of world events. Any statement as to the minutiae is apt to be outdated overnight, but the basic reason for being and the structure of this military airline will remain as they are described in this summary.

The changes that occur from day to day are most inconvenient for an author attempting to deal with them; he is glad nevertheless that they are made with such perspicacity by the men responsible for MATS' successful operation.

The author is deeply indebted to an extraordinarily large number of MATS men and officers for the help they have given in getting the facts and events of this book together. Since the list includes so many advisors from Washington to Thule and the Philippines and back again, who gave generously their time and other assistance, it is not possible to thank each individually.

Some of the people concerned in one way or another with the wartime Air Transport Command and the Naval Air Transport Service have also been more than helpful and these include: General Harold Harris, the Secretary of the Air Force, James Douglas, Harry Clark of American Airlines and Herbert Fisher of the New York Port Authority. Also, I wish to include thanks for the painstaking, stern assistance of Katharine Sturges Knight.

To all who have given this aid I offer my sincere gratitude.

CLAYTON KNIGHT
West Redding, Conn.
July 1957

LIFELINE IN THE SKY

1

IT WAS FIVE O'CLOCK OF A MONDAY MORN-
ing. Gusty winds carried smoke in long trailing patterns from
dozens of chimney pots in the suburbs of Birkenhead, across the
River Mersey from Liverpool, England. A slanting drizzle softened
the lights showing from a row of brick houses. Inside one of the
cottages a workman sat in the kitchen where his wife had just set
bowls of porridge on the table before him and their sleepy eleven-
year-old.

"Blimey," he growled, "another day of ryne."

The dripping windowpanes hummed to the beat of a four-
engined plane as it reached for altitude, heading westward.

The boy glanced up into the gray murk and grinned.

"There 'e goes . . . right on time."

The plane's appearance was something the people of the village had learned to check their clocks by, day after day, rain or
shine. Coming from the 53rd Weather Reconnaissance Squadron
of the Military Air Transport Service, based at nearby Burtonwood,
it was starting out on a triangular flight track that would take its
specialist crew halfway across the Atlantic before it turned on a new
leg. Twelve hours later it would fly back again, with 3200 air
miles logged.

❊   ❊   ❊   ❊   ❊

There were more lights than usual at Lowry Field near Denver,
at that very moment. More black limousines than usual were
parked alongside the unloading ramp, Secret Service men clustered
near the Base Commander and an Airman Honor Guard stood at
ease nearby. Newsmen who had arrived in an earlier plane turned
up coat collars against the chill breeze, their eyes skyward.

11

The voice into the tower operator's microphone intoned, "O.K. Air Force number one . . . you're clear to land . . . runway three four. . . ."

By the time the *Columbine* rolled to a stop before it the Honor Guard was at rigid attention and floodlights outlined the landing steps as the smiling President of the United States appeared in the Constellation's doorway.

*   *   *   *   *

At the moment the Burtonwood weather plane was leveling off on a 1500-foot flight path, an air-evacuation Stratocruiser was coursing through the intense blue of the skies between Hawaii and California. The plane's interior was almost fully lined with tiers of litters where twenty patients drowsed. The flight nurse bent over a sleeping boy with a glass of water in one hand and pills in the other.

"Here, my lad," she said, "take this. It's seven-thirty."

"Seven-thirty what?" he yawned.

"In the evening," she replied. "We'll be at Travis in another three hours and in a few days you'll be home."

TRAVIS AFB

*   *   *   *   *

At the same instant the young patient was relaxing at the prospect of being home, Captain Angelo Fortuna and his wife were having luncheon at the Clark Field Officers' Club near Manila with two airmen visitors. A slim Filipino mess boy wove his way slowly among the breeze-swept tables, tinkling a bell and holding aloft a small blackboard on which was scribbled: "Captain Fortuna report to the line at once."

The captain's quick attention fell on the message and, with the swiftly telescoped good-bys familiar to his wife and guests, he strangled down a last gulp of iced coffee and loped away.

Within minutes he had been briefed and an already humming SA-16 Albatross had eased off the runway with its crew of rescue experts. The wind was high and had whipped up the sea along the coast. Captain Fortuna listened to his radio operator confirming the position of the military jet ditched near a small island in the Lingayen Gulf.

A scanner pointed excitedly. Minutes later the Albatross had been set down in the swirling trough of the breaking seas and the crew was hauling aboard from a yellow rubber raft the jet boys they had come to save.

*   *   *   *   *

It was eight-thirty in the morning in Dhahran, Saudi Arabia, as Captain Fortuna on the far side of the world left his wife and friends. A big military transport plane stood blinking shafts of hot sunlight from its silver skin, its propellers flashing. Inside, settling into seats, a group of officers bent over briefcases of data they were to consider at a conference on new directives to the Military Assistance Advisory Group for Turkey and Greece, where they were headed via the Wheelus Air Force Base in Libya.

A colonel turned to shout over his shoulder, "Hey, Mac, I thought you were still in Tokyo."

"Mac," a battered but efficient-looking major, grinned.

"I was until last week," he replied. "On my way to McGuire after this conference. Ole Chuck Gordon who was in Alaska is in my job at Haneda."

Presently the major pulled a sheaf of reports from his briefcase and began to give the colonel a quick review of them. By this time the transport was well out over the desert and an airman flight attendant was taking orders for orange juice or coffee.

*   *   *   *   *

The same Monday dawn swept across the flat, featureless plains surrounding Sidi Slimane, in North Africa, and lit up the rugged slopes of the Atlas Mountains to the southeast. An operator in the tall white airport tower spoke quietly into his hand mike:

"O.K. to land, C-124, two-six-eight. Turn off the runway at the first taxi strip. I have a flight of 52's right behind you."

No sooner were the Globemaster's engines stilled than armed air police surrounded it and checked the security cards of all the crew members.

In the background there was the recurrent screech of rubber on the concrete as a formation of SAC jets landed.

Retrieving his security clearance badge, the young loadmaster of the MATS plane grinned at the SAC policeman and aimed a thumb at the B-52 bombers. A hot easterly *cherguis* wind ruffled his damp hair. "Don't forget, bud," he said, "those big boys don't travel far without we bring 'em the spare parts an' tools."

MATS, the Military Air Transport Service, which supplies airlift for the American defense forces, is the largest airline in the world and very likely the least known. Most of us hear, now and then, of sea rescues by plane, and of weather craft weaving their perilous courses into the depths of the most devastating hurricanes, and now and then of a bevy of wounded being flown from one part of the world to another. At times we read of spectacular flights of huge and swift fighting jets and bombers taking off from one hemisphere to land, a few hours later, in another. But it is not usually apparent to the casual observer that all these events are elements of two orderly, highly specialized Air Force organizations working toward a specific end. These are MATS and SAC—the Strategic Air Command.

MATS, like SAC a specialized sector of the Air Force, branches out from its continental home bases to flourish in Hawaii and points west, and across the Atlantic into the snows of the north and the deserts and jungles southward. It is a fixture of an age which is called peacetime but has little peace, functioning as a vital necessity to defense and as a trusted aid to a thousand enterprises having nothing to do with war or the thought of war.

This unarmed command was set up several years ago, when World War II had shown how costly and difficult it was to produce an airlift *after* hostilities had started, for men and cargoes adequate to the requirements of a modern military machine. Since its inauguration, the Korean War and other disturbances of peace have brought even more sharply into focus how important it is for this nation not only to possess a strong defensive striking force but also to maintain a back-up of air transport at peak efficiency at all times, available anywhere on earth. Warned by many difficulties encountered in the war in Korea, MATS has since strengthened all of its services and equipment which were not up to a desirable standard, and now stands a remarkably able organization profiting not only the western military world but incidentally many of the rest of us.

Although in peacetime MATS rescue planes have proved of incalculable benefit to those—whether military or civilian—who suffer calamity at sea, and its Weather and Communications Commands give our air enterprises endless advantages we did not have before, the reason behind every feature of the services is a training program in which each of its operational groups is learning its job by doing, time and again, those things it would be called on to perform in time of war. And in this training each is enabled to appraise and test equipment, to discover what is wanting or wrong or capable of improvement which, in case of extreme emergency, might make the difference between life and death for unnumbered people. Nothing in MATS is static; improvements in the planes and equipment used, in the dispersal of personnel and bases, in methods both of training and practice are subject to ceaseless study and, when necessary, change.

In several separate divisions defined geographically, MATS, one of the major U.S. Air Force Commands,* operates according to the needs and conditions of each area, its over-all operation controlled by a central headquarters at Andrews Air Force Base near Washington, D.C., under the final dicta of the Chiefs of Staff in the Pentagon. For *first, last and always, MATS is the logistics arm of the jet and bomber warhead of the American defense forces, the Strategic Air Command.* This is SAC, whose reason for being is that postwar international conditions have made it clear that any

---

* Continental Air Command, MATS, Strategic Air Command, Tactical Air Command, Air Defense Command, Air Matériel Command, Air Proving Ground Command, Air Research and Development Command, Air Training Command.

nation which respects the rights of nonaggressive peoples to live as they choose had better be prepared at all times to defend those rights instantly. But the defense lines of continents have been shifting lately and events have shown that since battles cannot be contained, they must be fought wherever on earth they blaze. In this air age it is planes that carry the burden of war, since they not only can reach any target anywhere but can rely on a fleet of support craft carrying those essentials which they themselves cannot do without.

SAC training, by the very nature of its mission and its necessarily extreme mobility over immense distances, requires the rapid deployment—in advance of, or following its squadrons—of such "housekeeping" items as replacement parts, tools, new engines, spare equipment of one type or another and especially trained maintenance crews to use them.

Supporting these missions is MATS' highest peacetime priority job.

In its ordinary procedures, about two fifths of MATS' work is in the visible form of flying transport missions—personnel and cargo carrying. The other three fifths is, like the greater bulk of an iceberg, submerged and consists of the Technical Services. These include the enormous network of communications systems using every kind of modern electronic device for speeding information and orders around the globe, the actual sea rescues that go on night and day all over the world and the gathering and reporting of weather from pole to pole and around the equator. Specifically they are: Airways and Air Communications; Air Weather Service; Air Rescue; Air Photographic and Charting Service.

MATS' peacetime services provide many benefits for the nonmilitary, especially for that part of the population that is forever crossing large bodies of water, but it is a military organization whose workings are part of a great and far-seeing plan for this country's defense in case of war. And big as MATS' airline is, so vast is the estimated over-all requirement of airlift for a modern war that military staff planning calls potentially for the additional services of at least forty per cent of the four-engined *civil* transport aircraft currently in use.

In recognition of this estimated need, two arrangements have been put into effect. One is the designing of most modern commercial airliners with quick conversion in view. With the Air Force footing the bill, fittings are built into many airliners so that they can be quickly stripped of superficial comforts and turned with little delay into rugged vehicles for transport of troops and cargo or for evacuation of wounded. The second arrangement might be called the confirmation of an interim working rapport with the civilian lines. During the great war, civilian and military airlines joined hands with commendable results and a satisfactory understanding of their mutual interests has survived. Partly to enhance this, partly because groups of MATS planes are sometimes fully occupied in support of one of the big SAC flight safaris, MATS turns over many of its hauling jobs on contract to both scheduled and nonscheduled lines: transport of cargo here and there and moving —usually small groups—of servicemen and dependents on geographical trajectories not easily fitted into MATS' more or less regular transport runs. Military people and civilian specialists working for the Defense Department are forever going in one direction or another these untranquil days and often to trouble spots not served by conventional routes and time schedules. MATS flies most of them but when it cannot do so, in emergency, hires transportation for specialists and its own people on other craft soaring to odd corners of the world.

In 1955, twenty-one million dollars were spent for commercial airlift of freight and passengers; in 1956, fifty-six million.

This contract work familiarizes the civil operators with, and keeps them abreast of, military requirements and procedures.

MATS' job, besides these duties, includes flying the President of the United States wherever he goes by air, and ensuring the last word in security and unequivocal safety of his planes and the routes he covers. This service, together with its Embassy flights into the Far and Near East and the transatlantic runs disrespectfully referred to at times as the "hot dog" or "blue plate" specials, are among the best known of the line. Security and high competence are no rarities in this well-planned organization—they have been in evidence for a long time, from the coal-grimed crews of the

Berlin airlift and the dripping paramedics hauling victims from the water, to the captain who snaps salutes from the door of the *Columbine*—but in some ways diplomatic flights are the elite.

The real bugaboo of all military activities today is the ceaseless departure of numbers of highly trained and most capable men at the end of their enlistment years. Although MATS operates through a large, sound core of devoted and extremely gifted regular officers and men, the loss of many of the highly experienced specialists cannot help but be felt, especially by executive officers whose distinctive commands must be kept up to a high level of performance. Perhaps this consequence causes the most inconvenience in maintenance, on which all safe and successful flying rests. It has been found necessary to train nearly 65,000 new maintenance personnel each year to make up for the loss of young men who decide not to re-enlist. The profitable side of the system, which was set up in the first place, of course, because it offers more advantages than disadvantages, is that it is creating a steadily increasing body of experienced technicians who will be available in case of a war emergency. That is partly what the elaborate training system is for. It is the individual officer who says a final good-by to his top-notch crew chief or electronics engineer or typhoon-scanning expert who suffers most, but in our traditionally nonmilitary way of life the career officer has become reconciled to such losses.

The head of the organization is Lieutenant General Joseph Smith, USAF, who directs the giant network of MATS lines from

the Andrews base near Washington—when he is not supervising some special feature of its operations at first hand, anywhere from Washington to Tokyo or Frankfurt. Cooperating on this complex air-defense project with the commander of SAC, who until recently was General Curtis LeMay, General Smith's ingenuity and familiarity with every detail of what such an air program is, must and can be, has brought the line to its present high level of success. He uses his authority with a lack of fanfare that keeps him farther out of the eye of the public than is usual among officers in such dramatic jobs.

Through Plans and Operations and Joint Strategic Plans Committees of the Joint Chiefs of Staff offices he moved in 1951 to his present post at the head of the Military Air Transport Service. Here his long experience in the field of strategy, bombers and administration is obviously put to its fullest conceivable use.

He is a West Pointer of the vanishing race who were graduated into the cavalry. Like many other young second lieutenants of the 1920's, he transferred quickly into the Army's air arm. In 1928 he transferred to the Air Corps and up to 1939 progressed through several stages of special training, teaching and building up service in the Bomber Command. This continuity was broken for a short time when he served as a pilot through the black months of March to May, 1934, in the Army Air Corps mail operations in which so many young fliers lost their lives.

After the war started, a large part of Smith's work lay in operational and administrative departments in planning, with the War Department General Staff, although this was interrupted in early 1945 when he joined the 20th Bomber Command in India and a few months later became General Doolittle's deputy Chief of Staff with the 8th Air Force on Okinawa. He was commandant of the Air Tactical School in Florida, later was commandant of the Wiesbaden Military Post, and for three months of 1948 commanded the Airlift Task Force (formed by General LeMay) which staged the Berlin Airlift.

2

M<small>ATS, AS IT EXISTS TODAY, HAS BEEN A</small> long time evolving. It came into being as a single grand-scale operation on June 1, 1948, with the official unification of the wartime Air Transport Command (ATC) and the Naval Air Transport Service (NATS), each of which had been improvised under the terrible pressures of the years of 1939-1945.

When the stable world began to blow up in 1939, with Hitler's first attacks on Europe, American government and military leaders were forced to take a hard comprehensive look at the probabilities that lay ahead for this country. By 1940, when it began to appear that England's continued existence depended heavily on American-produced war material, it was plain that the logistics of delivering those materials overseas rapidly and safely was an official problem which had to be solved at any cost and with no delay. The belligerent Axis powers, entrenched in the heart of Europe and using the war factories of the nearby subdued nations, had far less need of overseas transport than the newly formed Alliance against them. Britain's predicament was the ocean gap between the source of many of her supplies—the U.S.—and her battle lines.

It was soon found that sea transport under convoy which, with the greatest expenditure of heroism, suffered intolerable losses by submarine attack, was too slow as well as too hazardous for the shipping of badly needed combat aircraft. Transocean air transport was the most obvious solution but unfortunately in 1939 sustained overseas flying was not far beyond the experimental stage in this country. For one thing, crews experienced in long-range overwater navigation were scarce; Lindbergh, Post, Gatty, Byrd, Chamberlin and Kingsford-Smith were still regarded somewhat queasily by many of our excellent overland pilots as remarkably venturesome

20

fellows. Pan American Airways had already begun to operate an island-hopping commercial service across the Pacific and, soon afterward, a somewhat tentative North Atlantic schedule, but outside this airline and the Navy, U.S. pilots and navigators with transocean training were rare. Until the threat of war, only a small faction of the aviation world had seen any great hurry about pushing the evolution of the overwater phase of air transport beyond its normal pace and as a result railroad lines, rivers, cities and landbased radio beams were still thought of as very nearly vital assists to navigation by most flying men.

The air services of both the U.S. Army and Navy had behind them a number of illuminating overseas flight experiments but in 1939 neither branch had acquired enough trained crews or equipment to deal with the situation brought on by the irruption of an air war.

Immediately following the autumn of 1939 English flying crews were forced by the nature of the German attacks to drive ahead rapidly in the practice of overwater navigation; RAF Coastal Command planes ranged from Iceland to the Bay of Biscay and north to the upper tip of Norway, and by early 1940 a substantial number of British navigators had gained a lot of valuable experience.

As some possible phases of war conditions had been rather clearly foreseen in the United States, a number of plane builders, with the encouragement of both the military and the airlines, had been developing advanced ocean-spanning aircraft—land and seaplanes—of which several four-engined types were already well past the preliminary testing stage.

After a frantic production scramble, as more American bombers became available, a British organization was set up to facilitate the trial "cash and carry" stage of getting new craft into service by flying them to England from Canada, and when the need grew even more serious, RAF crews were sometimes taken off combat duty for this ferrying project. Through these teams, transatlantic bomber ferrying began and the British and Canadian crews were soon augmented by a number of volunteer American civilian pilots, experienced on multi-engined craft, who flew with British or Canadian navigators. After the terrible air losses during the Battle of Britain the flood of American volunteers increased sharply. In fair flying weather such direct air deliveries to England not only saved two or three months' delay but cut down on the frightful and mounting loss of shipments to German submarines.

While those early bomber deliveries were succeeding, though at considerable hazard, the flaming of the war into the Mediterranean demanded the establishment of a direct air delivery route to that new war zone. To build this up quickly Pan American Airways, as the sole agency with both experience and equipment, was commissioned by the American and British governments, on contract, to lay out a practicable new line across the South Atlantic. Official arrangements were made with the Brazilian government, and pioneering flights were begun from Miami, via the Caribbean to Natal, Brazil, then the ocean jump to Bathhurst on the African coast and across the waist of Africa to Cairo, Egypt. Although Pan Am's former ocean-crossing experience had been wholly with flying boats, their contract called for delivering some four hundred Martin medium bombers; and later, having seen the success of the bomber flights over both the North and South Atlantic, when they began transporting materials, they turned to two- and four-engined land planes, which carried greater loads.

With Germany barely checked in expanding her air war, England's need for all the combat aircraft she could get under the liberalized March 1941 Lend-Lease Act persuaded American Army Air Corps officials to set up a U.S. Ferrying Command of their own.

THE U.S. FERRYING COMMAND

General H. H. Arnold, head of the Army Air Corps, keenly alert to the countless difficulties of the situation, set to work forming a separate Air Command. His new organization, the remotest ancestor of MATS, was put under Colonel Robert Olds, a highly efficient and popular officer of wide experience. Colonel Olds had earlier been sent to Brazil by President Roosevelt to make arrangements for the use of Natal as a jump-off base for the South American crossings, and still earlier he had done some wide-ranging pioneer flying on a good-will tour around the southern continent.

Olds' official organization was activated on May 29, 1941, a little over six months before Pearl Harbor. In the beginning, the Ferrying Command had only one other officer and a civilian secretary besides its commander, but its mission and inspiration were:

"(1) To move aircraft by air from factories to terminals . . . designated by the Chief of the Air Corps.

(2) To maintain such special air ferry service or air transport service as may be required to meet specific situations."

The second directive was so broad that it ultimately resulted in an expansion of the Command's range of operations far beyond the scope anticipated by anyone at that time. The actual concept of supplying large quantities of critical items to distant armies by air had been insufficiently grasped, during peacetime air operations, even by the higher service echelons.

From the start, the infant service's responsibilities were diverse and included both an enormous amount of planning for expansion and the setting up of training programs for crews, which were put into training mainly in the southern states.

Washington, still technically neutral, felt strongly that Americans should confine their help to taking the new bombers only to U.S. ports of exit, from which crews under British command would fly them home.* But the war was at a stage that demanded the closest liaison between London and Washington, and for this purpose an overseas air service to carry diplomatic mail and special officials between the two countries was authorized under the directive of the new Command.

On July 1, 1941, Lieutenant Colonel Caleb V. Haynes, piloting a B-24 Liberator, started the operation and laid out the route to be followed. Leaving Washington, he refueled at Montreal and Gander Lake, Newfoundland, and flew the northern Atlantic route to Ayr, Scotland. From then on, an average of six round trips a month were made, despite some German air interference, until mid-October,

---

* Later on planes were also ferried to Fairbanks, Alaska, to be picked up by Russian pilots.

when winter weather brought U.S. crossings to a stop. During the next few months the British carried a few thoroughly miserable officials in the converted bomb-bays of some modified and winterized Lend-Lease Liberators at erratic intervals, but until improvements were made in equipment and experience was gained, North Atlantic winter flying was too perilous to be profitable.

Among other disturbances of that summer before Pearl Harbor was Hitler's catapulted attack against a deeply shocked Russia, when Stalin, angry and in desperate plight, called wildly for Lend-Lease. To conclude agreements between the leaders involved, Washington and London decided in September to send a mission to Moscow under Mr. Averell Harriman and Lord Beaverbrook. The flight offered many uncertainties and unpleasantnesses, so Mr. Harriman and Lord Beaverbrook proceeded by destroyer to Archangel. However, it was thought advisable to have aircraft under American control available while the visitors were in Russia. The Ferrying Command's two chief pilots on that mission made aviation history. Using Liberators, Major Alva L. Harvey and Lieutenant Louis T. Reichers flew across the Atlantic and, skirting the Scandinavian Peninsula, continued nonstop to Moscow—3150 miles—with much of the trip driven through abominable weather.

After leaving the Soviet capital, the crews of the two planes separated, both to pioneer in searching out new routes for wartime air travel between the Middle or Far East and the U.S. Major Harvey circled the globe, returning to San Francisco by way of India, Singapore, Australia, Wake Island and Hawaii. Lieutenant Reichers headed home through the Middle East, to Cairo, diagonally across Africa and over the South Atlantic, making use of the rudely laid-out fields Pan American was preparing. During the coming expansion phase, Reichers' civilian flying experience, which he gained as one of the more resolute experimenters of the 'thirties, proved to be continuously useful to the Ferrying Command.

The reports brought home by the exploring pilots revealed just how prodigious the job of aiding the war by such world-wide air operations was going to be. They had had few reliable weather reports to prepare them for flight conditions ahead; radio communications were negligible; runways were, for the most part, primitive;

facilities of every sort were inadequate or wanting entirely; and maps, in the sense of flying charts, were untrustworthy.

Since the prospect of the winter shutdown across the North Atlantic would result in a dwindling of vital supplies and aircraft to Britain unless new and more favorable routes could be substituted, the English Foreign Office and the U.S. State Department put pressure on Portugal for the use of the Azores as a refueling base, which would have made a *middle* Atlantic route through Bermuda possible. But with Hitler stomping almost unchecked across Europe, the Portuguese were unwilling just then to grant anything that might jeopardize their neutrality.

With this easier route denied, when the Nazi thrusts into the Mediterranean area of Greece and North Africa reached really dangerous intensity, the South Atlantic route became doubly important. Major General George H. Brett led a special mission to invigorate the line through to Cairo and the Middle East. On this mission he was flown from Washington through to Basra on the Persian Gulf and return by Colonel Caleb Haynes, with young Major Curtis LeMay as copilot and navigator.

The development of the route, with the help of the RAF Transport Command—although all too little had yet been accomplished in the actual large-scale delivery of matériel—proved its worth when the cataclysm of Pearl Harbor brought America into the over-all strategy as a belligerent.

AMERICAN ENTRY INTO THE WAR

The American entry as a fighting force demanded reassessment of all operations on a full-scale world-war basis. With the appalling advance of the Japanese almost unchallenged around the Pacific, the planning staff of the Ferrying Command had to discard earlier projects hastily, to alter and at the same time extend its routes. U.S. losses in Hawaii, and loss of the islands which had been used as steppingstones to the Orient, followed swiftly by the besieging of the Philippines, brought on a disastrous crisis; no adequate amount of air help could get across the Pacific until the Air Corps had prepared new island bases to take the places of those that were lost.

At the same time work was begun on enlarging small landing fields in friendly countries, two- and three-fold, to accommodate the rapidly multiplying traffic. Mountains of supplies, spare parts and unheard-of stores of fuel were moved into position at home shipping points and far overseas, while increasing streams of air crews and mechanics were rushed into training at every suitable base.

With America at war it was inevitable that many bombers and crews earmarked for air transport purposes should be withdrawn for combat duty. In addition, U.S. needs and Lend-Lease were swamping American aircraft factories with orders for fighting planes, which began to hold up the production of transport types. As a result, immediately after Pearl Harbor the government saw that it would be necessary to augment the resources of the ferrying fleets by making use of "in-being" plane equipment, and the Secretary of War was empowered by the President to call on the country's commercial aviation systems to fill the gap. The civilian lines were put under contract, and given supply routes and missions under the Ferrying Command, but the work was done by unarmed civilian aircraft manned by crews in airline uniforms. For the duration of the war this civilian armada constituted an important part of air transport. Fanning out across the skies far from their workaday routes, these and Air Ferrying Command crews eventually carried men and supplies to Alaska, Greenland, Europe and Asia—to what were, for most of the newly trained young American pilots, the uttermost ends of the earth.

Even with this help, the job of delivering supplies on such a scale, and returning ferrying crews from such distant points, put an almost superhuman burden on the Command.

THE NAVAL AIR TRANSPORT SERVICE

On December 12, 1941, to deal with its own vital supply needs, the U.S. Navy established a sister organization, the Naval Air Transport Service, and a smaller transport group which operated in its own localized battle zones was created by the Marine Corps.

Tremendous spurts of activity for the Army Ferrying Command followed the first months of the U.S.-Japanese war throughout the winter and spring of 1942. Desperate ways and means of sending help to forces under siege and heavy enemy pressure were used, first to the hopeless situation in the Philippines, then to China, to the British in Africa, and also Lend-Lease planes to Russia through Basra—all theaters of deep concern to America.

During the construction of new air bases from Hawaii through the mid-Pacific island of Canton—until then almost unheard of—to Australia, traffic to the Far East was routed two thirds of the way around the earth, over the South Atlantic, across Africa and through India—a costly and wasteful course. Eventually the route became only a little easier with the opening of a field on Ascension Island in the mid-South Atlantic.

THE AIR TRANSPORT COMMAND

On April 1, 1942, an organizational change in the Ferrying Command put Brigadier General Harold George in Colonel Olds' place at the head, and the group was renamed the Air Transport Command—known affectionately by a good many thousands from that time on as the ATC.

A reclassification of its multiple functions was issued on June 20, 1942, in Army Air Forces General Order No. 8, to wit:

"(a) The ferrying of all aircraft within the United States and to destinations outside the United States as directed by the Commanding General, Army Air Forces.

(b) The transportation by air of personnel, matériel, and mail for *all* War Department agencies, *except those served by Troop Carrier Units. . . .*"

In the new order the highly necessary provision was made that it was the duty of the completely separate group called the Troop Carrier units to move parachute troops, airborne infantry and glider personnel—men under direct orders of a theater commander—and to provide airlift facilities *within* all the theaters of operation. This clarified very nicely what had become a disastrously confused issue for the ATC. The new order gave a firm statement of policy for Air Transport, emphatically defining its independent character, which distressing experience had proved very few theater commanders up to that time had ever fully understood. With the crisscrossing of combat, transport and other air operations in various parts of the world, the vagaries of human nature had all too frequently interposed to create some first class *snafus* for the Command that, in the nature of existing pressures, ATC officers had found it difficult either to avoid or to control. A transport plane landing in a battle area and momentarily idle was an asset too heaven-sent for many a combat general to overlook. The result had all too often been that ATC aircraft and crews were taken off their legitimate missions and into actions for which they were never intended, sometimes for considerable periods. With the entire globe comprising the arena of its long-range operations, ATC orders might send one of its planes through as many as five separate war theaters to complete a mission, offering temptation to five separate hard-pressed ground commanders. It took stern orders from the War Department to hammer home the idea that if this sort of diversion went on, the usefulness of ATC and the whole system of strategic air supply would be destroyed.

Soon after Pearl Harbor, and in spite of dire conditions in the Pacific, it was decided by the American and British chiefs meeting in Washington that the first objective of the war must be the elimination of Hitler's power, which resulted in giving priority to the demands of the European allies. In accordance with this decision, early in '42 a large proportion of the U.S.-built heavy bombers and fighters was assigned to England to fly beside the RAF under American commanders, and still more effort was made to speed up delivery across the Atlantic.

New airfields at Goose Bay, Labrador, and two on the west coast of Greenland—Bluie West 1 and 8—were hurried to operational condition. To hasten the building there, Northeast, TWA and American Airlines, with some ATC help, ran flights carrying construction teams and supplies to the sites. With the use of these bases and another enlarged one in Iceland, overwater jumps for the shorter-range fighters were cut to about eight hundred miles. But another monumental job arose in the provision of accurate weather reports for the subarctic pilots, as radio communications on the route overtaxed the capacities of existing installations. To improve that condition, Lieutenant Colonel Milton Arnold, with authority from the War Department to perfect the job, set up and maintained a greatly expanded and constant vigil, and when mass flights of aircraft began, he monitored their movements throughout the mission's grueling length.

While the worrisome troubles of the North Atlantic supply line were being overcome, the ATC men who were bolstering military help to China were having different but just as vexing troubles. The Japanese occupation of Burma had cut off the truck road over the Himalayas which was then the only overland highway for moving in supplies to the Chinese.

By midsummer of '42 the South Atlantic ATC air route was operating more or less smoothly as far as India and, until the Burma Road was blocked off, had been feeding critical materials for China into its southern terminus at Lashio. When Burma fell, the 10th U.S. Air Force began an intermittent airlift of goods from India over the "Hump" into Kunming in China.

"Flying the Hump," like the Berlin airlift later, became one of the epics of flying history. A long succession of dedicated pilots and crews profanely but stubbornly left behind them everything they valued in the ordinary world to weave among the high, treacherous Himalayan peaks on flights that seemed to have no end, and many of them still lie shrouded in the mists of deep and unknown Himalayan chasms. The most distant theater from the nerve center in Washington, this action of the war has still, for most of us, as it had for those fliers, more the quality of myth than of reality.

The reason for getting war materials and official advisers into Kunming was not alone the need of Chiang Kai-shek's army for supplies to go on fighting the Japanese which, because of Chiang's fear of the Communists, he was doing only half-heartedly. It was the desperate need to keep the corrupt Chinese Army in the field at all and so prevent the Generalissimo from making a deal with the Japanese that would give them the airfields in China which were absolutely essential to the American Air Forces. The situation was already grim and the loss of the Chinese bases would make it far worse. Chiang distrusted General Stilwell's attempts to train Chinese troops for real service and in 1942 Stilwell was still struggling against serious odds to hang on to that part of Southern China which had not already fallen under Japanese and Communist control.

The Air Transport Command and other agencies stationed in the China-Burma-India theater to keep China fighting carried on the job with ruthless sacrifice. And the brunt of the sacrifice fell on the baffled crews and officers on the spot.

From April, 1942, when flights from India to China began, a long interim of grueling effort was made by the 10th Air Force and later by three ATC squadrons with such inadequate and poor equipment that any successful flight was a miracle. There was a perpetual shortage of gasoline and replacements. Communications systems were sketchy. Radio beams in the area were almost unknown. The mountain barrier crossed in daily flights was largely uncharted; air passage was for each pilot an exploration. Living quarters were as bad as any known to the military forces of the time. And yet those early crews laid the groundwork for a phase of the offensive against the Japanese that was considered vital to the whole Pacific war plan.

Local headquarters was in a large lush valley in northeast India in the foothills of the Himalayas called Assam—a district of tranquil tea plantations, remote from the vast, turbulent Indian plateau where the British still ruled uneasily. There were seven U.S. airfields near the small Assam villages of Sookerating, Mohanbari, Jorhat, Tezpur, in Simara, Dinjan and Chabua; the base at Chabua was the ATC headquarters terminal.

It was almost impossible for the transport commander to get enough accommodations or flying equipment and spare parts. The first planes sent out to the theater were any type procurement could lay hands on. Due to their condition the planes had difficulty in reaching the altitudes required to cross the high Himalayas and were so worn out that they could be kept flying only by cannibalizing spare parts from unsalvageable derelicts. Maintenance was at first pitiable; ships went down every day and few of the crews were ever seen again.

Brigadier General Edward H. Alexander, who was in command, ran the flights with a fierce determination and at last, when pressure on Washington reached a peak, a gaggle of newly produced C-46

Commandos was sent out before the craft had been developed to a safe level for this sort of service. Inherent weaknesses that caused carburetor icing and defective fuel pumps sent them down right and left in the chasms. To cut the casualties, Alexander ordered that they be used to transport cargo over the Hump but no passengers.

The pilots and crews were following orders with a sort of blank, hopeless fidelity; they said you could find your way to Kunming by following the smoke of burning wreckage rising from the gorges.

There were two ways into China: one was the high northern route over and around the highest summits, and the other was at lower altitudes, over northern Burma. The Japanese were then pushing into this wild jungle-swathed Burmese mountain terrain, following the river valleys northward, posing threats at a number of key points. One strong group had penetrated up the Chindwin River to Singkaling Hkamti, had established a camouflaged airfield and were known to be getting ready to push on India. To parachute into this country almost certainly meant capture by the enemy or by the headhunters whose villages were scattered across its great unmapped tracts.

Activated British authority extended from Assam over part of this wild never-never land of upper Burma, where it was maintained by highly experienced British agents and a few troops, with native auxiliaries made up in part of converted headhunters. But outside of these jungle posts were the savage tribes, often at war with one another, among whom the most aggressive were the Nagas.

In General Alexander's time the chief medical officer at Chabua was Lieutenant Colonel Don Davis Flickenger, who came out as Wing Surgeon for the ATC in late 1942. He was a pilot-doctor, thirty-five years old, slight, brilliant and a great one for following his own courageous instincts. Army discipline in Chabua and the other fields was then about what it is on any rough foreign base, but it was disrupted oftener than usual by circumstances that no field orders could foresee and provide for. General Alexander was a stern commander, as he had to be, and he and Flickenger were good friends and ordinarily worked well and very hard together to combat the terrible forces of discouragement, disease and unfitness that were all but insurmountable.

When the general issued his order that passengers were not to be allowed to make the flight into China in the faulty C-46's, a great backlog of officers, civilians and servicemen needed in China began to pile up in the Chabua base. Among them were the foreign news correspondent Eric Sevareid; General Stilwell's political adviser, who was the China expert (and Rhodes scholar) John Davies; OSS agent Captain Duncan Lee; and a couple of Chinese officers. They were all chafing savagely at the delay.

On the second of August, 1943, for some reason known only to the Command, one of the C-46 crews was ordered to carry a number of soldiers and civilians as passengers to Kunming. They took off from Chabua early in the morning. Less than an hour later first one of the Commando's engines gave out, then the other, and by nine-thirty the nineteen passengers and all but one of the crew had parachuted into an unsurveyed spot in the Burmese foothills and the plane lay in flames. The copilot, Lieutenant Felix, was killed but in the confusion of the hurried jump from the diving plane no one saw what had entangled his chute.

Reports of the C-46's imminent collapse, radioed back to Chabua just before the crash, set search plans into action instantly and a ship flew off to find the survivors, if there were any, and to drop food and equipment. Colonel Flickenger and General Alexander conferred quickly and prepared another plane to carry Flickenger himself and two medical aides to investigate the men's condition and parachute medical care to them if they needed it. The surgeon wanted to see for himself whether the survivors needed attention beyond the aeromedics' capacity, although he had orders from the general not to jump under any circumstances, since he was badly needed in his capacity as medical chief at the base. The two medics had never yet used a parachute; at that early period no such training was given. Flickenger, however, had already parachuted in his air-rescue work (wrenching a knee badly on one jump) and, all things considered, he intended to make up his own mind as to whether he would go when he saw what the situation was. There had been no medical man or jungle expert on the crashed C-46, and Flickenger had an idea things would go hard with the survivors.

When the passengers and crew on the stricken C-46 bailed out over the jungle they came down in scattered groups. Several, including Eric Sevareid, found themselves strewn over a rough mountain slope below a small thatched village about the size of a football field, that they could see a short distance above them. It was some time before the jumpers found one another but, after several precarious hours of warding off natives, separately and together they managed to summon enough strength and courage to get up to the cluster of native huts. There they found a second group from the plane, who had been less badly shaken up by the drop, who were already on some sort of terms with men of the village and feasting on chicken and eggs. Davies, Lee, and a young Chinese colonel were missing. The last man did not appear for several days, when he staggered in starving and almost dead, supported by a couple of savages.

After they got together in the village it was discovered that several of the men had serious injuries; the radio operator's leg was broken and it had been only by heartbreaking effort that he had been helped up to safety in the hut, for he was an enormous man. Sevareid was close to exhaustion, but he had sensed the need for direct action and making plans and had assumed command temporarily. The others seemed to have no idea how to act—how necessary it was to hide from Japanese planes, how to prepare signals for their own search planes and especially how to deal with the forays of clamoring natives who lashed out into furious chattering sub-battles among themselves, principally over the parachute silk and cordage. When the group settled in the central hut there was a confused atmosphere of menace and one band made meaningful gestures in favor of head-lopping at once.

The muscular, mahogany-colored savages, breech-clouted and sinister-looking men, carried spears and wore between their shoulder blades huge curved knives, called dahs, which they could whip out of the sheath with lightning swiftness.

The first rescue ship from Chabua came over not long after the crash; it dropped food and hastily collected equipment, including a few obsolete Springfield rifles, and during the day returned to make other drops and deliver messages. Among them were instructions for putting out signals in code which were to be panels laid out along the ground, whereupon the survivors immediately arranged

The nightmare of flights across the "Hump" to China.

signals asking for medical help. Orders from headquarters were stern: stay where you are, as you are safe there from the Japanese. A radio was dropped that afternoon and, though the receiving set reached the ground safely, the transmitter was smashed.

When Colonel Flickenger's pilot spotted the wreck of the C-46 at 4:15 P.M., he stared down uncertainly as his plane circled over the village and then read the message: "Urgent medical help needed." The two medics, Sergeant Harold Passey and Corporal William MacKenzie, also read the panels on the ground. "I'm going down," explained Flickenger, "but you stay put."

"Well, sir," said the two, "after you've gone there'll be nobody here with authority to stop us, will there?"

"Suit yourselves," said the doctor, buckling his chute. Clocked by the plane's crew chief, all three of them went off in quick timing. Flickenger landed first, on a clearing close to the village, and the medics some distance down the mountainside.

When he saw the victims, Flickenger had no regrets. The radioman Oswalt's leg was in serious condition; the others—among them, the older Chinese colonel—with leg and ankle fractures that badly needed setting and attention. All of the victims had abrasions and leech infections requiring careful asepsis. The group had settled in a sort of community hut, with a fire that did little to fend off the chill damp of the monsoon torrent that began to fall; at five-thousand-feet elevation the air was clear and sharp—hot by day, but far too cold after dark for ill men in tropical clothing.

Although their own troubles seemed almost more than they could manage, when one of the villagers offered a child to Colonel Flickenger for diagnosis he saw that it was suffering from mastoid and gave the father sulfa pills with instructions in pantomime about administering them. He was rewarded with an egg.

It was a night of almost intolerable discomfort and fear. A small .22 revolver that Flickenger always carried with him was their only dependable weapon, since they didn't altogether trust the old Springfields. Davies, Lee, the younger Chinese colonel and two soldiers strolled in with unfathomable cheeriness to join the others around midnight.

The next morning they received messages from headquarters warning them severely under no considerations to move from where they were. As soon as a way in to them could be plotted definitely (they were in unsurveyed country where there were no white men or stations), they were told, a British political agent would come with an armed guard; the agent later sent word that they were in unfriendly savage Naga country.

Colonel Flickenger was the top ranking officer. After the warning not to move had been discussed and stacked up against the chief's request to leave that evening, coupled with the erratic comings and goings of strange tribesmen who did not seem to be on especially good terms with their hosts, Flickenger decided at least to get out of the village. (The village people who cut their hair short with a bowl effect were known as Changshas; some long-haired, more warlike, visitors from another village were Ponyos.)

The Changshas accompanied the party to a small clearing high above the wreck of the plane and the villagers' hillside millet fields. The short uphill trek ended better than the colonel thought it could. The party had to move single file through the elbow-width track cut through grass scrub and bamboo thickets, and no one especially wanted to take the lead, not knowing what was going on behind him. Flickenger cannily intended to act as anchor man on the trail but the chief indicated with such firmness that *he* intended to take the rear that the colonel had no choice but to go ahead. The headman had brought with him a small boy, also armed, and as the two tramped close on his heels Flickenger expected momentarily to hear the swish of a dah aimed at his neck; what better chance would the chief ever have than this to teach his son how to hunt heads?

It turned out, however, not to be a head-hunting day. The crush of Changshas who followed the group up the hill fell to and helped their visitors put together new palm-roofed shelters.

From August third, the day after the crash, to the fifteenth of the month when, they were presently informed, the British agent would reach them, they existed in this precarious camp. Colonel Flickenger maintained order with considerable severity, and with Davies organized a barter business with the natives for food—both Changshas and Ponyos were possessed by an ardent passion for empty tin cans.

The stern warnings from Chabua continued, ordering the group to remain where they were until help came. By this time reconnoitering Japanese planes had also begun to be a source of anxiety, and the colonel ordered the party to keep themselves hidden when the planes came around. Presently the Ponyos brought news that the Japanese had moved ground scouting parties up toward the Americans' camp.

On the fifteenth the British agent Adams appeared. He was a thin, blond young Englishman, cultivated, unruffled, sharp, who ruled his wild jungle district with unshatterable nerve. He brought coolies and sixty naked Naga guards armed with dahs and spears. With Adams were an American radio officer, LaBonte, and John deChain, an extraordinary, bearded American sergeant who knew the jungles better than San Francisco, his home town.

Adams gave the Americans some interesting information that night; for one thing, this place was outside of British official jurisdiction, and Davies, on landing in his parachute, had floated down into a Ponyo village whose warriors last year had taken one hundred and six heads from surrounding villages. The head-hunters pursued their wars with some pride in their collections, Adams said pointedly, and most of them had never seen white men before.

With this promising outlook for the hike through the wild thickets ahead, preparations for the journey out were begun. This entailed using the radio transmitter Lieutenant LaBonte had brought to complete arrangements with headquarters for air coverage from Chabua along the route.

The tramp was over stony mountains and through deep hidden valleys, sometimes covered by sword grass and sometimes by enchanting tropical greenery. The men who could not walk were carried by Adams' coolies—over sometimes almost vertical slopes—in rude bamboo sedan chairs made by the natives under the direction of the two Chinese colonels. Flickenger says he hopes never to make exactly that kind of trip again. There were elephant herds and tigers. But planes came over every day showering supplies. It took seven tedious days to reach Mokokehung, a British garrison station deep inside Naga country, where Adams was stationed.

From Mokokehung the rescued party traipsed on blistered feet another eighteen miles along a safer track to a jeep trail, and at the end of this they were picked up by a plane and flown to Chabua and the hospital.

When General Alexander saw his invaluable surgeon safe again, he talked for a while about court-martial for disobeying orders, but that was averted and the two men set to work to begin the organization of a dedicated rescue squadron—although squadron is hardly the word for a unit of the size and quality that could be mustered then.

Eventually, in 1943 Colonel—later Brigadier General—Thomas Hardin succeeded General Alexander in command of the CBI Air Transport Command.

Hardin was taken off the Pan American-African division of the ATC operations and sent out to use his early experience in this Eastern Section of the CBI, and brought a new grade of ferocity to getting the cargoes across. In his old job he had been dealing with impossible situations long enough to know that the worst of them could be overcome if he drove hard enough and he started in on a tough, imaginative policy that was meant to get cargo through to its destination with or without the cooperation of nature and the Pentagon.

When Colonel Hardin came in he got brilliant help from his staff, who were no softer than he was. Colonel Tom Mosely was a veteran of the Ferrying Command, a blond, bright-blue-eyed dynamo of an officer who proceeded to drive himself and those under him at the rugged pace the situation demanded. That he was still a colonel was said to be due to his habit of telling his superior officers unpalatable facts which in the ordinary way of things they would rather have told him; his conversational timing was also said to be bad for a man who anticipated promotion. None of this, however, hampered his effectiveness on the job.

Colonel Harry (Red) Clark, who was Deputy Chief of Staff under Hardin, had been working as control operator in Prestwick, Scotland, at the receiving end of the flow of bombers and fighter aircraft being ferried into Britain. He was a highly experienced pilot with many hundreds of hours of flying time built up with American Airlines, and he had no sooner taken over his new job than he began day-in-and-day-out flights over the Hump himself, as an example to those youngsters under him, many of whom were fresh from training schools in the States.

Colonel Edmund O. ("Pop") Schroeder, with the help of Herbert Fisher, a technical representative from the Curtiss Wright factory—who finally corrected the fuel pump and carburetor troubles on the C-46's—and George McTigue, directed maintenance, hopping from one to another of the five stations on the India-Burma border from which the Hump flights started.

By the time the Hump run got into high gear Hardin was commanding between five hundred and six hundred planes, including elderly C-47's, Curtiss Commandos, and C-87's, which were a cargo version of the Liberator bomber.

Aside from the trouble caused by not having enough planes capable of flying the five-hundred-mile course to Kunming over this territory, it was always difficult to predict the weather accurately. During the monsoon season accuracy was no problem; it was habitually frightful, with thick, swirling clouds veiling the peaks and blocking the corridors between with dense fog. In cloud, twenty-three-thousand-foot Yulung Mountain, just off course, was especially difficult to detect, and the peak had many little less imposing rivals.

Under ordinary conditions Yulung's summit stood above the upper cloud stratum and, even with heavy loads, the C-87 cargo Liberators could climb over the cumuli when the courses through the valleys were closed. But the Commandos, without such power, had to grope through the valleys on instruments, the pilots sweating out their fear of Yulung and the other rocky eminences.

One condition that made trouble was the promise of "clear" weather at both ends of the run, with uncertainty, but most likely fog, to be met in the mountainous middle. And the condition that harassed Hardin most was "clear" at one terminal and "closed" at the other, which meant that planes *ought* to be able to get through, but could and would they?

It was the custom of some of the officers controlling the traffic to play it safe and ground planes when there was any uncertainty. One day in February, 1944, General Hardin stalked into flight control at Chabua base, fresh from a flight from Kunming with Colonel Clark as his pilot, to find *all* his planes standing idle on the field. Although the weather report on the Burma side was fairly bad, Clark had had no difficulty whatever flying through, since they had found no clouding over the better part of the run, and Hardin was infuriated by seeing deliveries washed out at the mere *threat* of bad weather. He stomped out and demanded a quick solution.

A new order was worked out swiftly with his deputy, Colonel Clark and staff. Clark did not ask his pilots to fly runs he couldn't do himself, but he was brusque about demanding of the seasoned fliers the best they had in them, both because they knew as well as he the urgency of the job, and as an example to the younger group, who would learn nothing from being coddled into thinking that they could expect to limit themselves to minimum performance.

Since weather watching and prediction were the key to keeping planes flying, the new order directed that a group of the most experienced pilots run weather flights both ways, day and night, at four-hour intervals, beginning immediately.

The weather crews flew to China and made a quick about-face return, turned in detailed reports, after which they went off duty for a twenty-four-hour break between working periods.

The terrain they covered was subdivided for reporting purposes as: 1, the Upper Assam Valley; 2, the Naga Hill Region; 3, Fort Herts Valley; 4, the high Hump (principally over the courses of the Irrawaddy, Salween and Mekong rivers). Both regular cargo and the weather flights were suspended when radio communication was eliminated by sunspots or other atmospheric phenomena, and when bad icing conditions were deemed inevitable. C-46 Commandos were to be used for weather flights on the theory that if they, the lower-ceiling planes, could get through, the high-ceiling cargo carriers certainly could. And in a very short time, the Commandos tracing their way just above the peaks discovered one other hazard. Japanese fighter planes sneaking up the river valleys from their fields in the south zoomed quickly up to attack before the Hump fliers knew they were there.

But on the whole, the weather runs did increase deliveries toward the level of Hardin's standards. Between the Japanese attacks and the sudden weather changes, conditions were something more than rugged, however, and grumbling in the ready room grew increasingly sour. It came to a peak when on one day thirteen planes were lost. While they were returning from Kunming, the weather suddenly socked in without warning; the pilots, blind and with insufficient gas to return to open weather, were forced to crash-land any way they could. Some made it safely and eventually walked out, and some did not. But the loss of thirty-nine crewmen and the planes seriously cut down on the quota of tonnage delivery, and it was necessarily some time before they were replaced. Any former Hump pilot reminiscing about those experiences will invariably refer to "Black Friday"—the day thirty-nine of their comrades crashed.

Losses were oftentimes greater on the Burma end of the course than in the mountain passes themselves. Immediately outside of the valley bases at Chabua, Jorhat and Sookerating there was cultivated land—open rice paddies and tea plantations. Beyond these flat, open tracts was the deep and fantastically fecund jungle, whose growth was so rapid that it immediately enwrapped any alien object injected into it. On one occasion a C-46 that left Chabua for Misamari did not arrive at its destination and when a search plane went out immediately, wreckage was seen crashed on a jungle-clad slope. By the time a ground search party could reach the general area, the plane had been so completely overgrown by vines that spotting planes overhead, guiding the ground detail, could not even detect a trace of the broken trees and the wreckage was never found.

Sometimes Hardin's boys had to be temporarily and suddenly hauled off the cargo routes to help out elsewhere. When the Japanese push into Burma threatened to cut off General Stilwell's troops, the ATC was asked to airlift the general's Chinese soldiers out of their mountain retreat at Yunnanyi. The C-46's managed to work their way down on the airstrip where the troops waited, and as soon as their doors were thrown open the horde of waiting Chinese began to crowd in. The doors were kept open and, without a count relative to the plane's capacity, slammed shut only when the plane was jammed full. The Chinese were small and expected no comforts; one hundred of them could jostle aboard on a single flight. Ten thousand were moved out to the base at Sookerating in India within three days.

Naturally enough, Hardin's home bases got as much harassment as the Japanese Zeros could manage. On one day Colonel Clark returned from CBI headquarters at New Delhi with a newsman, Lloyd Stratton of the Associated Press, as a passenger, unaware that a dogfight was swirling noisily over the field where he intended to land. Approaching the base, he asked the tower control at Chabua for landing instructions and received the laconic reply: "Ceiling three hundred feet; visibility half a mile . . . light to moderate falling parachutes."

The American fighter squadrons in that theater never did have enough fighter planes, but the 308th Bomber Group based at Jorhat made up for the shortage to some extent by the viciousness of the punishment they gave the Japanese Zeros in the vicinity. The 308th's Liberator bombers came to be so feared even by the most arrogant enemy fliers that it became plain after a time that the Zeros had begun deliberately to steer clear of them.

This sparked a bright thought in the minds of the C-87 pilots, whose cargo-carrying ships, aside from their lack of armament, closely resembled the heavily gunned Liberators. Following up the thought with action, they found bamboo poles the thickness of gun barrels, painted them black and thrust them out from their ships' nose, sides and tail. Thus protected, they soared off on their route across the Hump, happily assured that the Zeros would at least think twice before opening fire on them.

Weather, Zeros, clouded mountain peaks were bad enough; the most exasperating hazard for the pilots remained the gasoline shortage in China. With tanks drained at Kunming of every extra drop of fuel beyond the amount required for a swift direct flight back to home base, the last miles heading into the Assam valleys were always a nightmare of watching the gas indicators registering lower and lower. When flying conditions also dropped near the danger point no pilot knew for a certainty whether he could make it home. At intervals fuel supplies also very nearly ran dry in India. There were periods when a station consuming forty thousand gallons a day had no more than a twenty-four-hour supply on hand. At such times pressures were exerted by the tough, determined staff and somehow the gallons were piped or trucked in.

Losses during the bad weather of the monsoon rains gave added work to the rescue flights organized earlier by Alexander and Flickenger. B-25 Mitchell bombers were stripped down to carry food, medicines and warm clothing for drops to the crews who had had to parachute into inaccessible places, and they went out on their low scanning missions, ripe targets for Japanese fighters. One of the most expert veteran searchers, Captain "Blackie" Porter, was shot down and presumably killed, although his copilot saved himself.

A number of crews succeeded in the struggle to survive. Lieutenant Glen Norell, flying a C-46 northward from Chabua one day, reported engine trouble before he reached the high mountains, and asked for radio bearings. An unfinished message from him soon afterward said that his crew was going to jump. Three days later Norell himself walked out, damp and hot but unscathed, but with no idea of what had happened to his two companions. Nearly three weeks later both of them—Radio Officer Neal Dreyfuss and Private Elmer Vance—made their appearance at Shingbwiyang, even damper and dirtier and hotter, but also unharmed.

On May third a C-46 with a crew of six was reported missing; between the sixth and the eighteenth the entire crew had walked out.

It was only because many of the men did roam back unexpectedly from the oblivion of the gorges and forests that tension among the men was kept down to a bearable level.

In this same period there was a young Air Force corporal named Wesley Dickenson on the post at Chabua, whose preoccupation scared the daylights out of most of the other men there.

Colonel Flickenger always called newly arrived young airmen into his office to look them over and ask questions about such things as hobbies, in order to help the kids who were so often badly prepared emotionally and by experience to find compensations in their off-duty hours for being trapped in this alien, heart-shattering atmosphere. Dickenson reported to the surgeon's office, in his turn, with a python wrapped around his waist. Flickenger took a quick, startled look at him, and his questions were perfunctory. Yes, the boy liked collecting snakes and was ecstatic about having already acquired this fine dangerous specimen. "Can I keep him?" he asked.

"Not here," snapped the colonel.

But the corporal turned out to be an experienced and curiously devout herpetologist, who collected, studied and loved the snakes to an extent that fascinated Flickenger. His collection, by the chief surgeon's consent, was housed in boxes on the screened porch of Flickenger's dispensary and became so famous in the CBI theater that whenever VIP visitors—military or civilian—arrived for inspections the first thing they asked to see was the snake farm.

His collection grew rapidly until he had several species of the most deadly vipers in the region. Once Colonel Flickenger had a time of it, saving the young scientist's life when a much-loved black cobra bit him—by mistake—but the boy survived.

General Don Flickenger was later European Commander of Air Research and Development, USAF, stationed in Belgium. And the Don Flickenger Trophy named in his honor is awarded yearly to the best para-rescue team in the Air Rescue Command.

By 1944 General Hardin had done a magnificent job with first-class crews and contemptibly inadequate planes. His experience was badly needed elsewhere and he was moved on to the Central Pacific headquarters of ATC at Guam, and General William Henry Tunner took his place.

General Tunner was a West Pointer, commissioned in artillery in 1928, but he entered flight training three months after graduation and in the following year became an established member of the Air Corps. He went through training and tactical service, finishing up his own final burst of special tactical training just in time to join the Military Personnel Division of the Chief of the Air Corps as things began to break loose in Europe in 1939. Four months later he became personnel officer of the Air Force Ferrying Command.

He came to the China-Burma-India division after his successful handling of the involved process of the South Atlantic Ferrying Division operations and remained in the East until December following the end of the war. We shall meet him again in the transport arena elsewhere.

Tunner reacted quickly and adversely to the appalling condition of the planes with which he was expected to step up airlift. It was impossible, he said flatly, to increase the tonnage carried "with a lot of wornout equipment," and he promptly made his feelings known clearly in the Pentagon.

By this time the home factory production of four-engined C-54 cargo carriers had accelerated and, at General Tunner's demand for more and better craft, a reasonable number of them was ordered sent out to him by the Pentagon. With these longer-range planes his crews were not only able to avoid the more dangerous higher level routes over the Hump but to carry heavier cargoes.

In spite of all the breakdowns and hazards, the Hump operation made formidable scores. In one twenty-three-day period during which the run was passable for a total of only 290 hours, 1870 trips were flown.

ALASKA

A fresh disarrangement of Washington war plans came early in '42 when the Japanese, reaching out another arm of their beleaguering forays, suddenly occupied the Aleutian islands of Attu and Kiska. The ATC route from the U.S. to Alaska had then been only sketchily laid out. Such installations and service as there were ran through Canada east of the Rockies, recrossed the Dominion border beyond Whitehorse, passed through Fairbanks and Anchorage and loosely spanned the fogbound thousand-mile-long Aleutian Chain.

No one knew whether the clusters of Japanese on Attu and Kiska were making a simple diversionary feint or beginning an attempted penetration in force. The preventive measures called for, by Army defense and build-up of strength there, demanded more than the ATC facilities could cope with at a moment's notice, and the Command therefore promptly called on several of the national airlines to supplement its own services. Henceforth, until ATC could allot planes for this run, Northwest Airlines not only flew the long route from Minneapolis to the outer "williwaw"-swept stretch of the Aleutians but developed and improved bases at various strategic points along the way. United Airlines ran flights from U.S. depots to Fairbanks, Alaska, and Western Airlines as far as Edmonton, Canada, both carrying cargoes outbound and on their return trips bringing ferrying crews to Great Falls, Montana—the redistribution point from which crews were shuttled back to factories for new plane pick-ups.

In the pursuit of duty, these ferry crews often traveled from Great Falls to their factory destinations by continental commercial planes, coming aboard the airliners in their heavy flying gear and lugging parachutes. They amused themselves and disgusted the regular airline crews by whiling away the time finding fault with the flying techniques of the airline captains, which had a fairly disastrous effect on some of the greener civilian passengers.

Despite hindrances, the ATC operations grew by dint of imaginative improvisation, sacrifice and the diligence of both military and civilians. Toward the end of 1942 the Air Transport Command altered the status of Pan American operations; the war branch of the civilian company was officially absorbed by ATC and Major William Tunner was placed at its head. When Tunner met the Pan Am staff at Miami to effect the transfer, he was deeply impressed by the caliber of the staff he was to work with, as well he might have been. Afterward he said, "Many were men we needed badly. So I encouraged them to join the Air Corps and 'knighted' the best right on the spot, giving them the rank I thought they deserved in the light of their abilities."

In this way ATC drew steadily and heavily on civilian help. General George knew that no one could run a large airline better than executives who had already run large airlines, so he surrounded himself with officials who had had years of such experience. His deputies in the top command were C. R. Smith, who had built up American Airlines from its beginnings, and Harold Harris, an organizer of Panagra in South America. They in turn drew in many other trained airline people whose know-how helped surmount the peculiarly frenzied problems that could only occur in the fantastic exigencies of world-wide wartime air transport.

British experience had contributed a great deal when the Ferrying Command was exploring its way through a maze of immature techniques. But British factories were forced to concentrate on turning out war aircraft.* Also, during the war years, besieged by the Axis in their home island and fighting desperately in the Mediterranean, the RAF could spare only a restricted amount of help in transport to its own spheres in the Pacific areas.

There mainly ATC and NATS planes covered the long air hauls that were such an important element of the Pacific operation of all the Allies.

The NAVAL AIR TRANSPORT SERVICE and the SOUTHERN COMMAND AIR TRANSPORT (Marines)

The Naval Air Transport Service was distinct from the Army's and also from the smaller outfit flown into the wild blue yonder by the Leathernecks.

To support shore operations by the fighting Marine Corps, particularly during the bitter battles that raged around the Guadalcanal theater, the Southern Command Air Transport—SCAT—concentrated a group of eighty-eight DC-3's in that zone. They ranged the Pacific from New Guinea, the Solomons, New Hebrides, and Australia to New Zealand. Some of the pilots were youngsters with so little experience in ocean flying that their initiation in ferrying planes from the U.S. mainland and island-hopping across the widest part of the Pacific gave them the feeling of pathfinders. One of the survivors, Paul Lenihan, expresses it this way: "That first day, halfway between California and Hawaii, I felt like Lindbergh. When I landed my DC-3 at Honolulu, I fully expected a brass band and a cheering crowd to be out. What do I get? A blasé maintenance

---

* Immediately after the war, this was to count heavily against British aircraft industry, when competition for commercial transocean business found the U.S. in the position of possessing the only tried and tested airliners.

crew chief who just muttered, 'We'll have you refueled and ready to push on in an hour' . . . it sure was a letdown. . . ."

At first SCAT was made up solely of Marine "utility" squadrons —the 214th and 215th—but as the war moved from island to island and GI troops joined the Marines in the South Pacific, Army DC-3's were added to the earlier setup.

Colonel P. K. Smith, the original commander of the 2nd Marine Air Wing, was later joined by other experienced commercial air transport men, among them, Fred Angstadt formerly with United Air Lines, and Fiske Marshall of Northwest.*

Conditions of service in that South Pacific theater were well known for their almost complete lack of comfort, hygiene or safety. Until the last remnants of the Japanese were eliminated as a major inconvenience after the islands were secured, their presence in pocketed areas and their fighters and bombers overhead added to the daily perils of the Marine contingents, including the ground crews.

In the early months, flying off the short runways of Guadalcanal and Munda, the urgent needs of surrounding islands made it necessary for the pilots to throw to the winds most peacetime restrictions and stagger off in DC-3's that were shockingly overloaded. With Zero sneak strafing attacks sometimes, but not always, fended off by American fighter planes, SCAT picked up wounded and flew them across long stretches of the Coral Sea to base hospitals and in this period, at the peak of the fighting, evacuated fourteen hundred casualties a week in rough comfort.

The Japanese interceptions, the rough terrain of jutting mountains, unaccountable weather and steaming tropical conditions in general caused losses that could not have occurred in peacetime flying, when ordinary cautions could be observed. Flights were made because they had to be tried, in spite of every hazard.

One of the young SCAT doctors, Lieutenant Commander J. Miles O'Brien, who worked for many months on Guadalcanal, spent part of his time at the evacuation center there and flew with the wounded or rescue crews when he was needed.

---

* Angstadt some years before had been selected to fly Pope Pius XII around America during his visit here when His Eminence was Cardinal Pacelli.

He had just taken off one day in one of SCAT's pet planes called "Oh Five," on a mission to the hospital on Espíritu Santo, when a radio message intercepted the flight, calling him back to the base. "One of the boys has been badly hurt by a hand grenade. We need you here fast," was the order.

The plane went back, landed him and took off again.

Dr. O'Brien, on entering the service, had been a rising young eye surgeon, just out of Philadelphia General Hospital, and although most of the wounds he treated were not especially in his line, this one was. He was kept busy for some time with the emergency operation, which required removing the victim's eye. When he had finished, the plane "Oh Five" he had started on was already reported overdue at Espíritu. It never arrived and its burned wreckage was discovered sometime later, where it had run into the mountainside of the island of San Cristobal, to the south.

The grimness inherent in that kind of life was accepted by the Marines and SCAT men, who found, it must be suspected, their own ways to alleviate the deprivations and the lack of amusement and to relieve what every serviceman recognizes as the basic injustice of wartime life.

The freedom and the glamour of the High Brass, however invaluable it may be in the over-all picture of war, has always been an almost intolerable challenge to the man who is sweating it out in filthy and unspeakable jungle skirmishes when he is tied to his bloody job with no relief in sight. By the time Guadalcanal had been cleared of Japanese and its Henderson Field lengthened for the safe use of larger ships than the old workhorse DC-3's and the smaller fighters, the Marines and GI's who had effected the improvements were in no condition to have marked respect exacted from them by a show of authority.

Accordingly when the first of the new big ships, a four-engined Naval Air Transport plane was flown in, carrying a congerie of glittering high-ranking officers and a couple of congressmen, the enthusiasm shown in the lower ranks was less than torpid. The—for wartime—plush transport sailed down and taxied ceremoniously toward the deputation of clean staff officers drawn up to offer the VIP's a formal welcome.

The presentation of one level of Brass to another had just begun: "Admiral, this is our area commander . . ." when a loud explosion boomed in an ammunition dump at the far end of the runway. The ceremony began again, in a slightly higher tone: "Admiral, I want you to know . . ." The admiral leaned forward, straining politely to hear, and another detonation began which set off a chain-reaction upheaval that sent high and low into all available slit trenches.

Some hours later, when the tumult subsided, the ceremony and inspection were resumed with the decorum for which all our well-disciplined troops are so justly famous.

The story of the admiral's reception on Guadalcanal spread widely and pleasurably, for NATS crews moved across broad expanses of the world in those times.

Navy's VR-1 squadron made runs up from Seattle to Alaska and the Aleutians. VR-2 flew four-engined seaplanes (Coronados) from Alameda, California, to many of the Pacific islands. VR-3 ferried between the U.S. east coast at Patuxent River, Maryland, to Oakland, California. And the VR-4 and VR-11 outfits flew DC-4's (R5D's) with a fine disregard for particularity to all Pacific points, Africa, Iceland and England.

NATS crews, largely recruited from civilian life and painstakingly trained for service over limitless ocean wastes—and through enemy fighter patrols when necessary—were welded and dedicated to the business of keeping matériel and men moving. They became, in the atmosphere in which they moved, as salty as any crow's-nest lookout and as quick with the language of the briny deep.

NATS was, first of all, groups of crews, trusting one another and particularly their navigators. In the whole air world the navigator has a special niche in the emotions of his fellow crewmen, of which they are most keenly aware when he is trying to pinpoint an infinitesimal atoll surrounded by thousands of leagues of sweltering and empty ocean. The captain of one NATS plane flew regularly with a typical, rangy, bowlegged navigator from the Panhandle—not surprisingly known to his friends as "Tex." After many touchy navigational flights which turned out well—which means that the

island they were flying toward was just where Tex said it would be
—his captain came to know that Tex's "fixes" could be relied on.

But the outcome of long transocean trips in wartime was difficult to take for granted and at first the captain worried a little
when Tex came up softly behind him toward the end of each flight
and, with one cowboy-booted foot braced on the copilot's seat,
stood absent-mindedly humming a little tune that never varied. The
tune kept on during the throttling of the engines and the letdown
through the usual thick layers of cloud.

Sometimes, seeing only obscurity below, the captain would ask,
"You sure you're right, Tex?" and Tex would say, "You'ah O.K.,"
and the song would be resumed, *Mother put my little shoes
away. . . ."*

To this day that NATS captain recalls the calm assurance of that
hummed tune repeated over and over and sometimes wishes, when
he is beset by some civilian doubt, that Tex were there to sing it
over his shoulder.

The NATS crews faced the hazards of tropical storms, head
winds, dense murk and Japanese air patrols. Some of them were
lucky, however, in that a good many NATS runs brought their crews
home at frequent intervals, so that they had more or less regular
flying days at sea with off-time spent with their own families. Thus
their social lives were a great deal more normal than those of men
based on distant islands and girls were a less transfixing novelty than
to sailors and soldiers left for eons at distant spots without feminine
companionship.

One such NATS man was Lieutenant Frank Blair, now a news
editor on a widely known New York television program, who lived
then with his wife and family not far from his base near Alameda,
California. He spent a few days at home once or twice a month, and
counted on being there fairly often.

Blair piloted a PB2Y3R Coronado—a four-engined seaplane—
and an average sort of trip meant taking out about eighteen passengers and cargo, lying over for a rest at Honolulu while a fresh
crew flew the plane on the next leg of its schedule to whatever spot
it was destined for. When their names next came to the top of the

list at Honolulu, Blair's crew customarily took another Coronado on to Marcus or Saipan, awaited a turn-around and flew home by the same stages.

One deeply cherished, if quaint, tenet of the Command was that women were well-designed contraptions but that they did not belong on Navy planes any more than they did on destroyers.

And so it was when Blair's crew, on the way home from three weeks of island hopping in the line of duty, reached Honolulu and reported confidently for orders to pick up a plane to fly home to Alameda, they were badly jolted by the news that instead, their orders headed them back toward distant Australia. And infinitely worse were the instructions which revealed that their passengers were to be a contingent of English "Wrens." Women.

"Have a nice trip," was the operations officer's salute as he sent them off next morning.

As a matter of pure fact, it must be said that the attitude of the crew toward their passengers was not unanimously hostile. The Wrens were pleasant. "They gave us no trouble and when you got used to their British accent, they turned out to be a jolly lot," was the magnanimous consensus.

The long overwater jump to Palmyra was negotiated through towering black rain clouds and Blair concentrated on flying. He radioed their imminent arrival routinely, well ahead, and, recalling the advanced state of dishabille affected by the refueling men at such stations, he added cautiously that all his passengers were young women.

The plane broke out of a lashing downpour over Palmyra and as Blair circled down to land he spotted several jeeps just arriving, filled to overflowing with naval officers.

His schedule called for a one-hour stop for refueling and Blair groaned with the dead certainty of what lay ahead when the commandant leaped hospitably from the head jeep and other naval ratings sprang after him to help unload the Wrens.

What was called a "bang-up buffet lunch prepared and waiting for the ladies" was very obviously going to shatter Blair's schedule, but he stanchly held out for compromise and the return of the Wrens was promised within two hours.

Three hours later the ladies were escorted back from the Officers' Club, the American Navy's traditional obligation to entertain their British cousins whenever opportunity presented (as would have been the case, vice versa) having been lavishly fulfilled.

Espíritu Santo was the next stop and once again aloft, with the hilarity of reminiscence subsided, most of the Wrens were soon sleeping quietly. But that evening a crew member sidled up to Blair and said, "I think you better take a look at one of those girls, Skipper. She seems to be running a fever."

She was, with a constellation of red spots spreading warmly across her face, which any family man would have, and Blair did, recognize as measles.

The prospect of a return home, to that crew, was now dimmer than ever.

A forewarned Naval doctor appeared at Espíritu Santo with quarantine papers, and the period of waiting for release was spent by the airmen in one Quonset hut and the Wrens in another. News of measles in the Naval ranks was wired laconically across the Pacific and noted or forgotten at various bases.

No more measles ensued and, in the melee of the delay, responsibility for forwarding the British girls on to Australia was shifted to another crew.

Blair headed home with his men and found no repercussions from their ordeal worse than the expected light banter at rest stopovers. But the long arm of radio had outdistanced the PB2Y. As Blair looked down on the Alameda home base preparatory to landing, he saw etched brightly in the sunlight a line of ambulances all flying yellow flags. And as they set foot on home soil at last, a doctor crisply ordered them to regard themselves requarantined as of that moment. Radio and TV announcers are fast talkers, luckily, and Blair put everything he had into his explanation of the situation. But he would like to know the name of the joker somewhere out in the wartime Pacific who almost succeeded in putting the crowning blight on that long unnautical journey.

But there was definitely more business than pleasure and, by war's end, NATS had a smoothly running sixty-thousand-mile transportation system to move relief commanders, government officials, needed items and, on return trips, to bring wounded men home to Stateside hospitals.

In 1942, for administrative purposes, the Army's Air Transport Command was divided into five wings: the *North Atlantic, Caribbean, South Atlantic, Africa-Middle-East* and *South Pacific.* Until the end of the war occasional variations in the area of each field organization followed the unforeseen deviations of its course and the Pacific wing's relative importance increased after the collapse of Hitler's armies, when large numbers of men and supplies were transferred into the Asian theater from the victorious European battlefields.

Both ATC and NATS had sweated through the snarls of interservice ambiguities, shortages, time-consuming developments of suitable vital equipment as well as enemy interference. Unarmed, they carried out their missions efficiently—usually with a jaunty nose-thumbing at enemy bombs and gunfire.

In the Pacific the ministrant air traffic increased up to the very moment of the Japanese surrender near the end of 1945.

When Japan did collapse, one of General MacArthur's first directives was to call for ATC and NATS aircraft to move in the necessary military forces that were to take over and occupy the conquered islands. For this purpose, transport planes were sped in from every part of the world so that, on the eve of MacArthur's entry into Yokohama, more than two hundred four-engined C-54's were ranged on the hard-stands at one airstrip alone on Okinawa. To accept the surrender on September 2, 1945, shuttling planes carried the 101st Airborne and top commanders of the Army, Navy and Air Corps, headed by General MacArthur, across the now quiet intervening waters and wrote *finis* to the closing chapter of the long and costly conflict.

3

ALMOST IMMEDIATELY AFTER THE JAPA-
nese surrender ceremonies on the deck of the battleship *Missouri*,
the precipitate demobilization of America's overseas military millions began.

It was inevitable that once the final battles had been won in so
gigantic an affair as the Pacific war, every enlisted soldier, sailor
and nonprofessional officer in Asia should feel that he had finished
his job and clamor to return to normal life again. Any fortunate man
who could wangle priority and the prospect of a discharge crammed
himself into a home-going airplane as soon as he could.

A hard core of ATC and NATS career officers and men, now
wiser for more than four years of experience in their jobs, carried on.

In the multiplicity of war missions, NATS and ATC had been,
of necessity, flying more or less parallel routes, sometimes using the
same airfields, each branch devoted largely to its own people's requirements. That this dual service should produce at least a touch
of rivalry was taken for granted. One outcome was that men whose
priority gave them a free choice between the two lines were sometimes basely swayed by gossip that NATS served better in-flight
meals, even including first-class steaks and that nonpareil Navy
coffee which the entire armed world had come to revere.

One of the first postwar jobs of ATC and NATS officers, to
avoid duplication of efforts, was to merge their two services.

The reorganization, unhampered—or unspurred—by hard wartime exigencies, took a long time, demanding as it did a tremendous
shifting of powers, obligations and objectives. And at this time department work that had been under the jurisdiction of other authorities was transferred officially to the service, with the view that

it would contribute to the smoother working of the military air transportation system. This work was: weather reporting, airways and radio communication, air rescue, evacuation of sick and wounded—later, photography and charting.

The group which inaugurated the new world-wide air system was manned by both Naval and Air Force officers as well as such civilians as James H. Douglas, under the Secretary of Defense, James Forrestal. Recognizing the organizational genius of Major General Laurence S. Kuter of the Air Force, the council appointed him Commander Designate, with Rear Admiral John P. Whitney, Deputy Commander. And on June 1, 1948, in its final form, the organization was launched. It was now renamed the Military Air Transport Service.

It could never be called an infant service; its emergence was, rather, the coming of age of a command which had gained—as had many another stripling, through wartime experience—a right to take its place beside the senior services with their centuries-old traditions.

Both the permanent and incoming officers who were to be responsible for its plans had a great reservoir of experience to draw upon. Major General Harold McClelland took charge of Air Communications, and Colonel Richard Kight of Air Rescue. Air Transport was under Major General William H. Tunner, Air Weather Service was commanded by Brigadier General Donald N. Yates, and the Flight Service Commander was Colonel Nicholas E. Powel. Each had lived with the particular problem of his new job during the war. The new command visualized for itself a settling-down process, a smoothing off of rough corners, welding, perhaps shifting of emphasis from one function to another. Even with the quasi-peace that hovered over the world in 1948 there seemed to be plenty of time in which to get the new machinery oiled and adjusted for easy running. This idea was quickly shattered.

BERLIN AIRLIFT

On June 21, just three weeks after MATS went into business, a Russian edict drew the young MATS into one of the greatest sagas of air history—and the history of human determination to preserve the decencies.

On that day the Soviet Army permitted the passage of a Berlin-bound food train through the Russian Zone. That Red zone cuts Berlin off from the source of most of the supplies needed by the city's population of three million people. Without warning, the Russians then clamped down a blockade which barred all surface traffic by road, water or rail into the capital.

The entire world, and especially perhaps the Western Alliance, was rocked by consternation and shock. The three zones governed by France, Britain and America, cut off from Berlin by the Soviet orbit, were helpless to resist without knowing how far the Russian Army was prepared to go in carrying out its edict. And not only were the lives of Berliners jeopardized, but it was all too plain that the maneuver was aimed at the propaganda target of destroying Western prestige and terrifying all Germany into accepting greater Red control, especially the city of Berlin.

It took only a short time for the English and Americans to grasp the significance of the fact that the specifically mapped *air* corridors over the Soviet Zone connecting Berlin and the outside world, which had been agreed on by written treaty during Occupation negotiations, were still open to Western planes. Whether the Russian command would go on respecting that part of the treaty also depended on how willing it was to go to war to enforce its designs.

The corridors consisted of three twenty-mile-wide air avenues leading into Berlin from American, British and French occupation zones, passing directly over Russian airfields where squadrons of fighting planes were soon poised.

General Lucius Clay, then commander of all American Forces in the European theater, with his staff and the Washington authorities evaluated the situation and ordered planes into action to feed Berlin by air. The call went out to rush air transports from wherever they were and the airlift was on.

By June 26 at General Clay's order some C-47's,* then available on the spot in Europe, had made thirty-two flights over the cor-

---

* The Air Force designation for the commercial DC-3.

ridor from Wiesbaden to Tempelhof Airport, carrying in to the besieged capital eighty tons of food. USAFE, the U.S. Air Force, Europe, had at that time one hundred C-47's, which were put to work as quickly as arrangements allowed.

Approximately thirty-nine C-54 four-engined transports were immediately ordered to Germany from their home bases in the U.S., Hawaii, Alaska and the Caribbean.

Lieutenant General Curtis LeMay, who had become the head of the U.S. European Air Force, quickly organized an Airlift Task Force which was commanded by Brigadier General Joseph Smith. Although the operation was planned on a mighty scale, it was scarcely believed then that the Russians would be foolish enough to hold out more than a few weeks.

Pilots scattered across an arc of the Pacific from Panama to Alaska found themselves participants before they knew the facts. For example, Major Fred D. Macathee was relaxing in his off hours at a movie in Honolulu when the picture stopped suddenly about three o'clock and his own name was called out with the request that he report back to his base immediately. When he arrived there he was directed to fly his C-54 to Westover, Massachusetts, without delay. Since trick training flights were not unusual, he set off with minimum baggage and a light heart—still wondering how the movie came out.

Macathee and his crew flew the Pacific that night, refueled at Fairfield AF Base, near San Francisco, and arrived without incident at Westover. Feeling the strain of a twenty-hour flight only normally, Macathee went brightly in to the operations officer and jauntily declared, "There's your airplane, sir."

He was headed for the door with the idea of finding a bed and some rest when the voice behind him said, "The orders here are for you to deliver this ship to Lages in the Azores, via Bermuda."

"Tomorrow?" asked Macathee.

"No. Tonight." A tired pilot and his crew at that moment were of no interest to executive base officers—or anyone else except themselves; the business of MATS commanders was to get planes to Europe.

Before Macathee had ever set eyes on Lages' welcome airstrip,

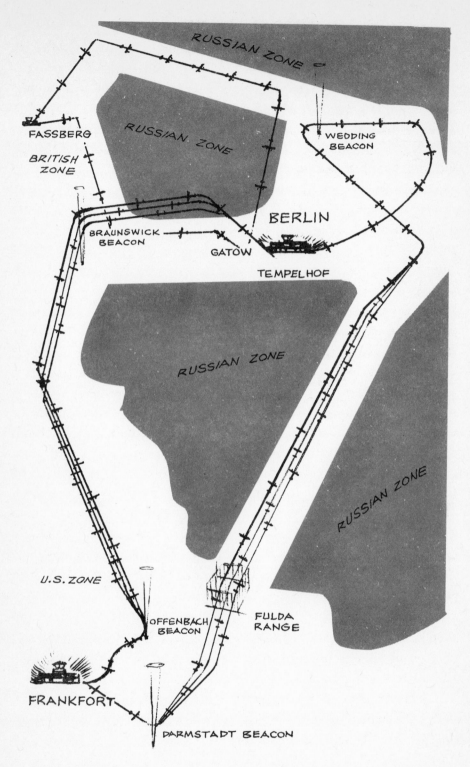

RUSSIAN ZONE

FASSBERG

RUSSIAN ZONE

WEDDING BEACON

BRITISH ZONE

BERLIN

BRAUNSWICK BEACON

GATOW

TEMPELHOF

RUSSIAN ZONE

RUSSIAN ZONE

U.S. ZONE

OFFENBACH BEACON

FULDA RANGE

FRANKFORT

DARMSTADT BEACON

Through 20-mile-wide corridors, in fair weather or foul, the Berlin Airlift
saved the people of Berlin.

an extension of his orders directed him by radio to refuel and go right along to Rhein-Main, Germany—ten hours farther.

By now the pilot and crew were feeling definitely seedy and they stumbled into "Operations" at Rhein-Main, glad to mutter, "There's your plane."

"Good," said a crisp executive. "Now just step over to this map. You follow out here and make a left turn over the Darmstadt beacon . . . check with airways control when you reach Fulda . . ."

There were not enough fresh crews on hand to take over. It was all the Air Force could do in those first days to bring machines and men and supplies into position, while mathematical schedules were being worked out. While coal—a critical need in Berlin—was loaded into Macathee's plane he had some hot coffee. Before that crew got to bed they had completed two round trips to Tempelhof, Berlin, with full loads which had to be discharged. After that they slept twenty-four hours.

In the rush to fulfill the airlift's requirements a crewman in Anchorage, Alaska, was summoned from a little joint where he was assuaging the rigors of local life with a glass of beer. Back at base he was soon in the air, headed for Germany, and as he said later, "Boy! by the Fourth of July I'm working regular for the LeMay Coal and Feed Company."

By July 20, following the sustained day-and-night delivery of planes to Europe for the lift, there were fifty-four four-engined craft in use and 105 twin-engined 47's. Their efforts were joined by forty RAF Yorks and fifty other twin-engined British Dakotas (C-47's). Deliveries of food and fuel rose to fifteen hundred tons daily by the U.S. and 750 tons by the British.

Operation "Vittles" had gone into high gear but it was not enough. Eight additional transport squadrons of C-54's with triple crews and ground personnel for servicing were ordered brought in.*

Major General William ("Bill") Tunner, directing the "back-up" of the lift from Westover, Massachusetts, received orders to replace General Joseph Smith as Task Force commander, with Lieutenant

---

* A squadron is usually twelve planes.

Colonel Robert ("Red") Forman as his deputy commander. Forman kissed his new wife good-by, they both turned their backs on Tunner's birthday party, promised to return in thirty days and took off for Germany.

Tempelhof Airport possesses, perhaps outside of Hong Kong, the worst approach possible for a terminal. Planted in the middle of Berlin, girdled by encroaching hills, frowningly surmounted by a brewery and seven-story apartment buildings, take-offs and landings demand piloting skill of an unusual order even in good weather. In the low-lying fogs and sleet storms that started before the lift ended—and during its later days when mechanical landing aids had been installed—it was a plane trap.

Since no one could read the minds of the Russians, the probable duration of the airlift was incalculable; it did not seem possible that the Russians believed they could outmaneuver the West with its dander up. Apparently, however, they intended to try and, as the blockade persisted, the stream of planes fell into precise, mechanical flight patterns that buzzed defiantly through the summer and into the storms of fall.

Spaced three minutes apart, at two hundred miles an hour, the loaded planes left Frankfurt for Berlin, and the pattern of their return was as exact. There were, most of the time, twenty-six planes in the corridor simultaneously. With such a multitude of ships following on one another's heels, landing techniques had to be faultless; each point must be passed at a precise height, at an exact time, at a predetermined speed. There could be no variations, no displays of individual temperament. There were casualties, but the deliveries went on.

By mid-August the cargo flown into Tempelhof had risen to a daily two-and-a-half thousand tons.

It was fortunate that proficiency in keeping so many planes in close flight through those narrow air corridors had been perfected in clear summer skies, for new problems rose thickly with the arrival of the August fog and storms.

The method installed to safeguard landings when these began was a radar monitoring system called Ground Control Approach— GCA. This consisted of tracing an oncoming plane's position by radarscope "blip" and directing the pilot's landing maneuvers through voice radio by trained operators on the ground. The operator's voice guided the pilot to a proper heading and gave him the exact amount of glide needed to descend "blind" to the last few yards before the approach end of the runway.

GCA had been thoroughly tested by the Air Force during the war and had been adopted for civilian operators.

In 1948, because most of the men who had been Air-Force-trained on the GCA system were demobilized, General Tunner found himself alarmingly short of seasoned operators for the airlift's needs. To fill this gap, the U.S. Civil Aeronautics Authority, which was now using Ground Control Approach methods as a normal function in its operations, sent twenty of its most experienced men to Germany. There, besides landing planes, they started a training school to prepare fresh drafts of Air Force men for the job.

As both the number of planes en route and the bad weather continued to increase, the incidence of "stacked" ships, waiting over Berlin for GCA to bring them in one at a time, built up to a point where deliveries were being badly slowed down.

When General Tunner and Colonel Forman flew to Tempelhof on a tour of inspection on August 12 they found themselves in twenty-eighth place in the landing sequence because of fog—with a plane reported on fire at the edge of one runway. General Tunner saw gas being uselessly consumed in the stacked ships kept helplessly aloft and ordered them all back to Frankfurt. If that sort of waste of fuel and time went on all winter, Berlin, despite the greatness of the effort already made, might well suffer seriously.

General Tunner put it up to Colonel Forman: "Some method of air traffic control without *stacking* must be worked out, and within twenty-four hours."

Colonel Forman obliged: Using the same three-minute spacing, henceforth each plane was to make a straightaway pass at the runway and if the pilot failed to make the landing he was to climb and return to home base from which he would make a fresh start.

It had taken an hour and a half to land nine planes from nine thousand feet by the stacking method; by the straight-in approach, in the same length of time, sixteen could be brought in.

The results were not all good. On one day of particularly vicious weather 214 planes attempted the straightaway and only one got in, but the system paid off. With day-in, day-out practice the crews grew as proficient at delivering their loads as freighting truck drivers.

As soon as a plane's landing roll had slowed, a "Follow Me" jeep swung in front of it to lead the craft to a waiting trailer truck, and before the pilot had finished yawning, unloading had begun. A rolling canteen brought hot coffee and snacks to the crew, followed shortly by an operations truck with briefing and clearance papers for the return flight. Within thirty minutes of its arrival the empty plane was headed back to home base, using a different corridor.

Because of traffic congestion in the corridors, P-47 fighters flew alongside, with the hard-boiled attitude of traffic cops, to make sure that the exact speeds necessary were held to meticulously.

The activities of these watchdogs, together with identifying themselves at many check points along the way * kept the pilots on their toes, particularly in "instrument weather"; in better weather radio chatter sometimes took on gayer strains, or if not gay, light.

On the westbound corridor one night, radio listeners heard:

> "Hello, Willies—along the way,
> Willie One Twenty has this to say:
> I'm over Brunswick, one-fifty-two's the time.
> But my feet are cold, my back is stiff
> I'm aging plenty on the old airlift."

On August 21, U.S. transport planes began operating also from Fassberg, a British base, which meant cutting the flying time to Berlin by half.

Shortly before, heavy engineering equipment totaling 57,500 pounds for new runway construction at Berlin was flown in by a new type, a C-74 Globemaster taking only two trips for the job.

---

* Eastbound was reported as "Easy"; westbound, "Willie."

Early in November the U.S. Navy sent twenty-four of its C-54's to MATS for "Vittles" and its support.

One Navy unit, VR-8, which was put under Pacific Command soon after the formation of MATS in 1948, with the Navy VR-6 Squadron, set an all-time airlift cargo record in the peak month of March, 1949, although flying fewer craft than some of the other groups on the Berlin run.

In spite of the almost continuous low fog and drizzle, the crews' flying technique improved with the steady rise of tonnage carried. But pilots do not live such lives without making known their opinions of it. The "fog-cutters" as they were called, were flying three round trips a day—twelve hours flying, twelve hours absolutely free.

The crews seemed to stand up under the strain, but the planes had to be sent back to Burtonwood, England, now and again, for complete overhauls; four hundred pounds of sifted coal dust was sometimes removed from between the flooring and belly of the aircraft.

Incidents occurred. A plane carrying two hundred bags of coal weighing one hundred pounds each had passed the last going-in check point one night when the propeller flew off one engine, bashing into another as it dropped away.

The plane's lights went out. The pilot, struggling to control the crippled ship, ordered the crew to jettison the coal and then, with a flashlight gripped between his teeth to light the instrument panel, made a try for Tempelhof. The crew, used to nothing more arduous than twiddling switches, turned to, heaving the ten tons of coal out of the lurching ship, not sure at any moment that it would not crash. Relieved of the cargo's dead weight, the pilot and the two remaining engines slid the plane safely down on the runway, but the exhausted amateur stevedores spent the following twenty-four hours in a hospital, resting.

Now came Operation "Little Vittles" and First Lieutenant Gail Halvorsen's rise to fame. Erstwhile of Westover Air Base, on his airlift trips into Berlin, Lieutenant Halvorsen had noticed the throngs of children that followed the progress of the food planes. He began to tie little bundles of candy into handkerchief parachutes to drop down to the children waiting below. The world's newspapers headlined the joy spread by the lieutenant's candy offerings, and a Movement to Increase the Scope of Children's Pleasure began to form.

Halvorsen's former home base, Westover, is near the town of Chicopee Falls and the citizens of that town wished to make the lieutenant's cause their own. They held town meetings at which a receiving depot for candy contributions was arranged and cartons of sweets began to roll in from all over the country. The lieutenant had found no difficulty tucking his candy floats away amid the heavy cargo items, but there was a limit to the number of extra pounds he could sensibly take on and the contributions quickly began to exceed that limit. When it came to packing in whole cartons he had to appeal to headquarters for advice.

But in its generous enthusiasm Chicopee Falls had got ahead of him with its own request to Pentagon headquarters to allot space in overseas planes for a weekly quota of candy. The stocks were now mountainous. An excited typist requested space for ten thousand pounds a week instead of the thousand she intended to write—which caused an outraged sensation in headquarters until a correction was made. Meanwhile no one ever thought to send Lieutenant Halvorsen the bales of handkerchiefs for parachutes this galaxy of sweets required and he had long since begun to make parachutes out of his own shirts.

The shuttle of allied craft swept along the corridors throughout the long dreary winter of 1948-49. No one in the old German capital was permitted to starve; though there was no luxury and shortages existed, people, stores and industries were kept going.

Twenty-eight American Air Force men lost their lives, as well as one Army and one Navy man.

Over a million and a half tons of food and coal had been lowered into the beleaguered city by American planes, nearly half a million by British.

General Tunner announced firmly, "We can keep pouring it in for twenty years if we have to," and shortly afterward the Russians began to believe it.

On May 12, 1949, they lifted the blockade.

4

THE SLOWING DOWN OF AN OPERATION
as monumental as the Berlin airlift had become took a little time.
The flights continued at a steadily reduced pace until the end of
July, 1949. Then came the disassembling. Squadrons had to be restored to home bases around the world, men reassigned to other
jobs, equipment rehabilitated and clearing-out details attended to
in the Air Force's most housewifely manner.

When this job showed signs of coming to an end, months later,
Colonel Forman arranged for leave in order to resume his interrupted honeymoon.

After what he had been through he should have known better.
He was still in Europe when, just before dawn on June 25, 1950, the
North Korean Communists, supposedly content with the territory
that had been consigned to them north of the 38th parallel, crossed
the boundary in an assault on South Korea. President Truman
quickly ordered out the Army, the Navy and the Air Force, including MATS, to stem the invasion, and U.N. nations took action.

Colonel Forman and General Tunner shot off from Germany
for Tokyo to command MATS' airlift of men and supplies in a new
war.

Fortunately some of the Berlin veterans had already been re-
assigned to bases in Japan—although their presence there so soon
after their Berlin experiences may have seemed more fortuitous in
the eyes of their superiors than in their own. Their response was,
however, prompt, audacious and resourceful.

And one of these, a captain and a seasoned aerial jockey from
the German airlift, may well have provided another historical
precedent in his first flight to Korea on the opening day of the war.
At least the battle he took part in was unique in air history.

66

He was ordered to fly forty Marines to Kimpo airfield, near Seoul, with the warning that nobody knew whether Kimpo or any other central Korean airstrip was usable. The unexpectedness of the North Korean invasion had created complete confusion across the waist of the peninsula and no one in Tokyo headquarters knew exactly how far south the enemy penetration had progressed at that time.

The captain was told to affirm the safety of landing at Kimpo by radio before he came in, which he did. His answer came back: Well, no, it wasn't safe. In fact, a pitched battle was going on across the runways . . . but if he circled a while . . . perhaps the Red attackers would be driven off . . .

His forty Marine passengers felt out of their element thus looking down from box seats at a battle and begged to be landed to help finish off the fight.

The captain received cautious permission from the tower to attempt a landing and the Marines began to buckle on their gear. As the plane wheels hit the ground and slowed, they slid out, fanning into formation with fixed bayonets, in a hail of gunfire.

The flight crew waited orders in the plane, a bull's-eye for the thick-flying shots, and were advised by radio to taxi to what questionable protection there was in the lee of the hangars. There on the edge of the battlefield-airstrip they fretted until the original defenders and the Marines managed to drive off the attacking group of North Koreans.

On the floor of the plane returning to Japan the captain carried many seriously wounded Marines whom he had brought to this new war only two hours earlier.

From the moment of the conflict's outbreak, MATS' share of the job was made difficult by the necessity of establishing supply lines and many other services under such chaotic conditions that the strain on the inadequate number of men and officers on the spot was unremitting. Getting troops and supplies into action, maintaining contacts under the fluid conditions on the peninsula, helping the ROK army under the authority of Syngman Rhee, caring for the wounded and setting up the necessary military order kept every available man working at fever pitch.

The South Koreans' situation was bad from the beginning since, when American Occupation troops were withdrawn earlier, it had been considered advisable to leave no heavy equipment which might have tempted President Rhee to start an invasion of the country above the 38th parallel, whose loss he so bitterly resented. Because of the lack of heavy arms, therefore, though the ROK army defended its territory heroically, the North Korean invasion, supported by Russian-built tanks and planes, had crashed through the northern border and rolled along almost undeterred.

Various other factors made defense against the Red invaders disheartening. The rugged terrain allowed Communist guerillas to infiltrate through the barren mountains almost at will and their whereabouts could seldom be detected until they had already created widespread havoc. The oddly clad regular troops and guerillas were largely indistinguishable from the civilian population; and some of that population was either afraid to refuse help to the Reds or cooperated with them willingly.

Into these confusions MATS hurried to set up the vital radio installations without which a modern army cannot work, particularly in air operations. Air traffic was heavy from the first, planes crisscrossing the open stretch of the Sea of Japan between the U.S. bases in Japan and the wildly surging battlefronts.

Because of the great need for dependable radio connections at the Korean end of the flights, a new communications device was tried out. This was a unit consisting of technicians equipped with portable radio transmitters and receivers, the operators trained to set themselves up at advantageous points and to withdraw quickly to other positions if enemy action loomed too near. The slogan of these Mobile AACS squadrons was "First In—Last Out," and they had plenty of chance to live up to it.

Even with such specially trained units functioning wherever conditions allowed, Korea-bound pilots reporting in code to airstrips on the peninsula, preparatory to landing, could never be sure of being acknowledged by their own communications men. But pilots and crews ignored the handicaps and delivered troops and cargoes in any way and wherever landing was possible.

The heavy lists of wounded from the first day opened the need for other quick and cogent action.

The limited Medical Corps on hand was immediately swamped by the appalling number of wounded who came out of the first hours of fighting. Without nurses it was impossible to give the men a minimum of humane care and on the second day it was decided in Tokyo headquarters that, whatever the hazards, nurses would have to be flown in. Those women would work the clock round under fearful conditions, always with the knowledge that no American unit could be completely safeguarded from the possibility of being overrun and captured by the Reds.

A nurse group was selected and on the second day of the invasion Captain Peter Bechtel was ordered to pick them up at Ashiya, Japan, and transport them to their destination. Captain Bechtel had been on the firing line the day before, and was a veteran of the Great War, in which before Pearl Harbor he had flown with the Canadians, later with the U.S., continuing his service through the Berlin airlift. He was redheaded, jaunty, unshaken by shaky circumstances and he knew the minds of pilots from A to Z.

When the time came to report to the Korean tower for landing instructions he turned the microphone over to a nurse with a particularly soft, lilting voice whom he had coached thoroughly in the proper way to make the routine check-in for him.

She opened softly, "TAEGU . . . This is Lullabye seven-two-oh-five . . . calling TAEGU . . ."

Ordinarily the air in a zone filled with planes in flight is noisy with official and other babble. In the split second after her call all this chatter ceased as suddenly as though an atomic bomb had gone off.

A long air silence, utter and complete, ensued.

Then cautiously the shocked sound of the tower operator's voice emerged: "Say again, seven-two-oh-five . . ."

In her soft, feminine soprano the nurse repeated her routine call and at this, every flight radio in northeast Asia broke out in such a hubbub that Captain Bechtel could barely detect his instructions from the tower rather uncertainly directing him in.

A new voice, that of a distant fighter pilot, rose gruffly above the others: "*Who was that?*"

That was what the captain was waiting for. "Oh," he replied airily, "just my copilot."

For a little while he had distracted the crews of many a plane from the horrors and strain they were going through. But, except for such moments, Korea left little time for fooling. Evacuating casualties from Japan to the United States by the returning MATS planes which had brought in troops and cargoes became a paramount mission. The possible need to convert its transport into flying ambulances had been foreseen long since by MATS planners and a technique devised. When a plane came in to the fighting front and ammunition, guns, radio equipment or heavy items had been unloaded, men slung webbed belting into position from ceiling to floor with fittings to support the stretchers on which the wounded men were carried aboard. On the quick return trip to base hospitals rode medical attendants and flight nurses to give pain-deadening injections, food, water or the simple solace of a cigarette.

After a short time the removal of wounded from the Japanese hospitals to the States became a substantial problem and the civilian airlines were again asked to cooperate. With their planes stripped of seats they, as well as MATS, transported to America postoperative cases who were fit to leave for home, the "walking wounded" and other men whose duty had been done.

MATS operations expanded daily with the war and the arrival of U.N. troops. The unstable battle lines and the menacing terrain never ceased to provide unexpected and unending complications.

The U.N. forces were driven to the very toe of Korea around Pusan, where operations became pure hell. With the landing of General MacArthur at Inchon and the recapture of Seoul, communications and airfield facilities became manageable again. When the North Koreans were driven back to their own mountains beyond the 38th parallel on October first, and the North Korean capital Pyongyang was captured on the nineteenth, the U.N. armies and MATS intensified their efforts and carried communication services forward with the front. There was little time, as the fighting progressed into enemy territory, to prepare proper landing strips for the planes bringing critical supplies that had to get through at any cost.

These conditions brought about one grotesque encounter between one air crew and the enemy, when a frantic call for tank shells came in from a U.S. outfit fighting off a guerilla attack fifty miles south of Pyongyang.

It was responded to by a three-man crew in a C-54 loaded with as many shells as it could carry. A precarious landing was made in an apparently deserted, barely cleared level space among rough, hostile hills and the door of the plane was flung open. Instantly a fusillade of rifle fire whined around the plane, spurting up dust.

The crew saw no sign of the Americans who had begged for the ammunition but, under fire, they began to off-load. They had made only a little headway when an American half-track driven by a single G.I. stormed up.

That ammo was needed in a hurry, the G.I. shouted—why didn't they get a move on? At the pilot's retort that he could unload faster if he had some help, the half-track and its G.I. driver slewed around and disappeared directly into the hills from which the Communist fire was coming. It charged straight into the pocket of enemy guerillas who, terrified of being run down, flung away their rifles and allowed themselves to be herded back to the plane where they obediently transferred the shells to the half-track.

This job completed, the G.I. driver roared off without another word, leaving the plane crew alone with the raggle-taggle clutch of bewildered Korean Reds, who had no more idea what to make of their plight than the Americans did. This unorthodox dilemma the pilot solved by tossing some boxes of C-rations out to the open-mouthed guerillas, slamming his plane doors and making a record take-off.

The northward push of American, ROK and other U.N. troops above Pyongyang carried the fighting steadily deeper into the ambush traps of stark and beetling mountains which were almost impossible for our wheeled armor to penetrate. As casualties mounted, the difficulty of saving the wounded grew more severe daily. The lack of roads and destruction of most of those that had once existed made ground evacuation, especially through the Red-infested gorges, incredibly difficult. Demands for better means of moving the critically wounded to hospitals rained on Operations headquarters. Compared to the orderly and safe evacuation from Japan to the States, the trips into and out of Korea were a nightmare.

During these days a call came for help from an obscure spot near Sinuiju, in rough territory about seventy miles north of Pyongyang. There was no airstrip near enough for use but headquarters was informed that a bulldozer had managed to scrape out enough space on a dirt road.

The crew of a C-54 was shown the location of the spot on a map and given open orders to bring out casualties any way it could.

On their arrival over the general area the bulldozed strip deep in the mountains was identified and the smell of cordite from shells being lobbed into a road farther north reached the crew while they were still in the air.

The pilot expertly brought the plane down on the crude runway surrounded by scrub trees and noticed files of weary, bedraggled Americans making their way slowly toward another group who were stretched out in the fringe of meager shade. There were no medical orderlies to care for these wounded, no stretchers, no officer in charge.

Those who were able-bodied carried the critically wounded aboard and the pilot soon saw that his plane could not possibly evacuate all the men there. He drew a chalk mark on the floor near the rear door of the plane and told the crew to lay men on the floor in close ranks up to that point but no farther, which was the only way he could think of to control the weight factor.

Then, having sent out a radio call for another plane, he took off with sixty-six severely wounded and no medical attendants. Fortunately the nearest ambulances were only twenty minutes' flying time away, where doctors would take over.

Such missions became typical as the battle lines zigzagged through the mountains toward the Manchurian border and wheeled vehicles became constantly less usable.

On October 25, with the sudden irruption over the border of the Chinese Communists in their padded coats and fresh political ardor, the whole Korean action underwent a violent change. The

U.N. troops were heavily outnumbered and their drive was reversed into a retreat. Cut off and trapped near the Changjin Reservoir, they fought their way out desperately toward the sea.

There, many were evacuated by the Navy, from Hungnam, and many of the wounded were taken out by MATS air-rescue helicopters.

Overhead, during this withdrawal and throughout the stalemate afterward, air battles blazed through the angry skies. Often outnumbered by the swarms of Russian-built Migs of the Chinese Air Force, the U.S.'s F-86 Sabre jets managed to bring down the enemy in a ratio of six to eight Migs to each one of their own planes lost. But even these losses meant that pilots of the U.N. fighter jets who had parachuted must be rescued from the valleys and gorges of the wintry mountains. They could not have been saved from capture had it not been for the almost unbelievable aplomb with which unarmed helicopter crews snatched them up and out from as deep as 125 miles inside enemy territory, under the very noses of the advancing Communists. It was the first time helicopters had been used for this most impertinent sort of action—a phase of war-making, born of necessity, which bred a new kind of airman.

More than ten thousand U.N. fighting men were picked up by the planes and helicopters of the 3rd Rescue Group—more than a tenth of that number from behind enemy lines.

The Reds drove down to Seoul by January 4, 1951, and took the city over for plunder. Later that month the drive was again reversed; U.N. troops recaptured Seoul and the Communist forces were once more pushed back over the 38th parallel. Here the war stagnated, although as the vicious fighting went on for more than a year, MATS' work also continued.

After the Armistice was signed at Panmunjom on July 27, 1953, MATS' mission slackened somewhat until the evacuation crews were again called on to carry home the 469 prisoners of war released by the Reds, a process known as Operations Big and Little Switch.

During the war Air Evacuation of the Military Air Transport Service had flown out more than sixty-two thousand men, or ninety-five per cent of all the wounded, taking them to the comfort of

American hospitals and families. The end of the Korean War meant an alteration rather than a lightening of the heavy burden MATS had been under, as it caused a shift back to a greater concentration on organizational details in the routines for which it had been set up—now in the light of the weak spots brought out by the war. Swift mobility, foolproof communications, maintenance where it was most needed.

Evacuation went on for a long time and was taken up with renewed impetus after the fall of Dienbienphu in 1954, when 508 French wounded were flown home from Indonesia by the MATS medical teams. The journey took them more than halfway around the world, over the entire Pacific, the United States, and the Atlantic, before they reached the France that many of them must have thought, as Communist captives, they might well never see again. By that time, with their accumulation of experience in evacuating wounded, MATS medics and nurses were able to take such missions in stride. French interpreters on each plane smoothed over language difficulties, and a special State Department dispensation overcame the lack of visas in crossing the United States.

5

As MILITARY ARRANGEMENTS INCIDEN-
tal to war were transmuted into nonwar status, MATS went on with
its part of the reorganizational work, moving troops and cargo at
peacetime pace to American stations overseas. That in itself is a
massive enterprise and may be easier to gauge if we follow a plane
on one of the innumerable similar flights going out everywhere day
by day.

MATS' headquarters is at Andrews Air Force Base, several
miles southeast of Washington. A typical journey on MATS for an
individual going anywhere in the Pacific on military or government
business would start not far from the Pentagon. The plane is apt to
be a C-118 airliner, similar in many ways to the civil airlines' popular DC-6B. It leaves MATS' terminal at the Washington National
Airport on regular schedule.

Until departure time the passengers mill around the waiting
room, as passengers always do, wondering what they've forgotten,
and what things are going to be like on the West Coast or in Tokyo
or the Philippines. But they differ from most air travelers in that
most of the men are in the uniform of the Army, the Navy or Air
Force. And if they are taking out flight insurance they are paying a
very low rate because of MATS' long safety record: fifty cents on
a $12,500 policy within the domestic zone and as far as Hawaii,
Alaska, Bermuda, Mexico or the West Indies, with a protection
clause of $625 for medical expenses.

Loading goes on as it does for all flight departures, here supervised by flight attendants—either a pair of airmen, or their feminine
equivalent, two WAFs. Inside the plane two more differences are
seen immediately: all seats face the rear, and quantities of safety
gear and escape equipment, such as life rafts in yellow bags, life

jackets, emergency radio kits, water containers and first-aid kits, are conspicuous. These safeguards are present on all overseas planes but in MATS craft are not tucked out of sight.

When the cockpit checks have been made, the craft takes off with every one of its sixty-two seats occupied. Space has been allotted, as on all such flights, by a priority system common to the three services; authorized civilians are always assigned under Defense Department orders.

On this trip a group of sailors who are being moved to a new ship in San Francisco cluster together like a flock of bluejays. There are several separate cadres of Army men who are being shunted to the West Coast, to Japan and tropical coral atolls.

By the time Pittsburgh has slid away under the right wing, the children of servicemen aboard bounce out of an initial state of awed inertia to make their presence felt, looking for more congenial companions than their drowsy parents. An Air Force sergeant urges his chubby two-year-old to slip quietly past her nodding Japanese mother in order not to disturb her, and join the other children. Some of the other service wives along the aisle know that the young Japanese wife, again pregnant, is returning regretfully to her native land on this reassignment of her soldier-husband's after getting accustomed to the supermarkets and general comforts of America.

A civilian expert is trying to concentrate on getting his papers ready

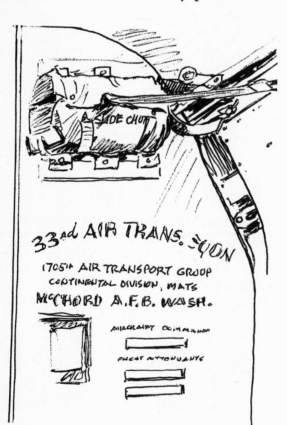

to present to an Air Force conference in San Francisco, but gives up when the appearance of flight lunch boxes brings the rising tempo of life aboard ship to a peak.

The two WAF stewardesses and the mothers juggle open milk and fruit-juice containers in a frantic effort to avert untidy disasters, at the same time trying to wedge cold fried chicken and sandwiches into unwilling little mouths ahead of chocolate bars and chewing gum.

The steel mills of Gary, Chicago's gray revetments, and the sedate, flat plains of Nebraska appear and retreat far below.

The plane crew has been shifting, one by one, from the powder-blue winter uniforms to sun tans, in preparation for landing in mild California, but the passengers follow no such ritual.

Capt. Richard L. Williams

A young Army captain on his way to Japan with his wife and eight-year-old daughter wonders how long he'll have to wait for a MATS plane going to Tokyo. A veteran of Korea, he is being re-assigned to a liaison post in Tokyo U.S. Army Headquarters after a stretch of intensified study of the Japanese language. On this job, according to regulations, he is permitted to have his family with him.

These people provide a typical cross section of a service flight in the transport division. Having crossed the continent nonstop, they land at Travis half a minute ahead of their ETA * without flurry, and presently, after a briefing, the Asia-bound passengers will set off for destinations farther west.

----

* Estimated time of arrival.

6

MATS' GATEWAY TO THE PACIFIC AND the Orient is Travis Air Force Base, set roughly sixty miles northeast of San Francisco in a broad, almost fog-free valley with little to hamper air traffic. Travis is the eastern terminal of the Pacific Division whose other terminal is at Dhahran in Saudi Arabia, nearly halfway around the world.

At Travis, MATS has established extensive repair and maintenance shops and all the facilities common to any bristling air terminal. There is also an especially fine, well-equipped modern base hospital into which the Army and Navy as well as the Air Force wounded and ill from the Pacific theater are often received until they are able to travel to other military hospitals.

The Travis Base waiting rooms hum at all hours of the day and night with incoming and outgoing men and women of all the services, their relatives and friends who have come to welcome their return from overseas or to say, "Well, be seeing you when you get back from your tour." It has its cheerful side and its quota of tears, like any terminal.

But one thing is remarkable. Nowhere else is the integration of the services more evident. Not only does the military personnel of every American service branch pass through here but also troops and technicians from innumerable friendly nations—especially those nations whose interests lie close to our own. The foreign visitors mill curiously together around shops and snack bars, their unfamiliar uniforms giving a touch of novelty to the familiar scene, their chatter usually gay and, to much of the crowd, unintelligible.

And behind the scenes, working twenty-four hours a day, is a great diversity of machinery which keeps the passengers moving, the planes in flight, the crews informed and alert. Under a traffic control director, all schedule requirements are planned; newly overhauled planes which have been flight-tested are assigned and, five hours before departure time, are spotted on the ramp so that priority mail and cargo can be properly loaded.

The crew puts in an appearance two hours before take-off time, when the captain is given a folder containing complete data for the trip ahead: a detailed, graphic weather map of the conditions he will encounter en route—the course carefully plotted so that he may take full advantage of helpful winds and avoid those which would delay—the radio call letters of stations or weather ships he may want to contact; the weight of the load he is flying; and a record of the quantity of fuel he will need in his tanks, an amount estimated as necessary to carry his plane to its destination, plus an extra supply for "holding aloft" or seeking an alternate field in case he finds unsuitable landing conditions at his terminal point.

All this information, made explicit on a few sheets of paper, is the result of the work done with the technical skill of MATS' Air Weather, Airways and Communications Services—the boys with the sharp eyes and ears and slide rules.

To provide one phase of this, seven strategically located weather squadrons stationed around the globe send out meteorologically equipped planes each twenty-four hours—or oftener if threatening hurricanes or typhoons are on the prowl. Following predetermined courses in which weather is sampled at levels between fifteen hundred and twenty-five thousand feet,* they compile data for the reports made available wherever men fly.

In order to obtain a world-wide picture, for accurate predictions, of the shifting masses of the upper air that bring storms hurtling out of Siberia or the empty ice wastes surrounding the Pole, the weather planes from all stations take off from their bases at the same instant according to Greenwich, or in military parlance, "Zebra time." Thus, when the oldest of MATS weather outfits, the 53rd Weather Reconnaissance Squadron, at Burtonwood, England, which is very nearly situated on Greenwich meridian, starts off its daily flight at five in the English morning, weather planes from

---

* Or, to get "winds aloft" information for SAC's jets, up to forty-five thousand feet.

Bermuda, California, Hawaii, Alaska, Guam and Japan start off simultaneously, whatever the local time of day may be for them. (There must be peculiar attractions in this early-rising Burtonwood job; ninety-two per cent of its men extend their tour of duty beyond the original time of enrollment and they hold the highest marriage rate of any weather squadron in MATS.)

Once the data on the elements from each of these seven squadrons scattered around the earth is amassed, it is taken in hand by Communications Service. That organization sends the reports by radio and teletype to master Weather Centrals. At Weather Centrals it is converted into world weather maps which are sent to every Air Force Base at home and abroad and made available to Army and Navy commands, as well as to civilian airlines if they wish. Such weather transmission makes up a large proportion of the work of Airways and Air Communications Service (AACS).

The work of AACS is never finished at any hour of the day or night. Even in the periods of general calm many, many thousands of messages in condensed weather code are received from the weather planes, by radio and by eternally clacking teletype machines whose coded yellow slips are one key to the safety of all Air Force flights. Since nothing is quite so transitory as a weather report, a prediction a day or two old is of no use whatever to a pilot many miles high in the constantly moving upper air strata. Typhoons or hurricanes increase the job of the weather reconnaissance squadrons and pile up more work for the communications men who must transmit the results of the storm's erratic tracks hour by hour.

Another duty within the province of AACS is supervision of flight control. Each aircraft aloft sends in a half-hourly report to be monitored by a terminal controller who advises and gives any help needed and in case of trouble hustles off the air-rescue crews.

The monitor at Travis Air Force Base, for instance, follows flights headed for Hawaii to the halfway mark, at which point monitors at Hickam AFB at Honolulu take over responsibility for bringing the plane safely in. Since the babble of voices reporting from the many outbound and returning planes flying similar courses at the same time would stupefy any monitor board, a simple rule of time control has been devised. The last numeral of the serial number which is assigned to each plane as its permanent identification for all purposes is multiplied by six and the number arrived at is the minute after the hour of that crew's reporting-in time; thus aircraft No. 2638 would report at forty-eight minutes after the hour, and half an hour later, or eighteen minutes after the hour.

These routine messages relay back to base the navigator's estimate of the plane's position, altitude, the amount of fuel consumed as well as the quantity remaining to that minute. Under ordinary conditions the monitor's job is merely that of a suspiciously watchful mother hen, but if the pilot has encountered unexpected resistance from winds aloft, thereby using fuel at a dangerously rapid rate, it is the monitor's responsibility to decide whether the flight should be about-faced before it reaches the halfway mark, since failure to return to the mainland before reaching the "equal time point" with a shortage of fuel would mean looking for the nearest place to land—in mid-Pacific terms, a very poor gamble.

If real trouble occurs, the monitor quickly clears the air of all chatter except the SOS.

The variety of experiences common to flight crews and monitors has no end and any flight that brings a crisis presents a need for quick decisions, taking into account new combinations of circumstances.

A huge C-124 cargo plane, a Globemaster, left Travis one day loaded with unwieldy airplane parts. It had already passed the point of no return when two engines became useless and a third began backfiring. With only one of the four putting out full power, navigational and other electronic circuits went out of action and in the murky weather the navigator had a job on his hands plotting a course to Hickam, six hours away. A request had gone out to Honolulu for a rescue intercept as soon as calculations seemed to show that fuel consumption would only keep the C-124 aloft five and a half hours.

Looking dolefully down at the sweep of the sea, one of the crew remembered the remarks of a couple of airmen who were spanning the Pacific for the first time. "Man, look't all that water," cried one and the other replied, "Yea, boy, an' that's on'y what's on top."

The Globemaster's situation was touch and go, with little assurance that the plane might not plunge downward hours before a rescue craft could arrive. To get near Hawaii, if that was going to be possible at all, it was necessary to jettison weight, while the first and second pilots struggled to maintain level flight. With enormous effort five of the crew eased bulky crates down into the elevator well and half the twenty-five thousand pounds of cargo was dropped.

Two Air Rescue SB-29's from Honolulu made contact within a minute of their predicted rendezvous time and guided the limping Globemaster in. During those tense hours the escort maintained a light cheering radio banter. . . . "You got new engines in that cargo. Why don't you use them?" a facetious rescue voice taunted. "We're saving the taxpayer's money," came the smug reply.

For saving half the cargo and valiantly bringing the valuable ship in, the crew were met and congratulated by the MATS deputy commander, Brigadier General G. S. Cassady, and other ranking officers who had come to the ramp to welcome them. . . . "Well, it wasn't any cure for ulcers," said the sergeant who had hefted overboard crates weighing more than he did himself.

During the last hour, when it appeared certain they would make it, one of the crew radioed an invitation to the rescue B-29 men to meet at Hickam for a drink, to show their appreciation.

"How'll we know you?" asked Rescue.

"You can't miss us. We'll be the boys with the scared white faces," replied C-124.

No line is drawn between civilian and military assistance by MATS Rescue squadrons, but the predominant calls are naturally in aid of Air Force planes. These are shepherded even when no great danger of having to ditch the plane exists. Where there is a suspicion of danger there is a hazard, and many times, as in the case of the Globemaster, no actual physical help is given, since knowing an escort is equipped and ready to render aid is sometimes all a harrowed crew needs to stagger home safely under its own power.

A routine report of an "intercept" by a rescue squadron added this note to its factual data: "The KC-97 was never unsure of its position and could have completed its mission without Air Rescue Service assistance if the psychological factor of Rescue escort can be discounted."

There are times when the psychological factor can't be discounted, when no amount of preparatory training can fully inure men to the strain of meeting hitherto unexperienced dangers.

The rescue men are in their jobs because they have been selected as particularly fitted to deal with all the factors involved.

7

FROM THE VERY FIRST GLANCE HICKAM
Air Force Base has the look of a soldier's dream. Hawaii's fragrant
reputation has floated so far and wide that a newcomer is pretty
well prepared for the lush beauty of the terminal's setting among

HONOLULU

the vivid, cloud-brushed hills that surround it. The building stands
green and cool around a center court where palm trees thrust above
the roof, soughing in the balmy air; around their feet the flare of
hibiscus, the tracery of giant ferns and begonias compete with the
herbaceous sports shirts of off-duty servicemen.

At this Hawaiian entry port the natural languor of the islands is quickened by the activity of planes arriving and leaving every hour of the day and night, loud-speakers announcing and summoning, and air police keeping order while fifteen thousand service people a year—ten thousand of them children—stream through the rooms and corridors. Here also military men and officers from Japan, Vietnam, Turkey, France, England, Australia and Nationalist China are an ever-present and colorful part of the passing parade.

Nearby, and part of the system of which the airport is the hub, stand some of the most severely technical modern installations of the age, and the operations and training that go on in them deal often enough with the somber matter of life and death. The illusion of casualness which is part of the Hawaiian atmosphere ends at their outer walls.

Hickam, as a main base of the Pacific Division whose actual headquarters are at Parks AFB near San Francisco, is the core of a great deal of wide-swathing activity. An extremely busy Rescue squadron, the ultrapowerful Airways and Air Communications complex, a vital Air Evacuations group operating in conjunction with Aeromedical Services, and an equally active Air Weather Squadron work out of here. And because so much transport passes through Hickam, maintenance work to keep the planes going is exceptionally important, even as maintenance work goes.

Because such hordes of travelers pass through the terminal, the airport has been blessed with the best of accommodations for in-transit families. Most of the facilities are duplicated at other MATS transfer points, varying only in proportion to the amount of traffic they cater to, but here they have a special glitter, not only on account of their refinements, but because of the enhancement of their lovely setting.

As a plane from Travis or the Far East lands, and parents and little children spill down the ramp, a rotating committee made up of wives of officers and local servicemen immediately takes the befuddled and travel-grimed babies and mothers to a special Dependents Lounge. And in an inner nook of the lounge, where no one, except an occasional father who has agreed to give the baby his next bottle, is permitted among the women and small children, the mothers are encouraged to stretch out for a much-needed rest

or nap while the children are watched over by members of the welcoming committee and a paid attendant who is always on duty. The hostesses bathe babies, change clothes, amuse the children and pleasantly fill in the tiresome gap between flights. The quarters have a special kitchen for preparing baby food and formulas, and equipment for any small family emergency. Sometimes stopovers cover only a few hours—oftener they are longer.

In the main part of the terminal building very nearly everything that is needed can be found: souvenirs, replacements for forgotten or misplaced toothbrushes and dungarees, Hawaii's exotic flowers and preserved fruits to be air-mailed home, air-conditioned lunchrooms, as well as all standard airport accommodations. This is the transient's zone—orderly, comfortable, prepared to speed the refreshed MATS traveler with his dependents on the way to duty somewhere over the horizon. The soldier or sailor who passed through Hawaii by ATC or NATS in the great postwar military dispersal would not recognize it; the present airport is an acknowledgment that service people have pretty much the same needs as the rest of us.

On a rise of ground within sight of the airport stands Tripler Hospital, a twelve-story structure of several wings, with a large staff of military doctors, medical attendants and nurses, many of whose patients are the wounded and sick from the whole Pacific Division. The Korean War wounded were rested and treated here on their way home.

MEDICAL EVACUATION SQUADRONS

There is a sharp memory here of the days when the wounded from Korea went through. Even though officers come and go, and the actual personnel who flew the mercy planes and tended the wounded men have to a large extent scattered to other duties and have been replaced, the impact of the war experiences on Tripler Hospital and MATS Evac elements at Hickam was so strong that

HICKHAM

they have powerfully influenced everything that has taken place since, in handling the wounded and ill.

Evacuation is, in fact, a word that is apt to make most of us who have taken part in recent wars wince with remembered distress. But in the hands of the men and women who give their attention to Air Evac today, that kind of transport has at least lost many of its grimmest features in the provision of infinitely better means and procedures than were possible during the war years.

The air evacuation that was originally begun in 1942 by the First Air Ambulance Squadron under ATC had five squadrons with a record of seventy-seven thousand wartime evacuations by 1945. When MATS was organized the five squadrons were consolidated in 1949 into the 1453rd Air Evacuation Corps stationed at Hickam under Major Lawrence Somlo.

To be historically correct it is necessary to admit that the first airlift ever attempted was in 1870—thirty-three years before the airplane was invented—with the hoisting of 160 patients out of Paris in a balloon, when that city was under siege. The lift certainly lacked many of the features now insisted upon by MATS doctors, and barely hinted at what such humane service could eventually be.

Present-day evacuation is not only concerned with the care of ordinary war wounds and transportation out of the danger zone, but is prepared to treat the most obscure afflictions incidental to troops who are exposed to all sorts of unusual conditions.

Bringing home the wounded from the two Pacific wars meant caring for patients who were not only intolerably war-weary and frayed to mental exhaustion but suffering from the ills of Asian and tropical backwaters and of prison camps—beri-beri, malaria and innumerable singular infections, diabetes, polio, and damaged hearts as well as wounds from every sort of shell.

In the rise of standards for such care, there has been a steady effort to improve equipment. For instance, the matter of a plane's going down at sea is an omnipresent subject for the consideration of all aeromedical staffs. Because it is conceivable that a plane full of wounded might have to ditch, methods of handling patients in such an emergency have been worked out to the finest detail, and one is the recent development of a new type of flotation gear for men in casts or other medical contrivances that prevent the wearing of a Mae West safety jacket. Better ways are being studied to tranquil-ize psychoneurotics en route, and new forms of on-loading patients in order to bring the ordeal to the very minimum of disturbance.

The interior of the Evacuation Squadron's planes is designed for easy adjustment to the comfort of patients requiring various kinds of treatment and for the convenience of medics and nurses attending them. The best layout has proved to be an arrangement of litters slung in single, double or triple tiers along both sides of the plane, with a curtained section forward in which removable seats are placed for ambulatory patients, and a small place aft for the nurses' desk and medical gear. An aisle between the tiers gives the attendants room to work, and lights are installed for illumina-tion where it is needed by the nurses and shaded for those who are sleeping.

Attendants for an air-evac flight usually include two or more medical corpsmen, a couple of flight nurses—Air Force, Navy or both—and when there are critical cases, a doctor or two.

Except when a doctor is in charge, the nurse's superior training over that of the corpsmen gives her the heaviest responsibility en route, but the psychological and physical well-being of the patients is to no small extent due to the remarkable patience of the medics, who watch over each one, not only as a patient but as an individual, and a helpless one at that. Besides doing the heavy lifting, and keeping a watchful eye on anyone in the litters who is especially restless or troubled, they meet querulousness calmly, comply quickly with any trivial request, understanding such things as a man's want-ing his small irreplaceable possessions right by his side where he can put a hand on them now and then.

When an air-evac flight is going off from Hickam the 1453rd Squadron is informed by the hospital of the number and condition of patients to be carried, and the plane is suitably geared to accom-modate that particular load. As the ambulances bring the patients to the loading ramp, corpsmen carry the litters aboard quickly and make them secure under the eye of doctor or nurse. All this is done smoothly, without the ado of an ordinary take-off.

As everywhere else, polio has brought its share of trouble to the Pacific Division. To protect respiratory cases, the aeromedical branch has stationed iron lungs at several key points and especially trained technicians and medical personnel to operate them. For the most serious cases a sixteen-hundred-pound Emerson respirator is taken into the transport before the patient is carried aboard, and carefully installed because its weight requires the most exacting placement to maintain the proper balance of the craft. The gear, including the generator, is thoroughly tested ahead of time, and in the event of power failure in transit, trained flight attendants work the lung by hand.

The shifting of patients from plane to plane, or hospital, can often be done with a newly developed smaller portable lung called a "Sam" and sometimes this is also adequate en route.

In early November of 1955 the illness of a serviceman at a base in Korea was diagnosed as polio and he was hurried from his station to Seoul by helicopter and from there in an iron lung to a hospital in Tokyo. With little delay he was transferred to the Emerson respirator in a Stratocruiser and, because of the precision with which such transfers are planned to the least detail, he was put down near his own home after a flight which went quickly through Hickam, Travis and Andrews AFB's.

A month earlier Gene Gruver of the Navy Seabees was flown in an iron lung from the Naval Hospital on Guam, where he had been under treatment for six months, to the Navy hospital at Oakland by way of Kwajalein and Hickam. A dangerous respiratory disability that was caused by a dislocated spine demanded the use of a respirator and at Guam the air evac officer, after consultation with the supervising surgeon, selected a MATS Navy Constellation as the most suitable craft because of its electrical power output for the long overwater haul. Sergeant Gruver was carried into the plane on the tray of the Emerson, protected on the short move from hospital to plane by the smaller respirator and made the trip, in the doctor's formal, detached, but obviously gratified words, "without incident." ("Without incident" in air-evac terms means "no worse" or "much better" for having made the journey.)

Increasingly safe air evacuation comes from ceaseless consultation and cooperation with plane manufacturers who use every re-

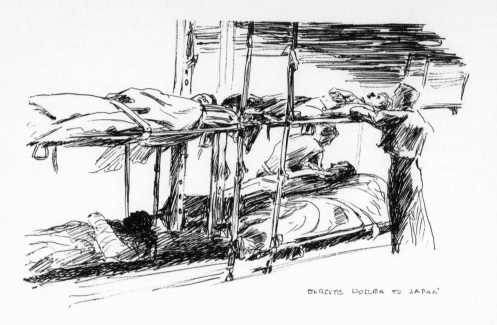

ENROUTE KOREA TO JAPAN

source to improve the equipment they produce, and from the skill of the medical officers and crews in using the equipment to the greatest advantage. The result is that a wounded or dangerously sick man can now be picked up anywhere in the world and set down safely in a hospital near his home within sixty hours.

The nurses at Hickam within the shadow of Tripler Hospital and the 1453rd outfit can never, by a very long shot, be considered usual women. Those at any air evac base are remarkable, but any one at Tripler can be taken as the prototype of her kind.

In her list of regular nursing accomplishments is the ability to take charge of a planeful of litter-bound patients and, in the unlikely but possible event of a ditching at sea, her authority over the means used in getting the patients safely out of the plane supersedes the aircraft commander's. But though this is part of her training, it is a theoretical matter. No evacuation plane so far has ever ditched and an evac nurse's duties are not ordinarily much different from those of a first-class nurse in any good hospital. She carries with her medical supplies for any sort of emergency, and palliatives, if not cures, for nearly every hurt, since drugstores or supply shelves won't be available en route.

When the day for going on flight duty comes round, she arrives well before the take-off with her list of patients in hand and looks the plane over to make sure that it has been properly set up. When the loaded ambulances arrive she supervises the medics fastening the litters into place, arranges for the comfort of men in casts, isolates contagious cases and keeps an eye on the occasional psychoneurotic who may require extra care. She jollies the ambulatories into their forward seats and pokes pillows in to ease damaged limbs, calms the weary and the uneasy, tucks in blankets and provides whatever other requirements are called for. Once in the air she doses, soothes, distributes food and liquids as diets dictate and watches over the condition of the more serious cases in her charge. And at the end of the trip she must have a written report of each case ready in duplicate—one for the receiving hospital and one for her own medical command, from which supervisors may draw suggestions for future improvements in evacuation service.

Air-evac landings coming in to Hickam are cheered along by the familiar welcome of Red Cross wives of officers and servicemen, bearing homely gifts of coffee and cookies and the pleasant novelty —for men who have never been stationed there—of slices of sweet, ripe pineapple. Wherever an evacuation flight ends, the flight nurse's duty for her charges also is completed on reaching the terminal hospital; if the patient's journey continues next day other nurses take over.

AIRWAYS AND AIR COMMUNICATIONS

As exquisite, as flower-bedecked, as languid . . . in fact, as Elysian as Hickam and the enveloping Hawaiian scene in general appear externally, the real work of the base, outside of its more lively services, is as sober a business as any great, modern, electronically controlled installation can conceivably be. There is no herbaceous coloring for the Communications Relay Center here, run by the 1957th AACS Squadron. The entire establishment is geared for rapid, alert communications concerned with serious MATS business.

The present service is an outgrowth of the Army Airways Communications System, which was activated on November 15, 1938, as one of the sudden Air Force needs foreseen in the light of war probabilities.

The purpose of the Hickam center is to receive and relay messages from all military headquarters to and from all the scattered land bases and airborne planes throughout the Pacific—a job that goes on day and night, 365 days of the year.

The messages are peculiar to Air Force wireless operation and are: ground-to-air voice circuits, cryptographs, two-way radio facsimile and tape-relay. The center's circuits are connected directly with Washington, D.C., through McClellan AFB in California, as well as the bases at Tokyo, Guam, Kwajalein, Johnston Island and the Philippines. Hickam Central is part of the global network which ties together in many codes all Pacific Division Air Force operations.

The main building, at the heart of the Hickam base, is an air-conditioned, windowless, "off-limits" structure under twenty-four-hour-a-day police guard; a visitor is admitted only under military authorization and after having proved he has an acceptable reason for being there. It is crammed with electronic instruments through which the endless streams of communications pass. And here are the cryptographers who decode the scrambled incoming classified dispatches and encode those going out. Four shifts of technicians complete a round-the-clock and round-the-week cycle of duty, passing on directives from the upper levels of the Defense Department in the Pentagon to the sprawling Pacific commands, receiving pleas for rescue from planes in trouble at sea, and generally making coherent the ether-borne chatter by which the Air Force and MATS conduct their manifold duties. (It is first, last and always at the call of SAC.)

The powerful, remote sending-receiving station for circulating messages is a transmitter standing amid its fanning forest of antennae in a lonely, ripe-smelling pineapple field about fifteen miles from Hickam, its security-curtained installation under the surveillance of a warrant officer and rotating staff of thirty-six airmen on twenty-four-hour coverage.

At the end of a winding road through the pineapple field the transmitting machinery is housed in long, air-conditioned, underground tunnels—a safeguard against any known type of bomb attack. The electronic equipment below ground is of extreme delicacy and to protect it from the slightest exposure to dust, all who enter are first relieved of their shoes. Inside the tunnels there is a startling lack of noise; the myriad voices from planes aloft speaking to the control tower, calling from Washington, Tokyo or from ships at sea, the sing of Morse code, the clack of teletypes are all converted into silence as they pass through the electronic tubes and spaghetti-like clusters of wires and cables in bank after bank of steel cabinets. Padding around to supervise and monitor them are the NCO and airmen specialists of this curious subterranean zone.

The earthy needs of these technician moles are supplied by a kitchen, refrigerator and pantry supplies cloistered there with them. And though thousands of pineapples are so extraordinarily available just outside the tunnel exits, the owners of the crop have no worries; it is only the newcomers among the men who have not long since reached a lamentable state of satiety.

A quite different duty of the dual installations is that directed by the flight controller at Hickam, also under AACS command, who is stationed in the Main Communications Building. That operator is in constant touch with all incoming and outgoing aircraft in the Hawaii area.

It has been explained that as a plane flies out over the Pacific from Travis, in California, it remains under the radio jurisdiction of the Travis flight controller until it reaches a halfway point where it is picked up by the controller at the destination base, and brought into the narrower zone governed by the airport tower of the destination base, the towerman then directing the actual landing on the runway.

The Hickam flight controller thus picks up all Honolulu-bound planes as they reach his midocean radio contact points and brings them in to the landing pattern of the Hickam Tower. The controller's job is to warn the airborne oncoming plane of the movement of other aircraft in its vicinity, and of weather conditions ahead—especially of weather changes.

The code name, *Blue Bark,* used by an aircraft commander when he reports his expected arrival time at the next base, is a compassionate warning that he has on board a bereaved person. On receiving this signal the flight controller on the field instantly alerts the commanding officer and the chaplain so that they will be on hand at the landing ramp when the parent or wife alights, to extend any courtesies found necessary.

The flight controller is the first to hear calls for rescue and intercept around Hawaii and, in fact, from an extremely wide part of ocean surrounding his area, and sets in motion the measures that send the relief planes off.

"THAT OTHERS MAY LIVE"

The generous sentiment adopted by MATS Rescue men pretty well defines the scope of their missions; it is a scope whose limitations are easier to see in the breach than in being.

The 76th Air Rescue Squadron at Hickam protects, officially, an expanse of five and a half million square miles of ocean, and when it is occasionally called on to go beyond those boundaries, it does.

An SOS radio call from anywhere in these millions of watery miles is overheard by Flight Control and immediately relayed to the duty officer of the 76th, where a crew is always on "alert" duty. Immediately notified, the commander of the 76th must decide if the emergency is within the jurisdiction of one of the other Pacific bases where rescue detachments are also kept in readiness—Midway, Johnston Island, or Kwajalein—and if so, a message is sent at once to that base in order to get local help on the scene at the earliest possible moment. If the disaster turns out to be one requiring extensive searches, all the island bases may be asked to send out planes. Often the call is for an intercept by a pilot who simply needs stand-by protection while he brings a crippled plane in.

The Coast Guard stationed at the Pearl Harbor Navy Base, which normally takes charge of civilian disasters at sea, is also notified of each SOS and in many cases the Navy at Pearl Harbor sends out its own rescue craft as well. Cooperation among the three services is swift and adjusted without confusion, to take the greatest advantage of the facilities of all. Because where lives are at stake no time can be lost in lengthy conferences, there is close liaison among the three branches, and admiration for each other's performance is more apparent than jealousy of prestige.

All the MATS' crews that enter into rescue work have a backlog of long flight training but before being assigned to squadron duty they are sent to Palm Beach AFB for specialized instruction in the handling of the newest rescue craft, equipment and techniques.

Air-rescue work operates on a fixed pattern, speeded to the highest degree of intelligent, practical action in any known kind of emergency.

When Flight Control relays an SOS, it gives the 76th all the details it has received pertinent to the accident: the latitude and longitude of the aircraft or vessel in distress, the cause of the trouble, the base the cripple is headed for and the number of persons involved. If known at the time, the position of other craft in the trouble zone is added to the report, especially of surface ships, which can often detect small objects in the sea more easily than do low-flying planes.

Armed with these facts, the squadron commander must decide on the plane best fitted to the emergency. Air Rescue squadrons are equipped with three types: long-range converted C-54 Rescuemasters; SA-16 Grumman triphibians, which can make water-landings; and H-19 Sikorsky helicopters.

As the crew on duty is being briefed, extra "back-up" crews are warned to be ready for a quick take-off. Ordinarily the back-up crew is not required to remain at the hangar, but its members must keep themselves cleared for action; this means no heavy parties or drinking, and telephone numbers left at their homes by which the men can be reached immediately, so that they can respond to any summons within a stipulated half-hour.

When the emergency warrants it, additional planes are sometimes drawn off from other missions.

The 76th ARS was recently commanded by Lieutenant Colonel Gene L. Douglas with the assistance, among other able officers, of his clever and likable Hawaiian-Japanese aide, Major Melvin K.

Ayau. They worked with strict attention to every facet of effectiveness.

A real effort has been made to provide comfortable quarters for the waiting hours of alert duty, since the fliers' performance is dependent to a degree on their physical well-being. Situated in a quiet part of the hangar given over to the outfit, the Alert Lounge has easy chairs, television and current magazines, and there are good beds in another air-conditioned room for interim naps. Here the men remain while they are on duty because many live at distant points on the base, or in nearby suburbs.

Colonel Douglas kept a watchful eye on housekeeping details and he has been known to point with some pride to the immaculate condition of the maintenance men's wash-up room. When, on inspection, a sergeant seemed convinced that certain grease smudges visible to the colonel's eye were not really there, Douglas ordered a larger light bulb installed and, when that failed to show up the last dirt particle, a still larger bulb, until that washroom at length gleamed in 200-watt spotlessness.

Until recently the Air Rescue mainstay for long searches was a fleet of SB-29's, and before that SB-17's. Both carried an underslung power-equipped boat which could be dropped by parachute at the site of a sea disaster. But the difficulty of placing the boat so that it could be boarded easily by victims floating in the water led to the substitution of C-54's with an improved rescue feature. Having been retired from transport work, the C-54's were rebuilt for their new purpose. Now renamed Rescuemasters, they carry four newly designed raft kits which have been found easier to drop conveniently to shipwreck victims, and in other ways more practical than the droppable power-boat. Besides which, the outmoded boats cost thirty thousand dollars and the expense of reconditioning one after a single drop was equal to the initial cost of a complete set of ARK's, as the new Air Rescue Kits are called. Also, each kit weighs only three hundred pounds and, with the four carried, can take aboard 160 rescued persons, against the droppable boat's capacity of fourteen.

The ARK is an arrangement of two twenty-man rubber rafts secured at each end of an 840-foot floatable rope, to which three bundles of survival supplies wrapped in yellow waterproof material are also attached at regularly spaced intervals. The rafts are automatically inflated by static lines as they are dropped up-wind of the victims in the water. The bundles act as sea anchors, and with any luck, the whole unit is carried by the wind in a giant U around those in the water, so that at least one of the rafts can be reached by a weakened man, hauling himself along the rope hand over hand, or tugging the free-floating raft to him.

While the victims are boarding the rafts, the Rescuemaster's crew, circling overhead, calls in help to complete the pick-up. The refurbished 54's have a staying power of more than eighteen hours without refueling and are fitted with every known sort of radar and navigational aid. A modified door, opening inward while in flight, is used to drop the ARK's, or by paramedics when there is need to parachute helpers to the victims.

One of the most demanding jobs is that of the lookout or scanner, on whom the entire success of a search may depend. It is extremely difficult to spot men's heads in a great tract of wind-tossed water, even if it is known in general where to look for them. In great searches the planes follow a mathematical pattern in order to cover every inch of the sea, but so quickly does a badly damaged plane sink and so illusive is the debris that it leaves, so unreliable an indication the presence of a wave-tossed oil-slick, that only the scanner's quick and ready attention may catch some clue as the plane roars by.

A scanner remains on duty only four hours at a stretch, seated in a comfortable chair looking straight down through a large B-36-type blister. At the end of that time, when eye-fatigue may make him less alert, he is relieved by another. In each ship there is an electric galley for preparing a hot meal, and bunks for rest.

In the Rescuemaster, scanners sit on each side of the plane and, near the left blister, smoke or light flares with a lasting time of forty-five minutes are discharged through an improved downward chute.

Since rescue demands are of such incalculable variety, the ARS schedule is designed to cope with any conceivable combination of problems. The Douglas SC-54 is winterized for emergency polar

use, and with its ARK units and great endurance potential, is valuable for circling and protracted escort purposes. The squadron's
triphibian Grumman SA-16 Albatross is designed for water landing,
on lakes, wide rivers and open sea, and is runner-equipped for snow
and ice. The Sikorsky H-19 helicopter snatches up victims from
difficult positions, in some cases too dangerous for parachutists.
While all this outlay is calculated as protection for SAC, MATS,
and Air Force planes primarily, its existence has been the salvation
of many a civilian victim.

The following is a small sampling of a long list of rescues
made in this area.

On February 16, 1955, the forty-eight-foot Japanese fishing
boat, *Heian Maru,* struck a reef at night south of Cape Kumukahi,
off Hawaii, and was partly submerged, her decks awash in five- to
six-foot waves and her mast swinging violently in the high wind.
Three of the crew clung to the mast, while two men on a hatch-
cover-raft, buoyed by the glass balls from their fishing nets, made
an effort to paddle to shore, several miles away. An SOS had sent a
Coast Guard plane out to search and a MATS SA-16 Albatross had
followed. The ship and raft were sighted after an hour-and-a-half
search. The raft was making no headway against the adverse drift
of wind and tide, and was surrounded by sharks, which were thrash-
ing optimistically around the paddlers.

Captain Frank M. Leese, of the 76th, in the air-rescue plane,
whose training had covered even this sort of malignity, decided he
could make a sea landing, which the Coast Guard plane was unable
to manage in such seas. Leese did so and hauled aboard the two
Japanese in the raft. Lieutenant Bonwit and Staff-Sergeant Lurie,
navigator and flight engineer of the SA-16, then boarded the
plane's rubber raft and paddled off to the *Heian Maru,* trailed by
the sharks—which by this time must have been somewhat baffled
—and rescued the three sailors still clinging to the nearly submerged
ship's superstructure.

With five extra men aboard, Captain Leese was unable to take
off but wetly taxied the twenty-three nautical miles to Hilo and
the haven of quiet water inside the harbor. Not a man was lost,
although there was damage to the SA-16's propeller. When this had

been repaired, the Japanese skipper and one of the sailors were landed at Hilo airport to make arrangements for salvaging their boat and the three others, with the grateful acknowledgments of Captain Nakamura of the *Heian Maru,* were flown to Honolulu.

An entirely different experience in rescue work, which was also undertaken with Coast Guard cooperation, involved a young lady named Mary Caroline Dunn. After the event, she called up the squadron one day, asked whether they remembered her, reminding the officer in charge that it was Friday, the *thirteenth* of the month, and announced that she was taking a plane to Molokai that day and just wanted to be sure the rescue boys were on the job. Well she might, although her personal safety was not, strictly speaking, the business of the 76th. The officer wished her well on her present jaunt and recalled without comfort her previous attempt to fly to Molokai, some three months earlier.

On that day she and three other passengers had taken off for the fifty-five-mile trip on a routine charter flight in a twin-engined Cessna flown by a civilian pilot named Emmett Kay. The weather was only fair; small-craft warnings—high winds and waves—had been out since morning, and two of the 76th's ARS planes were in the air on training missions.

Kay's call for help came in to Hickam Flight Control at four-thirty-five that afternoon.

Kay's Cessna was within sight of the jagged cliffs on the western side of Molokai when the right engine quit. Although the sea was running 12-foot waves, and Kay realized the difficulty of setting a plane down among them, he saw that he could not get his plane to land. He sent off his SOS and prepared to ditch. He got the passengers into their Mae Wests quickly and set the plane down skillfully in a trough. Since the Cessna carried no raft, he tossed out the buoyant kapok seat cushions, and when the craft sank five minutes later, all but one of the passengers were floating safely. One woman, in her panic, had swallowed so much sea water that she had lost consciousness and Kay was kept busy trying to hold her head above water.

Immediately after the call for help came through Flight Control, the Coast Guard at Pearl sent out two cutters and a plane. The

SOS was relayed to the 76th's two rescue craft that were already airborne—one an SB-29 and the other an Albatross SA-16, for a possible sea-landing—with instructions to proceed to Kay's aid. An additional SB-29 was sent off, and a slower-moving H-19 helicopter with Colonel Douglas and his pilot, Captain Richard R. Carpentier, on board.

As the light began to fail, the first SB-29 to arrive dropped smoke bombs to mark the position of the survivors. When the Albatross came on the scene it could not land because of the tremendous breakers. The Coast Guard P-49 dropped life rafts but as soon as the ditched victims clambered in they were washed headlong by the gale toward the rocky shore.

Pilot Kay had not been able to revive the unconscious passenger and, once in the raft, was afraid to stop artificial respiration. When Colonel Douglas and Carpentier arrived in the helicopter, the darkness, the wind and the condition of the inert woman combined to make a nightmare of hoisting the passengers off the tossing rafts by winch. But one by one, Mary Caroline and her companions were lifted into the 'copter and landed on the cliffs. Last of all, Kay and his patient were snatched up after Herculean efforts and the woman was hurried on to the hospital, although she was beyond help. One lost; four saved under highly adverse restraints.

It is not only the drama of saving lives that makes the accomplishments of MATS Air Rescue Squadrons notable wherever they work, but the beyond-the-call-of-duty quality of performances of both officers and men whenever they are summoned to fight against time and space over the wet and windy ocean.

Colonel Gene L. Douglas moved on to command the 3rd Air Rescue Group at Nagoya, Japan, in April of 1956, where he completed nine years in air rescue. He was not a West Pointer but, looking for combat when the war began, learned to fly and found himself an instructor on B-17's; he tried to get to the South Pacific or China and turned up as a flight commander making raids on Germany out of England with the 398th Heavy Bomb Wing. As a deputy commander with the DFC, Purple Heart, Croix de Guerre, Silver Star and a spangled theater ribbon, he made one last raid— his twenty-sixth—which ended abruptly and he spent the rest of

A 'copter from the 76th Air Rescue saves four near Molokai.

the war as a guest of Hitler's at Stalag Luft III, from which the Russians rescued him, after which the 8th Air Force rescued him from the Russians. His re-entry into the Air Force as a regular officer in 1947 took him back to B-17's and, from 1948 to 1951, he worked with the arctic expert Colonel Bernt Balchen in Alaska, during this interlude making the first nonstop flight with Balchen over the North Pole to Oslo, Norway. In that chilly setting he got into air rescue. After spells out of active duty for those schools created by the Air Force for providing itself with specialized officer material, in 1954 he was assigned to command of air rescue at Hickam.

EMBASSY FLIGHTS BY NAVY-MATS

The Navy's part in MATS operations is not easily segregated, because the Command is officered by both the services; a generous sprinkling of Navy men appears in operational and executive positions in every branch, except in a unique few which are all Navy.

At Hickam there are two wholly Naval transport squadrons, VR-7 and VR-8, which, working closely with the Air Force, are happily ensconced close to the base of their natural parent at nearby Pearl Harbor.

V-8, the elder in point of service, we have already seen whacking away at the Berlin airlift. Its backlog of tradition and accomplishment in fact dates back to World War II, when it was stationed at Oakland, California, under the Naval Air Transport Service; from there it was moved on to Hawaii in order to give its brilliant support in the final assaults of the Navy's great Pacific battles. After the Berlin airlift, in 1949, it was returned to Hickam just in time to begin rushing critical materials to Korea and to start bringing back the first wounded.

In April, 1953, its sister squadron, VR-7, was recommissioned and assigned to Hickam also, and after eighteen hours of existence was out over the Pacific in support of U.N. forces in Korea.

The Navy's cherished dream of flying the fastest military transport was realized at the end of 1953, by an assignment of Super-Connies—C-121's. These craft, with MATS-NAVY markings, henceforth carried seventy-five passengers in comfort and haste and, when converted to evacuation of wounded, sixty-seven patients, or on all-cargo missions, fourteen tons.

The Navy's Embassy runs are a quite separate, distinctive Hickam feature. Planes which carry important people and missions, State Department personnel with diplomatic mail, priority patients and cargo through the Orient, must be somewhat more choicely fitted out than the ordinary transport ship, and Embassy flight planes are both faster and more comfortable.

Taking off from Hawaii each week, they pass through Tokyo, Manila, Saigon, Bangkok, Calcutta, New Delhi and Karachi, finishing at Dhahran. The stops in Indochina, Siam, India and Pakistan, where there are no MATS bases, are necessary for refueling and also for the convenience of official passengers who have business in those countries. Passage through these exotic countries gives the Embassy flights a slightly glistening aura which is denied the more workaday MATS units.

Because it is necessary for diplomatic craft to give impeccable performance and because there are no maintenance technicians to rely on at several points along the route, Embassy planes carry double crews, fifteen hundred pounds of spare parts and extra Navy mechanics along with them. Repairs may thus be made en route, and delays because of man- or machine-failure are usually avoided, which is a vital factor in the timing of high-level processes. The chief reason for maintaining flights of this kind, however, is to insure reliable service throughout the long stretch where American bases are not permissible.

SIMULATOR TRAINING

When airmen are assigned to MATS crews they arrive for service with a backlog of training as thoroughgoing as it is within the power of old-hand instructors to give. They have been trained in both practice and theory. But beyond this training there is a demoniac range of trouble that any crew may sometime have to deal with, and can deal with only if their responses are so instantaneous that the margin of safety is kept to a good gambling level.

The Air Force has provided at Hickam a couple of devices called simulators which, without leaving the ground, accustom crews to coping with every kind or combination of flight perils. The simulators here are of two types: one is an exact replica, with full instrument installations, of a C-124 Globemaster; and the other, of a C-97 Stratocruiser. Seated inside them, with the cockpit windows frosted to counterfeit blind-flying conditions, crews are put through engine and propeller malfunctioning and every other emergency they are ever apt to meet, by means of electronic flight controls, under two check instructors—an engineer and a pilot.

Pilots, navigators, flight engineers and radio operators are all required to pass through this ordeal, each performing his duty during a realistic flight plan that may last through a session of two or three hours. When the men have finished a course they come out looking a good deal as though the ordeals *had* been real, and no amount of theory could take the place of the simulation of the realities they have endured and learned to beat.

An added advantage in the use of simulators for training is that the replicas obviate much of the expense of flying real, heavy-fuel-consumption planes. Operating a C-124 simulator costs fifty-five dollars an hour, against eight to nine hundred dollars an hour for a real Globemaster flight, and thirty-five dollars for the C-97 replica machine against four hundred and fifty for the airborne Stratocruiser.

For three years the chief director of simulators at Hickam was Master Sergeant Hugh J. Mullaney. He badgered crews so, in practice tests with such diabolic inventions as engine failures of ingenious sorts, fires, fuel leaks, icing conditions and jammed controls, that his pupils came out all but sweating blood.

Joseph Conrad once wrote about taking such a test to attain a master mariner's license. When he was brought to the last of a series of calamities and one he felt was beyond human solution, his examiner smiled at his hopelessness and said, "You could always pray." Sergeant Mullaney assumed that his pupils would pray in the face of dire disaster, but he was determined that their reflexes were going to be working satisfactorily, too.

He is remembered at Hickam, though he was retired by a severe attack of polio in June of 1955, when he was paralyzed and began a long course of treatment at Tripler Hospital. At the entrance to the C-124 simulator hangs a brass plaque which reads, "Mullaney's Pride." It is a tribute of gratitude for his ardent efforts, from students who had learned to appreciate what he had done for them, whether they liked it or not.

WEATHER SQUADRONS

MATS' weather flights at Hickam are as important as the weather reconnaissance at any of the other bases where such missions are routine. But because Japan lies within the typhoon belt, the 1st Weather Central's flights there perhaps represent most completely the full scope of that MATS job and the characteristic exploits of such reconnaissance can best be watched from the Japanese base.

One event typical of the odd variations of weather flight service, however, was a Hickam affair that began when a call came from a cable company in Sydney, Australia, saying that one of their employees stationed on little Fanning Island was desperately ill of a rare disease and would die within thirty-six hours if he did not receive treatments of cortisone and ACTH drugs, which were not available locally.

Fanning is a minute spot in mid-Pacific fourteen hundred miles south of Oahu and three times that distance from Australia. It was not far off the 57th Weather Squadron's daily course but had no airstrip on which a plane could land.

The message came in to Hickam at eleven o'clock at night and was given to the deputy commander of MATS Pacific division. Colonel McDonough, surgeon of the division, got the drugs from Tripler Hospital, the 57th packed them for a parachute drop and at 7:25 A.M. the weather plane took off with them. At 3:10 that afternoon a wire came back from Fanning: "Parcel received. Wonderful drop. Many thanks to all."

The matter was significant in that there was no other way by which those special drugs could possibly have reached the sick man in time to save his life.

8

Westward of Hawaii the next big MATS terminal is at Tokyo, Japan, at the airfield which was originally known as Haneda. The flight from Hickam is through Wake Island and the return via Midway, on a more northerly course. But since the eastward flight benefits seasonally from the high, fast winds of the jet stream, which often drive along at two hundred or more miles an hour, planes returning from Japan are sometimes able to overfly Midway and reach Hickam nonstop.

An alternative Pacific connection is from Hickam through Guam, the Philippines and onward to the far Far East, with diversions to the restricted atomic proving-ground at Eniwetok near Kwajalein. These are all long ocean hops of from fifteen hundred to more than two thousand miles.

While the transportation of personnel to the far Pacific with its human problems and complications is the most eye-catching of MATS jobs beyond the embarkation port at Travis, cargo-carrying is in actual fact one of the line's most important activities.

In order to fill quota weights to capacity, even passenger flights are loaded with crates of electronic equipment, tires, small plane parts, medical supplies and special articles being hurried along to fill some sudden important need. All of these shipments are scheduled by a priority board made up of Army, Navy and Air Force officers.

The mainstay of the cargo carriers is a fleet of planes that carry most of the heavy, bulky material; in their vaulted caverns only an occasional passenger finds himself rattling around. Presently the newly tested, giant Douglas C-133, turboprop craft (jet engines driving propellers) will be brought into use but the real workhorse of the freight-carrier business, as it has been for some time, is the C-124 Globemaster. Though dwarfed by the new Douglas, the

108

Globemaster in turn dwarfed its bold predecessor, the C-74, and is itself far from puny.

The C-124 carries a long-haul payload of seventeen and one-half tons at a cruising speed of only slightly less than that of commercial airliners and, as the pilots say, it has "long legs"—that is, it can cover more than two thousand nautical miles nonstop.

Perched on the airstrip, the plane's pilot compartment stands at about the second-story of an office building. In fact it looms so high that the commander in the cockpit must use an intercommunication phone to direct the ground crew when they are standing by below with fire extinguishers for the engine-starting routines. For the same reason, during the testing of elevator and rudder controls a member of the crew using a portable microphone is stationed in a tail compartment to report on how they are functioning.

The wings of the Globemaster, long and tapering, look too small for the bulky fuselage, but they have enough thickness at the leading edge to allow a flight mechanic to work within their structure. Squatting inside the wing while a propeller is feathered, the mechanic can make adjustments en route to rear accessories or wiring and repair a balky engine.

Wing repairs saved an awkward situation for a C-124. After leaving the ground with a mixed cargo, the pilot had warning of a leak, of the sort from which fires start, in the fuel line leading to No. 4 engine during a thickening fog. With landing fields reported closed everywhere nearby and with the destination a third of the way off across an ocean, he feathered his No. 4 propeller, shut off the fuel line and sent a man into the wing. In the wing cell at eight thousand altitude the air was icy and the silent engine glowered sullenly in contrast to the others humming with power. But while the plane cruised on at its normal altitude the repair was made and the trip was completed with all four engines working perfectly.

Because of the time and distance elements of the Globemaster flights, their crews are larger than usual: three pilots, two navigators, two and sometimes three flight engineers, two radio operators (who may be superseded by an automatic-tuning radio gadget for the pilot's use) and a loadmaster.

Loading is done through clamshell doors in the nose or by elevator hoist at the after end; through these, into a cavernous cargo cabin almost as large as a basketball court go completely boxed piston engines or jets in tanklike containers, sections of wings, jeeps, trucks, disassembled helicopters and inevitable queer-shaped objects and crates marked "urgent." The floor is closely encrusted with "tie-down" rings in long rows for lashing cargo, and fittings have been installed for quick conversion to meet any stretcher-bearing, air-evac emergency.

Below the forward pilot compartment is the loadmaster's area and it is he who, using his weight-and-balance computer like an impressive slide rule, determines how cargo is to be stowed in position and secured. And it is his responsibility to see that it does not shift through any degree of turbulence. In this eerie maw inanimate objects of colossal size—two city buses can be wheeled aboard —travel from continent to continent.

The connecting link between the cargo deck and the crew's quarters is a frail aluminum ladder which few in their right senses would choose to mount on steady ground. Rocking in bumpy weather, it conveys the illusion of suspending the climber alone on a spider web in the uneasy air, clinging to a swaying guide rope for support.

The rarefied atmosphere of the upper level having been reached through a trap door, the climber enters another world. This much smaller arched compartment contains the crew stations, and aft of the trap door, three full-length bunks for off-duty rest periods. Forward, the two pilots are hemmed in by levers, knobs and instruments on flickering panels. Immediately behind the pilots, to the right, the flight engineer works constantly at his console flanked by a battery of dials and throttles, while the navigator opposite him concentrates over his charts, with the radioman busy at the navigator's back. A kitchen counter with handy electric outlets for heating

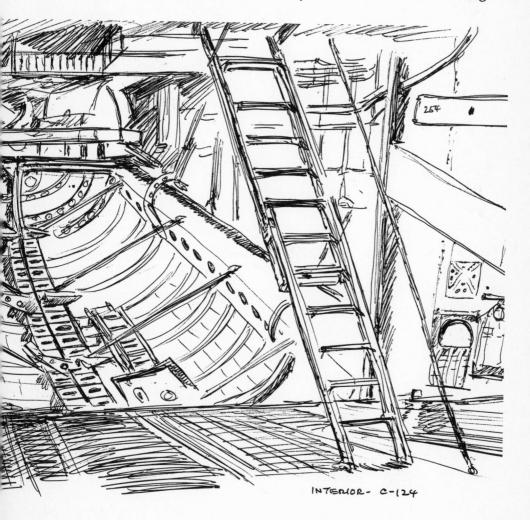

INTERIOR — C-124

coffee or soup and with lockers below fills the space beside the flight engineer.

The most singular thing about the outward appearance of this plane is the long aggressive thrust of the black radar dome in its nose. Almost all MATS ships carry a radar installation forward of the fuselage, but on none of the others does the protuberance seem to prowl, Pinocchio-like, snooping and sniffing through the oncoming clouds. The nickname "Nosey" fits it neatly.

The Globemaster has a gargantuan portage record: a dismantled stone-crusher from Westover, Massachusetts to Thule, Greenland; a complete caterpillar tractor weighing 47,500 pounds from Thule to the Danish weather station at Nord, Greenland, a few hundred miles from the North Pole; an eighteen-and-three-quarter-ton electric armature containing miles of copper wire, from Pearl Harbor to an American naval vessel laid up in Yokosuka, Japan.

A recent three-hop MATS transportation job was to move a massive—in fact, twelve-and-one-half-ton—Westinghouse generator from Travis to Tokyo. Beyond a few niggling crates and bags of mail, no other cargo was put on that particular flight because of the big machine's weight and size. The dull red bulk was placed in majestic isolation in the center of the cargo deck and lashed into place by an enormous web of chains secured to many tie-down rings.

The sight of it brought to the mind of one of the officers present the comment of a Mississippi loadmaster during the catch-as-catch-can days of the Korea-Japan airlift when he was sharply criticized for the sloppy tie-down of a heavy load: "Why, they's so much rope there," he protested, "the tangles'd hold it."

Nonchalantly mentoring the huge and wayward generator was a giant of a loadmaster named Robert Williams who, in earphones and a blanket, cat-napped during most of the trip with one eye ever fixed sleepily on the lashings he was responsible for.

Accompanying Colonel Jacob Bigham and the rest of the crew were three officers: Major Roger D. Lowe, the MATS information officer at Hickam, a colonel from the Inspector General's office in Washington, who were both fliers, an Army courier lieutenant, plus the author. They made do with the bucket seats except when

GENERATOR
EN ROUTE HONOLULU TO WAKE TO JAPAN
AT 8,500 FT.

the two flying officers went up to spell the pilots now and then.

After some hours Colonel Bigham phoned down to the load-master as the plane cruised on at 8500 feet to say that the radar indicated turbulence ahead, and added, "Let me know instantly if that thing starts to shift."

The big man downstairs said "Roger"; with what presumably was a superradar sensitivity to air conditions, he had already checked and tightened his turnbuckles.

At the end of the leg from Hickam to Wake Island, ten hours and 2200 miles from the take-off, "Nosey" eased down smoothly on the six-thousand-foot concrete runway that skirts its way between the islet's outer rim, where it dips two thousand fathoms deep into the sea, and the blue-green iridescence of the encircled lagoon.

Wake Island, now an important link in trans-Pacific travel, has only recently shaken off the impact of its historic role in the Great Pacific War. It is an American possession in the middle of that

WAKE ISLAND

ocean, made up of three islands forming a U-shaped atoll around the lagoon into which there is only one narrow passage from the sea. At twenty degrees above the equator, its climate resembles southern Cuba, although the sun blasts down on the unshaded sand almost uninterruptedly.

The American Government took possession in 1899 and its jurisdiction was turned over to the Navy Department in 1934. They, in turn, granted Pan American Airways the right to establish a seaplane base on Peale, one of the atoll's three islands, as a stepping-stone for the new line that was to run from San Francisco to China. By mid-1941, when Japan's intentions began to seem ominous, a Naval force under Marine Corps Major James P. S. Devereux was put in charge of the island and as soon as a landing strip was laid down, a squadron of twelve Grumman F-4F Wildcats under Major Paul Putnam was sent out.

Four days after their arrival both Pearl Harbor and Wake were attacked—Wake by a softening-up raid, through which a China-bound Pan American clipper, turning back from Guam, was strafed, but managed to land at Wake and take as many civilians as it could carry on to Midway. Before the last of the twelve land-based American Grummans was destroyed in the air or on the ground, they had sunk eleven Japanese Naval ships, some of them transports loaded

WRECK OF JAPANESE SHIP ON WAKE IS.

with troops, and had shot down twenty-nine attacking Japanese planes. The garrison held out until December twenty-third and for twelve hours after the first enemy troops were landed.

The fate of the forlorn band of Japanese who occupied Wake after that was not a triumphant one, for they were under such attack by air and sea that supply ships could not get in, and many of them very nearly starved. Even now the hulk of the Japanese transport *Suwa Maru* lies impaled on a coral reef not far from the end of the runway, where she was torpedoed by an American submarine when she tried to land food supplies.

Today, Wake is a calm and lovely place, where the cooling trade winds come sighing in off the ocean every evening, and tiny wavelets riffle along the lagoon's shore just outside the door of the neat little tropical hotel run by Transocean Airlines. No point on the island rises more than twenty-one feet above sea level and twelve feet is more usual. The entire land area is less than three square miles, sprinkled with scrub trees rising around the remains of derelict Japanese installations. Below the surface there are solid concrete shelters, and two great, long-range cannon, believed to have been brought by the Japanese from Singapore, still look emptily out to sea.

To a Northerner, the tropical night sky of this pleasant spot is as startling as it is brilliant, with the lower edge of the Great Dipper resting on the horizon, its reflection sparkling in reverse in the waters of the lagoon.

The roughly five hundred permanent residents have bathing, tennis and some of the finest fishing on earth for recreation. They also find diversion in the steady stream of travelers who flow through the airport from Pan American's almost daily flights, as well as other international airlines, and the heavy military traffic. Besides the regular forces on duty there are airline personnel, Civil Aeronautics Authority employees who man the tower, Loran and homing beacon; U.S. Weather Bureau officials and Standard Oil men.

The Transocean Airline, whose installations are an important factor on the atoll, is a nonscheduled service which made a name for itself during the Korean War by providing eleven percent of the trans-Pacific airlift, as well as servicing military and contract carriers en route, feeding and housing the in-transit passengers and crews while they were on the island.

MATS does not keep maintenance men or repair depots on Wake. Any necessary overhaul work is done on contract by Transocean's mechanics, an arrangement that has proved thoroughly successful. The maintenance crew got a workout on the C-124 when "Nosey" taxied out at eight o'clock on the morning after her arrival, to resume her travels. Before she reached the take-off point the crew noticed her No. 3 engine was smoking badly and she was rolled back for repairs. A second start two and a half hours later showed up trouble in the hydraulic system.

"Gentlemen," said Colonel Bigham coldly, "we're going back to the barn again."

Eight hours and two thousand miles of cloud-blanketed ocean after the third and successful start, "Nosey" reached her goal and, figuratively speaking, the waiting arms of the Navy officers who had ordered the generator brought halfway around the world.

9

THE DELIVERY OF THE TWELVE-AND-ONE-half-ton generator by Colonel Bigham's C-124 at Tokyo International Airport was carried out by a routine that looked as simple as the grocery boy's entry through the back door with the vegetables. The handling of all Oriental-bound and outgoing MATS freight is by now typically well managed, and scale and weight have few horrors for the cargo men.

The cargo hangars stand a little to one side of the giant new airport's monolithic mass of stone and modern chromium, and its fine, long runways. Through these hangars pass countless tons of freight and mail moving to east and west.

Because of Japan's geographical position, Tokyo Airport is the focus of Far East traffic of all sorts, and necessarily all U.S. Air Force installations in the country are large. So is the list of personnel. But service in Japan is, far from being considered a hardship by the average service individual, a remarkably congenial experience. The Japanese people, who are going through one of the greatest social readjustments that have ever torn the traditional habits of any race apart, have such a warm eagerness, such a real appreciation of many things that came to them willy-nilly as a result of the war, that most Americans have found residence here both pleasant and rewarding. The exquisite Japanese Kabuki and other theaters in Tokyo, the grace and novelty of the native arts and lingering customs are of more than passing interest to many servicemen. And unlike some foreign bases, Tokyo is closely surrounded by beautiful recreation spots not noticeably damaged by the war. The docility of Japanese wives, so favorably advertised by innumerable astounded American men, has perhaps added something to the situation, too.

KYOTO

Unlike the compact arrangement of MATS installations at Hickam, those at Tokyo are scattered widely around and outside the city. The newcomer finds them first in the big cargo hangars and at the handling center in the Airport Terminal building where thousands of MATS transport passengers are attended to separately from civilian traffic.

The Command's chief administration headquarters are some distance from the airport and until 1956 were installed in a tall, modern building bristling with radio towers, pleasantly overlooking the park and the moat surrounding the Emperor's lovely old palace in the heart of Tokyo; the palace and its environs were spared from bombing during the war because of the Emperor's presence. After the capitulation, because of their importance to the build-up of postwar stabilities, various branches of the U.S. Air Force were housed in readily accessible buildings in the city—the famous Daiichi, the Meiji, the University Club and others. Here were the offices of the Far East Air Force (FEAF), Air Communications, directional departments of several MATS activities and the service Officers' Club.

Now, however, following a policy of returning as many as possible of Japan's office buildings to their former owners, some of these departments have been moved out of the center of Tokyo to less crowded areas. The flight squadrons work out of a number of satellite airports which were once wartime landing strips, rehabilitated since for heavy postwar traffic. They are used jointly by U.S. Fighter, Tactical and MATS outfits. Many of the Headquarters directional staffs, which until recently occupied the Meiji Building, now function from Tachikawa AFB.

All civilian and military traffic, through Peace Treaty agreements, was to be supervised by the Route Traffic Control Center at one of these fields, Johnson AFB (not to be confused with Johnston *Island*). It is reached by an hour-and-a-half drive through an endless tract of almost completely new suburbs on the bomb-devastated rim of the densely congested old city.

Control of air traffic over Japan is in the process of being shifted from the American military to Japanese administration in compliance with the agreement that American control was to continue

FUJIYAMA, JAPAN

until a Japanese civil aeronautics group was prepared to take over. Inasmuch as air-traffic control over Tokyo and its environs encompasses safeguarding the movements of such large fleets of aircraft, the transfer meant the development from scratch of a modern system and the training of sufficient personnel to manipulate it. U.S.-trained Japanese traffic-control men now work much of the supervision, and the change-over will be completely made as full staffs are brought to the necessary high level of experience and competence. In this sort of undertaking it should be remembered that a new generation of Japanese is gradually assuming responsibility for the country's enterprises, the continuity of experience in aviation having been largely broken by the postwar years in which progress almost came to a standstill.

The area controlled by traffic central at Johnson AFB extends eastward nearly to Wake Island at the 160th parallel, and southward through the Ryukyus and the Philippines. Except for the fact that it contains mountainous territory topped by Fujiyama, it somewhat resembles the New York air-control system, governing not one central airport in the heart of a city of millions, but a number of peripheral fields.

The Control Center directs aircraft en route and up to the actual

KYOTO

take-off and landing zone just beyond the runways, where the Tower at Tokyo International takes over and directs the planes' movements by the same method used at all well-run airports.

Although the animosities and conflicting interests of the war years have become for the most part vague, unhappy memories in the genuine effort made by all concerned to strengthen the realities of Japanese ties with the outer world, it is natural that the Japanese people should not forget husbands and brothers and sons who made great sacrifices and whose loss is a lasting sorrow. A memorial in the form of a "BAKU" bomb, to the men of the Kamikaze squadrons once based on this field, now stands in a small park in front of the Johnson Officers' Club; more than any other emotion, it evokes a recognition of the devotion of young men, many of them barely out of childhood, who gave themselves to a duty without hope of reward or personal salvation, for some a sacrifice they knew to be useless.

Operating out of Johnson AFB is a unit of the 1808th Airways and Communications Service, the 1st Airways and Communications Mobile Squadron, which we have already met trying itself out under the worst possible conditions during the Korean War.

This remarkable outfit, whose slogan, it will be recalled, is "First In—Last Out," is distinguished for one thing by being the only organization in MATS in which all men are permanently on continuous alert, no member ever getting more than six hours away from his base of operations. Even so brash a slogan gives little indication of the kind of duty the squadron is prepared to do at the drop of a hat—or oftener, the drop of one of the typhoons that are the bane of that blustery region.

It is the Mobile Squadron's responsibility to hurtle itself into the teeth of the trouble when a marauding enemy force or disaster has wiped out any existing military communications facilities, and to set up a new system—leaving the shortest possible gap in contact between headquarters and the trouble spot or planes flying to that spot. To do this they are always ready to move quickly with portable packaged equipment for providing temporary machinery to be used until permanent installations are again in action.

The Japanese Mobile Squadron has ready three such packaged

equipment units and between emergencies the company engineers spend much of their time correcting and improvising in order to reduce their matériel to the lightest and most compact form possible without sacrificing serviceability. No manned rocket to the moon can conceivably be sent off, they point out hopefully, till they get there and set up communications for landing instructions.

One of their critical tests came in 1955 when a vicious typhoon swept northward across the western Pacific and leveled to the ground military buildings and utilities on the island of Iwo Jima. The 1st Mobile Squadron at Johnson AFB packed into seven C-124's transmitting and receiving units, generators for power, a fully equipped airport tower, radio beacon, tents and a five-days' supply of rations, and took off. It landed on Iwo's barely usable runway a few hours later, and within twenty-four hours and fifteen minutes had a communications center in business. From that moment it was sending out weather reports and bringing in the badly needed relief planes.

The operational end of the Communications Wing in Japan is at Johnson AFB, its directional headquarters at Tachikawa. This center is one of the vital links of the global communications chain by which the Defense Department directs military movements and policy enactment throughout the Far East. Stemming from Andrews AFB in Washington, D.C., its orders are relayed through McClellan, following the same process as at Hickam. The Japanese station is linked with bases on Guam, Kwajalein, Midway, Iwo Jima, Johnston Island, Okinawa and the Philippines, as well as Travis.

One of its best customers in the MATS entourage is, of course, the omnipresent, omniactive Weather Wing.

WEATHER FLIGHTS

Headquarters of the 1st Weather Wing of Tokyo Weather Central is also now in Tachikawa. The organization directs all USAF weather stations in the Far East and Hawaii; its local squadron is the 56th, stationed at Yokota airfield.

The business of the 56th is to search out and record weather conditions in a wide circle around Japan, both for long-range scientific research and the day-by-day meteorological maps of air movement in the western Pacific for the practical use of all fliers.

The records sent in by the WB-50 weather planes are formulated into charts by the Tokyo Central bureau and promptly distributed to all craft, either civilian or military, converging on the Asian hemisphere.

The Research Department is working on long-range studies of characteristic Far East weather tendencies and habits. (Half a million punchcards containing research notes on the subject have been sent for study to home headquarters at Asheville, N.C.)

The daily reports are circulated through the communications system to craft already in the air or planning flight in areas which show any threatened change of weather.

The ornithological terms "Buzzard Delta" and "Buzzard Kilo" would not appear to have much to do with a plane flying around Alaska or Siam, but the findings of the local weather flights so named often furnish the key to the successful completion of air transits in such faraway spots. The names are code words for two

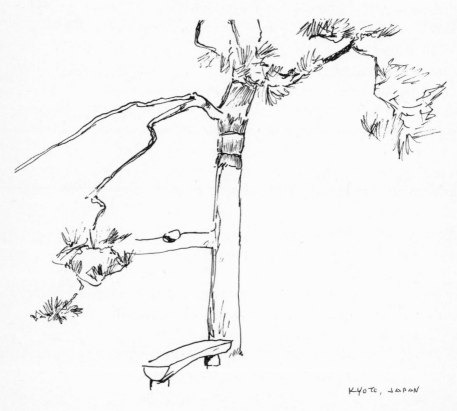

KYOTO, JAPAN

simultaneous missions performed by the 56th to collect information that goes into the daily weather charts.

"Buzzard Delta" is a triangular, 2600-mile overwater track, its first leg skirting the (now Russian-held) Kurile Islands. On daily flights over this leg, temperatures and wind readings are taken at the *lower* air levels. Then the ship climbs to the 500-millibar level, or about 18,000 feet, turns out into the Pacific and, at 100-mile intervals, drops an extraordinarily precise and accurate instrument called a Dropsonde to sample a vertical cross section of moving air masses.

In a timed drop the five-pound instrument descends by parachute to the sea surface and transmits back to the plane a coded record of the temperature, humidity and barometric pressures it encounters on its fifteen-minute downward plunge. Five such drops are made on the leg back to base.

These knowledgeable little servants are not recovered but by the time they touch the water they have completed the job for which they were created. The internal humidity detector of their mechanism is provided with a series of the finest human hairs obtainable, stretched tautly between ultradelicate registering devices, and Dropsonde experts say that only the previously unshorn locks of an auburn-haired girl will work. If so, the supply problem must be an interesting one because all seven of the MATS weather reconnaissance squadrons use a very large number of Dropsondes day after day, *ad infinitum*.

As the instrument is so delicate in structure and its scientific purpose so essential, delivery to the squadron's base is made in triple-sealed, shockproof cartons which are stored in air-conditioned rooms until the day before the Dropsondes are to be used. Even when they are treated with this extreme caution, to assure absolutely perfect functioning the calibration of the working parts of every instrument to be carried on a mission is double-tested by the Dropsonde operator one day preceding a scheduled run. Fifteen minutes before the instrument is to be released in flight, the operator places it in the drop chamber, attaches the parachute static line, closes the chamber and leaves the device in the belly of the plane to become adjusted to the outside temperature.

As the drop begins, the operator's attention is rigidly concentrated on making an accurate record of the radio code readings transmitted back.

"Buzzard Kilo," the second of the two operations, flown at the same hour, covers a tract southward across Korea and down the China Sea, gathering similar readings by identical methods.

These are the weather boys' routine jobs. Typhoon watching is a sort of superimposed exertion with its own regular danger-paced routine. Storms gathering in the Indian Ocean and other typhoon-breeding climates of the Orient produce early warning signals and with the first swirl of abnormal air movement, meteorological test readings are stepped up and widespread preparations begun. Roving planes and Air Force squadrons stationed along the winds' probable path are warned to get clear. Bases are told to batten down and, in addition to flights from Japan, Weather Reconnaissance planes at Guam and the Philippines fly out to sniff at the typhoon's track like mettlesome hound dogs.

Readings gathered from Dropsondes used in the "eye" and turbulence play a vital part in fixing, for charting purposes, the power and course of the storm.

A typhoon wind, whirling around a 1500-mile expanse at 150 miles an hour, drives masses of turbulent black cloud with immense violence into 30,000- to 35,000-foot towers circling around an ominously quiet funnel of clear air. Sunlight filters into the tunnel in eerie shafts as the dusky walls boil upward and spill down to be caught again by the lower forces of the wind.

In a storm called "Grace" the disarmingly calm eye hovered for nine hours over Okinawa while the outer winds lashed with dreadful destruction around it. But more characteristically a typhoon rages steadily along in a northeasterly direction, spinning from island to island while the weather planes pass to and fro through its funnel, relaying homeward a record of its progress and intensity.

Although routine weather watching is a well-ordered process, its methodical rounds are sometimes interrupted by unscheduled and alien events. Weather wing aircraft habitually fly over the less-frequented tracts of the ocean fringing the regular air lanes. When a plane is reported in trouble, therefore, or an SOS sets up a search, one or another of the weather craft is often closer to the disaster area than other ships, and is sometimes called in from its regular program to lend a hand. In the great searches, when every possible plane in an area is needed to comb many square miles of ocean, the weather watchers turn to with the rest.

The long-range surplus WB-50 Superfortresses, built during World War II and modernized and refitted for the job, perform so well that by late 1955 the 1st Weather Wing had run up the remarkable record of forty thousand hours of all-weather flying without a serious mishap. Five ships out on reconnaissance make up the daily average, and six more are added in typhoon-chasing times.

ATOMIC TESTS

No other MATS group has a greater responsibility than the weathermen who fly reconnaissance to help prepare for the great bursts of the thermonuclear tests in Bikini Lagoon at the Pacific Proving Grounds. The First Weather Wing, with three aerial reconnaissance squadrons—the 54th, 56th and 57th—in cooperation with the 55th Special Task Force Squadron, chart winds and atmospheric conditions over a very wide sector of that part of the world to determine the possible extent of a particular "fall-out."

They make the long and thorough air surveillance of the prescribed area by taking samplings by Dropsonde from sea level to more than forty thousand feet above the sea; this information, together with additional weather soundings from Australia, Hong Kong, Singapore and the Aleutians, governs the decision of the military officials responsible for the exploding of each test bomb.

Sentinels of the air, the weather fliers go their way largely unseen by most of us and, except in their own field, the value they give for their monthly pay is seldom fully acknowledged.

EXTRACURRICULAR WORK OF AACS

American airmen have been in the Far East in such numbers, often for years, at the very heart of every major event outside of politics, that it would have been all but impossible for them not to have developed a strong personal feeling, perhaps inarticulate but real, of closeness toward both the Orient and its people.

It is a peculiar characteristic of many Americans that they carry with them wherever they go, and on whatever errand, a need to set something or other right which they feel is not as it should be according to basic American precepts—those with a strong strain of Puritan upbringing having it worst.

The American Air Forces in Japan and Korea—like many other U.S. soldiers—have found plenty of things to get into and mend during and since the two wars. And stirring this latent predisposition is an absolutely overwhelming need to make up for the lack of family life on the part of men who are separated from their own young children and homes.

The military has done what it could to supply diversion for its members in Asia. There are excellent libraries at all of the main bases, and for individuals who have been prevented from getting ahead with their education, college courses are made available and a good many take advantage of them.

SEOUL

But the "off-base" limitations set up by the Army to prevent difficulties stimulated by the less controllable elements which exist in any army, together with language and cultural differences, tend to increase in some of the youngsters stationed abroad for a long time a desire for fuller emotional outlets and the human touch.

These are not the soldiers who, when you ask them how long, out of their prescribed 365-day term of overseas service, they have been on duty in Asia, will tell you the exact number of months, days and hours yet to go. In Korea they are the ones who see the people not as alien souls with whom one can barely exchange the simplest ideas, but as a people torn and divided, living in a dreary country in poverty so profound that hope seems an illusion.

The MATSmen stationed in Korea find little warmth in their own military installations since, for reasons of practical policy, they are crude and uncomfortable, lacking amenities found in most other bases. The Korean climate is incredibly harsh at most times of the year, the roads bad and transportation scarce. The dramatically beautiful mountains are too vivid still with the bitter memories of war, and many of the towns and villages, once also beautiful, are shattered.

It is the children who, to a great many Air Force men, present the most heartbreaking appeal. The thousands of orphans who roam the streets in feral ugliness and filth, hopelessly cast in a mold of deceit and ignorance from which they will never be saved if it isn't done quickly, offend every humane instinct. In the struggle to survive at all, Korea has found place for very few of them in its reconstruction plans.

Their plight has stirred numerous Americans to help as many as they can, and among the Americans who have worked to do this are the men of the 1818th Airways and Air Communications Service Group stationed at a base about thirty-five miles south of Seoul. This galaxy of airmen represents one of the best examples of men who make an effort to overcome an intolerable condition which is almost, though not entirely, beyond control.

WAR ORPHAN

Just before Christmas in 1950, some of the members of the 1818th discovered a crowded orphanage in Seoul in desperate need of help in order to keep functioning, and they more or less took the institution over for the holiday season. Clothing, shoes, blankets and food were moved in through the usual army legerdemain. And the children got their first glimpse of the wonder of a glittering and laden Christmas tree.

This satisfactory beginning was only a warm-up for a thorough investigation of what else could be done. Korean babies, like all little Asians, have an almost unbearable appeal with their bright, observant, sober black eyes. The acceptance of what was for these

children a singular experience in the aspect of love which the men
had given them, and the unexpected smiles of pleasure bound the
1818th to them with iron bands. Following the lead of former
AACS men who had fostered the "Fathers-for-a-Day" movement
in the States, the 1818th Headquarters group decided to found an
orphanage of their own and invited all other AACS personnel to
join in a "Fathers-for-a-Year" project. They decided to finance an
orphanage for as many Korean children as possible, and collected
eight thousand dollars for it in the first seven months.

It was not easy to find a house. Seoul was so badly smashed up
and so little restored that there were almost no houses available on
any terms, but a group of three suitable buildings was at last secured.
The buildings had been the home of a Japanese in the prewar
period of Japanese Occupation, and were surrounded by a wall
which protected an ample play yard. Situated on a steep, narrow,
hillside street not far from schools and downtown Seoul, they were
ideal except for their decrepit condition. They had been occupied
by, and then shelled by, the Communists, and the water, sewerage
and electrical systems were shot.

This was not daunting in itself. Radiomen and other trained
specialists tackled the job. By March
the buildings were livable and all
utilities functioning.

KOREA

To help the project along on a
sound basis, the 1818th enlisted the
advice of Dr. Helen Kim, President
of the Ewah Women's University at
Seoul, and an untiring worker for the
country's restoration. Two experienced social workers, a nurse and
cook, were engaged through her to
care for the children.

Dr. Kim's ideas about the suitable upbringing of the little strays
were entirely congenial to those of
the men of the 1818th. Both believed
in the importance of sustaining the

children's faith in their own ancient and noble culture. "These children," she said, "have a long and honored Korean inheritance. They must be brought up as Koreans," and the sponsors heartily agreed.

In the middle of March, 1952, fourteen children, between four and eight years old, were brought together into the protection of the rehabilitated houses. They came from an overpopulated orphanage, and the experiences of all had been sordid—of some, horrifying. All were undernourished, ragged, and generally afflicted by war injuries and the diseases of neglect.

Insecurity had terrified them and none spoke—to one another, to the attendants and least of all to the strange American men. They sat or struggled to their feet when told what to do, without a flicker of expression.

The children were given a hot Korean meal and when they were warm and fed, each soldier took a child in hand and scrubbed, soothed and got his charge into clean, warm clothes.

The flow of trust between the men and the children began soon after that. As the children began to thrive, they looked on these new uncles as a miracle in a life which they had learned through helplessness to take for granted—at least a miracle that brought a rewarding answer to yearnings too deep to understand.

As individual airmen were rotated out of the base, others took their places and responsibility for the orphanage has gone on. Title to the property now lies with the Ewah Women's University, under the aegis of Dr. Kim. Earlier, when the buildings were presented to the government they were promptly resold and the 1818th had to raise money hastily to buy them back again. Since that time Dr. Kim has signed a formal agreement to take over the active management if and when the MATSmen are withdrawn from the country.

"Some of the children," she says, "haven't the capacity to go far with formal education, but we'll see that, they learn a useful trade, so that they can take care of themselves."

Though most of the 48 children attend nearby schools, Ewah College sends student teachers to the orphanage to help with the nursery-school group.

SEOUL
KOREA

The visits of the airmen are still the highlight of events. When Major Howard W. Jones shows up at the door with an armful of clothing and toys, he is immediately overrun by the little ones. Major Jones goes through a list of important matters with the resident director.

"Sweaters?" he may ask.

He is shown sweaters that the teachers have knitted. But this or that child could do with a new one. A soldier will soon be over with the required number.

"Dolls?" Major Jones shakes his head; that means writing to the States. It will take time; however, they'll come.

When the major gets ready to leave, the children begin to squirm with nervous excitement.

"They have been rehearsing a song for you," the nurse explains.

The five- and six-year-old stars line up and bow and then burst out full-throated, shaved heads tossed back, and little new teeth just peeping through the gums are exposed as the folk song rolls out.

Some of the littlest girls hurl themselves into the ritual of putting on the shoes that the visitors have shed outside the door when they arrived, in compliance with custom in Korean houses. It is something they can do themselves for their uncles.

On the twenty-five-mile drive back to Kimpo Airfield Major Jones speaks of the satisfaction he found in the orphanage. "I've got a kid of my own at home," he says.

The story of the AACS orphanage is well known around the Far East, and voluntary offerings keep ahead of regular expenses.

The children's answer to all this is, *"Domo, ahli gado, honto desu."* . . . *"Thank you very much, for sure,"* and a smile.

KOREA

36TH AIR-RESCUE SQUADRON
JAPAN

The method of air-rescue work doesn't differ much from one MATS arena to another, but the

geography of each place presents the various units with a decidedly
diverse brand of experience in pursuit of their calling.

Water probably figures as the major hostile force but around
the Tokyo area, Mt. Fuji's nineteen-thousand-foot peak rising high
above exquisitely beautiful mountains supplies some formidable
hazards. Mt. Fuji, stubbornly retaining its historic, mystic domina-
tion of its surroundings, spends most of its time well hidden behind
thick layers of fog and sometimes clouds of snow.

On March 5, 1956, snow and a gale whipping around it blan-
keted the slopes. A pilot and his copilot from Tachikawa AFB, in a
C-47, crashed into the mountainside at the eleven-thousand-foot
level and wrecked their plane, though they were not too hurt to
walk. They started laboriously up the slopes to the nearest shelter,
a weather station on the top.

A short time later they were sighted by a passing jet, and a 36th
ARS plane with two para-rescuemen aboard hurried to the scene
and dropped warm clothing and medicine kits, which the gale
promptly whisked into oblivion. After the two victims had managed to climb to the weather station, the para-rescuers themselves
made a successful drop at a base near the foot of the mountain and,

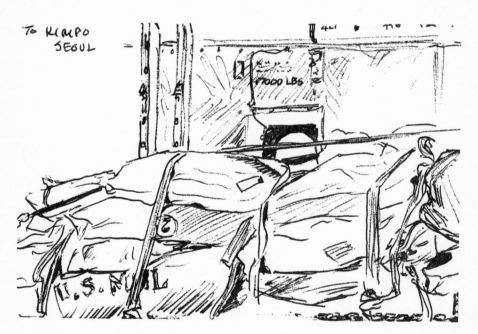

supplied with climbing paraphernalia, scaled the mountain and brought the exhausted pilots down.

It is a little difficult to discuss objectively the paramedics and para-rescuemen of MATS. For one thing, their spruceness is such as to draw the eye of the least impressionable. Their uniforms are distinctive, designed for practicability, and no one has ever seen one of them mussed up—presumably they remain neat whether working in the desert in a temperature of 125 degrees or climbing out of a twelve-foot trough beaten up by a typhoon. With all this, they have had time to learn a great deal about parachuting and first aid of a very high order and are first-rate medical attendants in any sort of calamity. Their courage is as svelte as their looks. One of them jumped into the Arctic Ocean a few months ago, to hold up a drowning airman, knowing that the odds were against the chance that either of them would be picked up in time. (The odds were wrong, thanks to the determination of others; both were saved to thaw out in hospital.)

The 22nd Crash Rescue Boat Flight is a slightly off-beat element of Tokyo MATS in that, though airmen, they have nothing to do with flying except to fish other airmen out of the bay area surrounding Tokyo when by some untoward chance they fall into it. The crash-boat crews are on twenty-four-hour alert, and primarily devote themselves to protecting all, of whatever nationality, who fly in and out of the terminal airport.

It is perhaps not precisely accurate to say the 22nd has nothing to do with planes, because their light crash boats are driven by an airplane engine and air propeller mounted on the stern, which send the unorthodox "swamp buggies" racing around Tokyo Bay at thirty-five to forty miles an hour. The boats ride so high, drawing little water, that the boys say all they need to coast on is a good heavy dew. Besides shooting out to planes which ditch close to shore, they spend their time rescuing overturned small boats in the bay and bringing back swimmers who have overestimated their endurance. The appearance of the smart small craft and a larger conventional twenty-four-foot boat suggests, however, that the 22nd also spends some little time in polishing brass and using that time-honored Navy pestilence, the well-loaded paintbrush.

10

L EAVING TOKYO BEHIND ON THE PACIFIC quadrant, MATS routes lead to the next big Air Force Base, Clark Field, near Manila in the Philippines.

Between Tokyo and Clark there are two islands, Okinawa and Formosa, into which goes a certain amount of MATS freight and passenger traffic. Operations concerned with Formosa are too infrequent and untypical to be included in the over-all picture without pointing up their specific nature.

Formosa, about seven hours' flight below Japan, is a handsome, mountainous island which, although astride the Tropic of Cancer, cannot make up its mind whether it is tropical or only inclined to tropical vagaries of climate and herbage. Lying within sight of the Red China coast, its problems as the haven of the Chinese Nationalist Army are manifold and often close to insoluble. It is, moreover, a sovereign island, and while the American Defense Department maintains an understanding with its government, U.S. commitments do not call for a MATS installation there. MATS flights into Formosa are for the larger part diplomatic, or for the delivery of training personnel or matériel and, oftener than not, use contract transport flown by private companies, among them General Claire Chennault's Central Air Transport—CAT.

An example of one of these flights follows: The CAT plane leaves from the *civilian* loading gate at the Tokyo International Airport, whereas Air Force planes use MATS departure facilities. The CAT plane is spotless and has regular commercial airline seats. The pilot, an American, wears a typical airline uniform and the stewardess is a slim young Chinese girl. Seats have been removed from the forward third of the cabin to make space for an extra cargo of mail, crates and packages.

The passengers this time are a dozen or more U.S. military personnel, and four or five Chinese civilians, probably lesser officials and couriers.

Having left Tokyo at midnight, it lands at Okinawa for refueling about five in the morning. There is a slight, sleepy shuffle of passengers leaving and new ones boarding. The stop is only forty-five minutes long, and the plane lands two hours later at Taipei, on the northern end of Formosa.

During the evacuation of the Tachen Islands, two hundred miles to the north, which was accomplished between the eleventh and seventeenth of February, 1955, extra MATS teams—air communications and air rescue—were sent in to Formosa on a temporary basis to ensure the safety of the operations. Inasmuch as the USAF had despatched, for precautionary air cover, a Wing of F-86 Sabre jets, there was the ever-present possibility of some kind of water disaster to the jets or evacuation ships. Clark Air Rescue at Manila was asked to provide protection and, since it could not spare its stand-by crews for long at a time, the crews rotated, returning home for duty after a week's stay.

The ARS crew were based at Tainan toward the southern end of the island and enjoyed the assignment, in spite of fairly crude living conditions, no special facilities being handy. Between flights they built themselves a clubhouse of native bamboo. Around this extended the gray tile roofs of the Formosan farmers' villages, spreading rice paddies and patient, yoked water-buffalo plodding their way through what, for all the buffalo knew, was still one of the earlier medieval centuries. The airmen, to remind themselves perhaps that the village mores were not necessarily their own, set up a tall pole alongside the club and mounted on it signs reading, "Top of the Mark, 7200½ miles" . . . "Stork Club, 9498 miles" . . . "Teahouse of the August Moon . . ." and various others.

TAI PEI, FORMOSA

There was no great excitement about the rather routine intercepts which the

CLAYTON
KNIGHT TOWER AT
CLARK A.F.B.
PHILIPPINE

crews were called on to make but they were not devoid of a few minor shocks. Ground Control Approach had been set up to bring in the planes during filthy weather and was run by Chinese operators, not all of whom had won complete mastery of English. One pilot jotted down a typical landing-direction exhortation by one of these native GCA operators: "Li'l high . . . velly high . . . drop!—DROP!" . . . a burst of pure high-pitched Mandarin and, when the pilot had got himself under control and his plane back on the glidepath, a final, loud, triumphant "ROGER!"

While MATS' ties with Formosa are not routine, with Okinawa they are eminently orthodox and a part of the over-all defense plan. Air Force occupation of a considerable tract on Okinawa is an important project, but little of it is actually under MATS control; compared to the installations at Tokyo and Hickam, the MATS Okinawa offices are infinitesimal. There is of course a communications unit, a subsidiary weather station and a full complement of rescue planes, the 36th ARS, having all resources needed for the usual wideranging rescue action.

Air communications and rescue squadrons are posted here, the former because MATS needs a sound communications setup at such an important defense outpost, and as a link in the global system, and the latter because the island is a strategic arena of operations in the direct long overwater haul between Japan and Indochina. The seas around the Ryukyus and Japan and Formosa are busy ones; surface ships ply thickly between the northwest Pacific and the spice islands, and in that bed of winds, shipping accidents are a recognized hazard in the kind of life that is closely bound with the riches and habits of the sea.

In the late evening of a day in September, 1955, a Dutch freighter, the *Shouten,* sent out a call for help for her captain, Jan Janker, who was desperately ill. The call came in to the 33rd ARS Control Center stationed at Naha, Okinawa. An ex-army nurse, a passenger on the freighter, radioed that in her opinion the captain would die if he didn't get help immediately. It would have been impossible to land a plane on the water near the ship in the darkness but, with the first streak of light, an Albatross SA-16 took off and intercepted the freighter, then 160 miles at sea. The captain was picked up and flown to Mercy Hospital on Okinawa, where he could receive excellent care. This rescue was attributable to biological rather than meteorological conditions, but the life saved was chalked up just as significantly as though it had been that of a MATS officer.

Most of the 33rd's rescues in this zone, however, are in support of its own. The value of intercept in doubtful situations plays the same important part in its work as in every rescue effort. A twin-engined Flying Boxcar—a C-119—was on its way from Guam to Okinawa one day, under the command of Colonel C. A. Stark, when one engine suddenly quit and the other set up ominous sounds of complaint. Colonel Stark was still 260 nautical miles from land and at once reported that he was losing altitude. When he got down to three thousand feet he radioed he would begin to bail out his passengers and ditch the craft.

The 33rd's Air Rescue scrambled a plane in seven minutes and the mission commander also dispatched a sixty-foot crash boat to the Boxcar's path and asked both a British and an American Naval vessel to divert their courses to the scene. A Navy helicopter was asked to stand by for pick-up if the ditching was made within the 'copter's sixty-mile off-shore range. Sixteen minutes after the first call came in, a second, stand-by SA-16 went off and, inside of an hour, a third.

The second Albatross to leave base was first to locate the Boxcar in the clouds and guided it to open weather, where the other two Albatrosses swung into escort position.

The sight of all this equipment had a strong effect either on Colonel Stark or on his rebellious surviving engine, for the plane staggered on as far as Kadena Airport on Okinawa, where it made a safe landing with all passengers still comfortably dry inside.

THE PHILIPPINES

Clark AFB, which spreads its many homes and installations over a tropical valley about sixty air miles north of Manila, on Luzon, the largest of the Philippine Islands, is the last large base at the far side of the Pacific Division; the next one of comparable size,

Dhahran, the Saudi Arabian terminal, is in another sort of world. Both are important halts and working spots on MATS' round-the-world route—Clark, because of its strategic position as a jump-off point from which the Embassy flights thread their way over the Indo-Chinese, Hindu and Moslem countries.

The Philippine base is administered under unusually pleasant conditions, as foreign bases go, because of the wholeheartedly amiable relations existing between the Philippine and American governments and the real accord this makes possible between U.S. officials and those of an independent foreign country. The easy exchange and mutual respect enjoyed by American and Filipino officials make Clark Field an especially sought-after assignment for all Air Force ratings. The almost equatorial surroundings are hot but they are also lush and, now that the "HUK" guerilla troubles have been finished off, the Philippine Islands are a charming place to be.

Clark Field's structures are not of a squared-off glassy modern type; many of the buildings are old, or elderly, but they are built for the tropics and delightfully habitable. Set in a blaze of brilliant flowers, under palms and mammoth, spreading trees, with large playgrounds for the children, they probably offer a better chance to provide a homelike atmosphere than most military posts. And the

OFFICER'S LIVING QUARTERS — PHILIPPINES

Philippines are one of the few places left on earth where it is possible to employ excellent and happy household help; there have been Clark wives who did not want to go home. The chief handicap to domestic easiness here is overcrowding.

Life is made lively and natural by a lavishly stocked commissary and a Post Exchange that can supply every known article for contemporary living, by air-conditioned clubs, swimming pools, an excellent library, schools for the children, college courses provided by the University of the Philippines and churches of every denomination. And beyond the ordinary needs there is a leave-hotel at Baguio, four thousand feet up in the mountains a short distance off, for anyone who needs to get away for a time from the continuous lowland heat and humidity.

The land on which Clark Field stands is under lease from the Philippine Government and the arrangements with local people seem to be of a satisfactory character from all points of view. For one thing, Filipinos are employed in any number of different jobs, ranging in aptitude gradation from gardener to expert airways and air-communications radio operators. A Filipino expert is expert indeed and the participation of Filipinos in American Air Force work has produced excellent results and good feeling. Some of the Filipino assistants in responsible positions in MATS administrative of-

CLARK AFB
PHILIPPINES

fices have been there longer than any of the military personnel.

"Operation Native Son" brings Filipino builders, with their fine, knowing craftsmanship, into the construction work on the base, although a particular carpenter may not always fully grasp the real purpose of the work he is doing.

Mahogany is simply a good workable hardwood in that land of mahogany forests and is used for floors and anything else intended for long, hard use. One of the newer buildings at Clark is a windowless Airways Communications edifice to shelter sensitive electronic equipment similar to the Hickam installation. Air-conditioning machinery, plastic floors laid over mahogany and other complicated devices required nearly a year to construct and install, and one of the skilled carpenters who toiled with immense interest at the work observed all these miraculous innovations with the keenest delight. When the building was at last done he stood back to appraise his own handiwork. "Such a nice building," he commented sadly. "But why no windows? Nobody can see out!" A house is a house is a house, as any sensible person knows.

MATS' tenancy of the field is shared with regular Air Force jets and SAC's restless squadrons, which liven things up by appearing now and then. Things are also enlivened by a wide variety and number of ground-level transportation vehicles, since the distances

NEAR SUBIC BAY
PHILIPPINES

between flight lines, living quarters, shops, clubs and other establishments are great. Among the array of personal cars of every vintage, Italian Lambretta motor scooters are extremely popular, especially where the two-car family problem arises; they are a quick and uncumbersome means for the men to attend to duties, while the wives shop or round up little Willie at the swimming pool.

With its own predominantly military preoccupations, Clark Field is pretty much of an American island, its occupants not mixing very closely with the Spanish-speaking people deep in their own preoccupations. This is probably due to the fact that so large a base must have self-containing facilities for its huge population, which keep them well and happy but tend to discourage exploring around.

QUARTERS ON SANGLEY POINT, U.S.N. PHILIPPINES

The flying crews here are less restricted. Many of them visit the sister Naval air base at Sangley Point, a narrow strip of land jutting out into the harbor from Cavite and the outskirts of Manila. As they fly training courses the crewmen can look down on the rusting and deserted installations of Corregidor and the scene of the great naval battles of Subic Bay. The Lingayen Gulf waters lap peacefully nowadays on the Hundred Islands basking under the

blazing sun and the sound of Naval guns and tumult of landing
parties have given way to the slapping of waves against the sides of
the fishermen's outrigger *bancas* drawn up on the edge of the slum-
bering sands.

Rumors of HUK's still hiding among the upthrust mountains are
largely small talk for leisure hours, but the memory of their raids is
very much alive. There is a mountain which rises from the floor of
the valley on the far side of the runways and, though it must once
have had a name of its own, it is now referred to only by the one
it has earned—HUK Mountain.

The subject of venomous snakes is one whose fascination is always fresh, as it is apt to be at that latitude. One Clark story is that,
on account of the crowded conditions on the base, a newly arrived

CAVITE
PHILIPPINES

airman and his wife decided to live in a small, picturesque but shabby native village hard by. One night the young wife reached out to push back a belt she thought was falling off a chair and stopped her hand just out of reach of a hooded head that reared up suddenly. A loud scream, an awakened husband, the bang of a gun, a dead cobra and a move back next day to any little old house on Clark Field where snakes are discouraged, followed quickly.

The Philippine Islands are vividly fascinating, even beyond the intensely moving drama of their history of Spanish-galleon invasions, American reconstructions and the Japanese devastation that was ended by battles so heroic that they left behind a trail of ineradicable glory. Humid mountain gorges dripping with wild begonias; jungle-clothed hills in which charming, if primitive, tile-roofed villages squat; the slim, handsome people; women drifting like butterflies through sunny, palm-shaded avenues; rebuilt public buildings glittering and up to date; streets seething with chromium-festooned jeeps refashioned into groaning buses; business redolent of all the industries of the earth, make up the physical scene beyond the base. And skirting Luzon are the outlying islands in a sea theatrical and ever-changing under the impact of boisterous winds that stir up a cauldron of weather rarely matched elsewhere.

Along the eastern shores it is an immensely deep sea—34,400 feet, the greatest known depth of any ocean—and since it is the realm of a big fishing industry, its currents and winds are wont to bring on calamities.

The Clark Rescue Squadron is kept very busy, accordingly, not only with day-by-day disasters, but also with watchdog duty on a good many long overwater air routes.

The 31st ARS, which is adept in handling its craft in the most violent of weather changes, is poised at the end of the flight line at Clark AFB, its operations closely dovetailing with sister services on Okinawa and Guam.

Especially during the seasonal monsoons, shipwrecks among the islands require the attention of every possible rescue force. The Philippine Government, the U.S. Navy and the 31st ARS are on constant alert, but even then the diabolic forces of nature cannot always be successfully fought.

A rescue attempt to save the crew of a freighter failed in November, 1955, when a lumber boat of the Madrigal Shipping Company went aground in a storm near the mouth of the raging Cagayan River at the northern end of Luzon. After the cargo had been jettisoned, the swift current carried the listing hulk into deep water; and though the crew leaped overboard before she sank and some managed to climb onto floating timbers, they were lost to sight in the churning brown tidal race.

The 31st sent three planes to the scene and the Philippine Air Force sent three C-47's, in relays. A Philippine Naval gunboat went in to scan the boiling surface and a long watch was kept. Nine of the sailors were washed ashore on their timber floats, but not one had been detected in the muddy waves by the searchers and nothing was ever known of the fate of the rest of the crew.

In the line of rescues the 31st's pickup of passengers from a Cathay airliner, when it was shot down by Chinese Communist fighter planes in 1954, was the 31st's most horrendous and outstanding experience; fortunately actual hostile attacks on airliners at sea are rare enough to spare some of the dreadfulness undergone by the crew and passengers on that hapless ship. Less harrowing was the shepherding of a Pan American Clipper unharmed into port when it required intercept because of the feathering of two of its four propellers while it was yet a good distance out over the water.

"Mission accomplished" is the proud *finis* of every successful rescue report. Now and again, it is written sadly but with a genuine sense of having won a personal victory over circumstances.

Another kind of search conducted by rescue teams is heroic, civilized and ineffably tragic. It is the search for a plane that is believed to have left no survivors after crashing. Until the disaster site is reached it must be assumed that some of the crew may be alive and suffering for lack of help, so that even though the chance of saving anyone may in some conditions seem remote, every ounce of effort must be put into finding the wreck at any cost to the rescuers.

On the morning of the sixth of March, in 1955, an Air Force

plane, a C-54 that plied transport missions regularly in the south-west Pacific orbit, left Kadena Airport on Okinawa to fly a new en-gine to a disabled MATS plane in Hong Kong. Its course lay across the southernmost tip of Formosa. About ten o'clock the Joint Opera-tions Center * at the Chinese airport at Taipei received a regulation radio report from the plane's captain and about 10:45 the captain again reported, this time through a Chinese radio check point which he identified as Heng-chun, well down at the southern tip of the island. That was the last time he was heard from.

When no radio signal was received after the 10:45 call, the plane, which had been due to arrive at Hong Kong about one o'clock, was reported missing by Joint Operations at Taipei and a review of all contingencies was begun.

It was discovered immediately that the station at Heng-chun was not operating at the time the C-54 radioman believed himself to be in contact with it, but that a beacon at Taitung, sixty miles north of Heng-chun on the east coast, was, and there was a separa-tion of only twenty megacycles between the call signals of the two stations. The deduction made was that the C-54 was in error when it reported itself over *Heng*-chun. The sinister implication was that if it was on a course that passed over the *Tai*tung beacon instead, it was flying dangerously close to the high peaks of a mountain range called Minami-Daibu.

But that the plane was flying over that course was only con-jecture; it might equally well have gone down over the ocean any-where between Formosa and the Chinese mainland.

The "plane missing" report to Clark Rescue Control Center was relayed through the Sangley Naval Air Station near Manila about two in the afternoon, and meanwhile several British planes, which had learned that a craft was overdue in Hong Kong, had flown out over the China Sea to look for it in that vicinity.

On receipt of the message, the U.S. Navy also diverted ships on patrol in the Formosa Straits to the search.

But in some quarters the belief that the C-54 might have hit a

---

* Manned by both Chinese Nationalist and U.S. military officers.

mountain on Formosa persisted and at three o'clock the 33rd Air Rescue at Kadena sent off an SA-16 to assist in the Chinese search over the mountainous tract.

Another SA-16—"Dumbo Charlie," † 1002—was stationed on detached service at the Chinese Air Rescue Service at Chiayi, thirty-seven miles north of Tainan. After being recalled to that base from another mission, the "Dumbo Charlie" commander reported that he needed a replacement part before he could enter the search.*

During the night surface ships continued to reconnoiter but the British planes, after returning to Hong Kong, could not go out again because of bad weather.

While next morning the Navy ordered the water-scanning to go on, searching the course the missing plane would have followed if it had reached the open ocean, the feeling in the Clark Field 31st ARS briefing room was that the mountainous tip of the island was a more reasonable place to look. An all-out effort was ordered, every plane and crew of the squadron going out to cover both sectors.

"Dumbo Charlie" 1002 was repaired by dawn and took off from the base at Chiayi on what was the beginning of its long and useful part in the endeavor. Its first direction covered a specific sector of the search pattern with orders to examine particularly the "contours" of the mountains above eight thousand feet.

By now the Royal British Navy and Royal Air Force, the United States Navy and Chinese Air Rescue, as well as the American Rescue Squadrons, were engaged. But it was para-rescue technician Verl Linford, aboard "Dumbo Charlie" commanded by Captain Matthias, who spotted the wreckage of a large aircraft on the side of the 10,138-foot mountain Nan-Ta-Wu-Shan. Captain Jack Woodyard, flying as on-the-scene commander, came in to dive his plane close and affirmed that the wreckage was probably the lost C-54. There seemed to be no chance of survivors. The 31st and 33rd search planes returned to their bases—"Dumbo Charlie" and the para-rescue men to Chiayi.

----

† "Dumbo" was a wartime name for rescue craft and "Charlie" stood for "C."

* A new fuel-selector valve was flown up from Clark that night, arriving shortly after one in the morning.

The wreckage lay high on the peak's steep, craggy slopes banked in tall, rugged cypresses. The terrain made para-rescue drops impossibly dangerous, although the para-rescuemen were more than willing to try it, and at that altitude no helicopter could be kept properly under control, even if there had been any level space on which to land.

Arrangements were quickly made to send the para-rescue technicians on "Dumbo Charlie" as a ground party up the mountain and they were hurriedly cleared by the Joint Operations Center; the men themselves were so eager to start that half an hour from the time "Dumbo Charlie" had brought them down a C-47 had taken off with the men fully prepared and briefed. The technicians were commanded by Master Sergeant Verl Linford. Their plane landed at Taitung, as near the foot of Nan-Ta-Wu-Shan as they could get by air.

At Taitung the group picked up trucks to carry their kits, a body of thirty-six Nationalist Chinese soldiers for protection in the somewhat wild country, porters and an interpreter (who was accepted hastily, to the men's considerable regret later on). They started walking toward the mountain at five o'clock and climbed until three the next morning, having crossed one river fourteen times.

When they reached the village of Biero the interpreter said the party would have to wait there for supplies. It was an exasperating wait. "Dumbo Charlie" appeared overhead to drop water and rations, a D-1 kit and some Taiwan dollars. Captain Matthias reported down by radio that he would be back next day with more supplies and at ten the following morning he showed up with work uniforms, medical kits and more water, all of which were recovered safely.

The crash had occurred on the sixth; this was the ninth. The trip up was resumed and a stop made for lunch at another small village, the Chinese porters going on ahead to set up tents, which was lucky because that night rain fell heavily and after that the going was tougher.

"Dumbo Charlie" had made a drop of supplies at the crash site and the rescue party asked the pilot to bring cigarettes and gasoline for their Coleman stove. On the tenth, a reporter for a New York newspaper, who had started off energetically with the rescue team, now completely done in, gave up and turned back.

By this time Sergeant Linford had discovered that his interpreter was so much afraid of the Chinese porters that he repeated whatever the coolies told him to, and the result was that the porters took the party almost to the top of a ten-thousand-foot peak before Linford suspiciously took compass bearings and discovered that they were on the wrong slope. A full day was wasted climbing down that peak and up Nan-Ta-Wu-Shan.

That morning when "Dumbo Charlie" 1002 came over, reception was too poor to understand and as the water was all gone, Sergeant Linford ordered the porters to fill the cans at a waterfall. The porters then went on ahead to set up camp. The para-rescuemen and soldiers reached the camp shortly afterward, to discover that the water cans had not been filled and that no water was available.

That night it again rained, which at least provided drinking water. One of the para-rescuemen became ill, with indications of pneumonia, so that preparations had to be made to evacuate him as quickly as possible.

At six the next evening, after dreadful climbing conditions on the slippery trail, they reached the crash site and discovered that the C-54's entire crew of fourteen men had been killed instantly. As Captain Matthias again passed overhead word was relayed back to Chiayi that the C-54 was found, with no survivors.

A succession of planes from Chiayi and Clark gave all possible aid during the next two days, advising, bringing equipment for recovering the bodies of the crewmen and delivering supplies.

The rancorous feeling between the interpreter and the Chinese porters broke out over the subject of where the best place to cut a trail down the mountainside would be, as it was not considered possible to descend, burdened by the bodies, the way the party had come up. The squabble was settled by orders from the rescue squadron commander, flying overhead, and the work of preparing for departure began.

It was discovered at this time that most of the money had been stolen from the wallets of the dead men.

Captain Baker was now flying "Dumbo Charlie" and flew the usual support as the trek down began. At 10:30 A.M. on the thirteenth the porters took the bodies down and returned for the rescue party's gear. That night the rescuers slept at a little village in quarters provided by the local police, who also produced some food.

The men were passing through villages where Americans had never been seen and at one halt the visitors were treated to a welcoming ceremony which consisted of seating each one in a chair and tossing him vigorously into the air.

In the morning, after reaching the village of Ku Lu, when final arrangements had been completed for shipping the bodies to Manila with all due care and honors, the para-rescue team was picked up at the end of a truck trail by one of their own planes and flown back to base at Chiayi, where Sergeant Linford made his report.

Part of his statement read: ". . . I'm going to make sure I have a competent interpreter the next time. . . ." Another passage, ". . . tried to find out who took the money from the bodies. . . ." for the only money found was in wallets hidden under some of the victims.* The report continues: "Tremendous hazards were experienced by the men. . . . They lost an average of seventeen pounds. . . ."

The tragedy of the attack by Communist fighting planes on the civilian Cathay Pacific airliner flying peacefully from Singapore to Hong Kong occurred on July 23, 1954, near the Communist-held island of Hainan. Nine of the eighteen people on board were killed. Several died when the Communists' bullets riddled the plane without warning, others in the crash of the completely disabled craft in very rough water; one died stretched out in the 31st's SA-16 rescue plane on the way to the Hong Kong Hospital.

A regular SOS report was relayed to the 31st Rescue Squadron that morning, through the civilian Manila Rescue Control Center. The report said that a Cathay Lines' DC-4 passenger plane had reported an engine on fire at such and such a position and requested

---

* Formosan native coolies, such as the sixty-one who were hired for this job, were paid the local rate: thirty-three American cents a day.

help. Nothing was said about the shooting; no one knew that the plane had been *shot down* until the Rescue SA-16 reached the nine survivors and snaked them out from under the guns of the Communists on Hainan.

The liner, which was marked by its name and a three-and-one-half- by five-foot Union Jack painted on its side, was proceeding along its course, still four hundred miles from Hong Kong and just outside the twelve-mile off-shore limit which the Chinese Reds on the mainland claim as their own. One of the pilots looked out and saw a Chinese fighter plane closing in from above and behind. The Cathay's captain, Philip Blown, then saw another Red fighter coming in on the other side but had no time to move before the Red planes opened machine-gun fire, which set an engine blazing, ripped through the cabin and killed several of the occupants and crew. Captain Blown managed to order some of the people into life jackets but there was no question of bringing the plane down safely with the rudder controls and the instrument panel shot out. Water gushed into the hull as it struck, scattering the living and the dead among the heavy seas.

Nine managed to keep above water for an hour, when one of the pilots discovered that the box one of the women clung to was the container for a twenty-man rubber raft. Wrenched open, the raft was inflated and all were pulled aboard it. Some of the badly hurt occupants were shielded by a tarpaulin. So they drifted and they were safe only because the Communists apparently did not think it conceivable that anyone could have lived through their murderous machine-gun fire. There was one small survivor, a little six-year-old girl, whose two small brothers and father had been killed. The passengers had been: six Americans, five British and seven Chinese. One of the badly shot-up Americans was a representative of the American Defense Department, who was worried for fear of being given an anesthetic because he was carrying his instructions in his head and was fearful of anything that might loosen his tongue.

When the SOS call came in to Clark Field ARS, Captain Jack Woodyard was about to take off for a practice flight in an SA-16

Albatross with one of his copilots who wanted some refresher training on water take-offs. They were on First Alert, but intended to stay close to the base and were not off the ground when they were told to divert. The captain, on a hunch, ordered all his tanks filled and was away within twenty minutes, though the position of the DC-4 in trouble was not exactly known, as nothing had been said in the first report about the chance of ditching. The captain tried to compute how far the DC-4 would have flown toward Hong Kong on three engines, in order to intercept it as quickly as possible. At the most likely estimate, Woodyard was four hours away but he knew that British search planes would have gone out from Hong Kong, which was much closer than he was to the airliner's course—or ditching, if the DC-4's trouble had come to that.

Thirty-five minutes after Woodyard left Clark another SA-16 commanded by Captain Dale Baker took off and the two Albatrosses raced forward, keeping in communication, though intercepted radio messages from Hong Kong reported that nothing more had been heard from the damaged liner.

Forty minutes after Woodyard, in the first SA-16, had left Clark Field he heard a relayed message from Hong Kong stating that a British Sunderland flying boat had reported sighting a raft in the area in which the Cathay plane had in all likelihood gone down. Assuming that the British flying boat would pick up the people in the raft, the Albatrosses planned to search further for other survivors who might have been scattered in the heavy seas.

The liner's situation now seemed more serious but there was still no intimation that the plane had been disabled by gunfire.

Woodyard's navigator estimated the probable point of ditching and a short calculation showed that the raft on the water must be inside of the twelve-mile territorial limit claimed by the Red Chinese. Shortly afterward, word came to Clark from Hong Kong Government radio that no rescue planes were to fly anywhere near Hainan Island. Sometime later—at 12:30—Clark Field radioed its Albatrosses to stay outside of the limit.

Even before midday there were several planes in the search, including a Cathay Company PBY flying boat. They were all in radio communication and Woodyard asked one of the planes—a French craft from Tourane, Indochina—to give him the location of the raft and to drop a smoke flare near it.

The raft was four miles from Hainan Island and two and a half from another rugged little island, seaward of Hainan.

Woodyard let his SA-16 down toward the water near the survivors and saw that nothing but a ship like an Albatross with reversible propellers, could land in the large swell caused by a stiff crosscurrent and so he decided to try it.

A hasty survey had shown that as usual the lee side of the smaller island provided safer landing conditions than the open sea around the raft, and after making the most careful calculations, he set the plane down in the slightly more protected water and taxied out around the island. By maneuvering, the Albatross was brought in a position close to the raft so that a line could be passed to it quickly, and the desperate nine, including the little girl, were tenderly helped up to safety. Most of them were badly hurt, one Chinese girl too seriously to be lifted to a bunk, and she was made as easy as possible on the plane's floor.

It was then that the Cathay's Captain Brown explained that Communist planes had deliberately shot him down. "Watch out for yourself," he added. "There may be other fighters in the area."

Captain Woodyard now realized he'd better get away fast.

The SA-16, with its extra thousand pounds aboard, was helped to rise by Jato bottles, hastily jammed into position after a radio warning that more fighters had been seen in the air. The Albatross was airborne before it was discovered that the fighters were Americans. The nine Cathay passengers were flown to the nearest hospital at Hong Kong and when he got back to his own base at Clark Field Captain Woodyard learned officially about the Clark controller's warning not to go into the Communists' twelve-mile zone.

There is no real explanation for the deadly attack on a civilian liner quietly plodding its legitimate course from port to port over open seas. The Red pilots may have noted only the first three letters of CATHAY and thought it was a CAT Nationalist airliner, then, discovering their mistake, determined that "dead men tell no tales." There is one peculiar circumstance in connection with it which may or may not be significant. It became known later that William "Bill" Donovan, formerly head of the American wartime OSS and at the time the American Ambassador to Thailand, had expected to fly over this region on General Chennault's CAT Airline about that time. Whatever the purpose of the attack, the men of the 31st Squadron have very strong feelings on the subject.

An observation at this point might be made, since the names Cathay, Singapore, Chiayi, Taipei, Tourane, may seem strange and remote, and the rescue teams working there almost equally unfamiliar and far away. Americans are fabulously generous in contributing to lifesaving causes, especially those for which they have deep sympathy, but to most of us, taxes are altogether another matter. And yet to each tax-paying American the cost of supporting the rescue squadrons which are such a vital feature of MATS is probably no more than an average citizen's yearly donation to the Red Cross.

The 31st ARS and their collection of lifesaving craft are but a small segment of the activity along the Clark flight line; Tactical Air Command's jet fighters, SAC's visiting bombers, MATS' freighters and passenger craft, and local traffic keep the tower busy with their landings and take-offs, high-lighted by the arrivals and departures of the Navy-run Embassy Constellations.

Embassy flights moving through the Philippines, headed out for Asian countries where there are no MATS bases, are prepared for the journey by the 1506th Squadron under Colonel Clayton Doherty, much of whose business is the welfare of those flights. Since the diplomatic climate is touchy in several of the countries where the flights halt on schedule, it is necessary to prevent misunderstandings by having an unusual number of travel documents in absolute order. The 1506th, therefore, makes sure that all regulations pertaining to entry into those countries have been complied with and tries to ensure that there will be no embarrassment either in connection with the condition and handling of the planes or in the status of the passengers.

To avoid on-the-spot confusion, MATS has stationed extremely skilled and tactful official intermediaries at each stop for the express purpose of steering American nationals through the intricacies of the numerous newly made government decrees encountered en route. It is Colonel Doherty's responsibility to be sure that each plane and passenger leaving Clark Field for the 4500-mile passage through Vietnam, Thailand, India and Pakistan is properly prepared for *any* emergency that *could* occur.

Before the flight takes off from Clark, passports, visas and records of required immunization shots are scrutinized; visa regulations vary a good deal among these countries, religious affiliations barring their issuance in some cases. Every passenger is briefed on what otherwise might be perplexing requirements as to customs and health regulations. Since such regulations are often changed, all Embassy crews are interrogated in the "debriefing" routine on their return to Clark, and their comments, together with the weekly reports sent to Colonel Doherty by liaison officers stationed in those countries, keep the 1506th's information up to date.

Such adjustment is no novelty to Colonel Doherty. During the Pacific War he not only flew 394 combat missions himself through this part of the world, but supervised an air-cargo task force that supplied the British 14th Army in Burma with some of its needs.

Its documents and business cleared, the Embassy flight leaves

Clark Field for Dhahran every Friday and returns, to pass through the Philippines on its way home, on Wednesdays. Another, shorter run called the "Bangkok turnabout," is made by two types of planes—a Navy Constellation and a C-124 carrying cargo. Coming from Hickam, it also goes through Clark once a week, drops off its cargo and passengers at the Bangkok terminal and immediately flies back to Hawaii.

Although elaborate preparations are made, by having aboard extra parts and crewmen, to keep the longer flights on schedule without incident, a special unit is maintained by the 1506th Squadron to go off at a moment's notice to correct any serious breakdown in these services which may be beyond the capacity of the Navy crew on the ship. Like a country doctor, this unit packs its special kit into its special C-47 buggy the instant a call comes in, and is off for the stranded aircraft without fuss—a mission that requires the possession of innumerable crew documents kept up to date for immediate use. (This precaution is another in-case-of-war measure when such runs would be especially important in the global scheme.)

All these provisions are complicated and sometimes confused by political conditions and relationships. Many of the countries touched on are new, their governments only just trying out independent participation in the turbulent field of international relations, and their sovereignty is as precious as we felt our own in the eighteenth century. Beyond Manila lies, first of all, the short refueling stop at Saigon, and then Bangkok with its fantastic Wats and the jungles of Thailand.

11

THE EMBASSY FLIGHTS' DISTINCTION IS
that they are a Navy project, and when the Navy runs a thing its
partisanship is rarely much disguised. Naval *esprit de corps* is a
sort of Everest among such phenomena; translated into words by
an Embassy pilot it sounds like this: He points down to a continent
under him and says, "Here we fly like the Air Force . . . follow
rivers and railroads and get lost when their leads go into a tunnel."
(Quoted verbatim.)

In Navy eyes, overwater flying is its ordained province, the
training of nautical airmen is such that they feel themselves masters
of any kind of action related to the presence of a large body of
water. And like the Marines, what they *feel* they *project*. The end
result of this emotional attitude may be biased but it works out fine.

On taking off from Clark Field on an Embassy run there is a
sense of leaving a real-life background and heading for the more

nostalgically romantic atmosphere of Conrad and Kipling and Maugham, or perhaps among the younger passengers, of
Michener—at least of Ezio Pinza and
Mary Martin. The passengers help this illusion along. A group of young Vietnamese lads who are going home after a
seven months' training course as flight
mechanics at Sheppard Air Force Base
near Wichita Falls, Texas, are chattering
excitedly and their display of Texan tricks
and speech makes them seem infinitely,
delightfully and colorfully more South
Asian; not even a Texan would wear so

many ball-point pens, sun glasses, notebooks, cameras and other gear. The knowledge of having mastered the new techniques of their own age gives them a bubbling self-confidence and gaiety; being almost home lifts their spirits to a high pitch.

There is also an investigator named Stanley traveling to Rangoon to get information wanted by a U.S. senator tied down to some current problem in Japan. There are two brisk young women secretaries from an Asian department of the Army, who are making use of a short leave to see India. One member of the crew who is not on duty takes an appraising stroll down the aisle; it turns out he was once an "Our Gang" child actor in Hollywood but there is no childish pitifulness about this slim, balding, keen-eyed officer. The flight engineer also appears and curls a rude lip at the secretaries' admiration for Oriental scenery; the camera in his pocket belies his own blasé air.

SAIGON

The Vietnam halt is no more than a fuel stop. This is the only MATS flight, except that to Rio de Janeiro, which comes so near the equator and the heat beats up as the Constellation swings down into Saigon. Palms and lush, tropical hills rush up and rice paddies and the white glitter of the city swirl in the landing pattern and settle into perspective. The Vietnamese lads from Texas have prepared themselves and tension rises. The youngest, Nguyeň Chăn Giám, pulls on his newly acquired fur-collared Air Force flight jacket in such a way as to expose to the full his battery of pocket equipment. Noses pressed to the windows, the youngsters identify relatives straining at the customs barrier, and not many minutes later are wrapped in waiting arms.

Tropical vegetation and sun-baked buildings border the field and the humid heat increases as the passengers file past a slender, straw-helmeted, Vietnamese peasant girl languidly at work edging the lawn. They go quickly into the restaurant for croissants and *café au lait,* for which there is barely time while the plane is being refueled. This is gastronomically a French restaurant and the atmosphere is Eurasian. A fresh horde streams in from an Air France liner that has just landed. There is a babble of French, Vietnamese, Indo-Chinese, English and half a dozen other languages, for this is an air crossroads, as it has been a crossroads of civilizations for centuries.

Pressing through the hot mobs, Major Christiensen, the MATS liaison representative, gets his job over quickly, as he must—supervising the dispatch of incoming and outgoing diplomatic mail pouches, checking the refueling, assuming responsibility for the correct dispatching of cargo, watching over odd passengers or VIP's. In the unusual event that a spare part which the crew does not have on board is needed, he must quickly borrow, scrounge or otherwise find a replacement; in a rare emergency he has had such things made in a local machine shop. He receives and sends off six planes a week.

In the five-hundred-mile tract of jungle between Saigon and Bangkok covered by the flight, the crumbling brown turrets and serrated spires of the temple of Angkor Wat can be seen deep in the universal green, quietly surviving in their isolation the centuries that have passed them by.

BANGKOK
NOV. 25

BANGKOK

BANGKOK

Entering the Thai capital, the two young women secretaries are agape, as is anyone seeing Bangkok for the first time. Thailand is a fertile country, able to feed both body and soul and, despite centuries of invasion and war, to sustain a rich and complex culture which rises into ebullience here. The population of more than a million live in weathered wooden houses verging on a tremendous skein of canals, or *klongs*, that web out from both sides of the Chao Phraya River. Along the river the countless truncated tiered spires of temples, or wats, sparkle gold and multicolored in a glitter of semiprecious stones, bright broken pieces of crockery, enamel and ancient glazes. Like many old-world places, it is a city of mazes packed with humanity, but there the tone is one of endless good nature, though poverty is no less apparent than in other old-world states.

RIVER RAFT-HOME
BANGKOK

The canals are crowded with barges and slim, graceful canoes that loaf or skitter along in that part of the city's activities which are inseparable from the existence of the bankside people. Carrying lumpy cargoes of rice, vegetables and fish, coal, machinery and oddments of Oriental living, both ancient and new, the barge owners give loud outcry in pursuit of trade; they exchange gossip and noisy, gay sallies with their friends, with great gusts of laughter, and carry on domestic disputes with strident candor.

Tooth-brushing, laundry, bathing—of which the Thai are very fond—and such acts as children feel momentarily called on to perform, are some of the uses to which the waterways are put—casually, without a snap of the fingers for germs.

Paralleling and rivaling the life of the canals is that of the narrow streets. Speeding *samlors,* or bicycle-driven rickshaws, bicycles and cars contend with pedestrians for space. Crowds of predominantly Asian but polyglot strollers and tottering vendors bent under the weight of overfull baskets suspended from long shoulder-poles vie for right-of-way with the wheeled traffic, though the concept of a right-of-way is in itself a ridiculous assumption. The pale golden people are small and for the most part delicately beautiful and as brilliant as tropical birds. The king, especially from the time of the SEATO Bangkok Conference, decreed that all his subjects, even the little tots, must—at least in public—be fully clothed. Swinging signs of the Chinese shopkeepers banner the walls and open doors offer both beautiful wares and the headier and

BANGKOK

smellier objects of commerce. The Thai have always been fine weavers, colorists, woodcarvers and goldsmiths and the rich invention of their ancestors has not deserted them. Thailand is one of the few Asian countries that produces more rice and staples than it needs, and the effect is everywhere evident in a relaxed sense of well-being among the population in general, if not always in particular.

The lighter touch also appears in the love of theatricals and

BANGKOK.

especially the tiny dancing girls who have been trained from child-hood to enact, in pantomime, and with the grace of flowers in a light spring breeze, stories drawn from Sanskrit poetry. It is a little disillusioning nowadays to see a troop of them after a show, reduced to slacks, sport shirts and head bandanas, climbing into a jeep to go on to their next performance, but such things are managed today much as dancing troupes are handled in the commercial West.

One rather surprising kind of entertainment in this hothouse heat is ice-skating, for which the Siamese have recently developed a craze. Conceivably *because* of the climate, the stadium with im-ported refrigerating machinery that has been put up in the center of the city for ice-skating shows is one of the most popular places in Bangkok. And, while the skaters describe their Spencerian spirals and whorls in the rink, the heavily arabesqued golden barges of the king and queen float in stately royal procession down the river, and candles and incense in small leaf cups are set a-sail on the *klongs* in the centuries-old *Loy Krathong* ritual.

Although Thailand has no permanent U.S. military installations, an officer who is diplomat, engineer and administrator, with a large knowledge of flying techniques, is stationed here, as at the other MATS stopover points, to keep the transports going at efficient and economical speed and capacity. He has an assistant, an airman who is assigned to the job, is rotatable and often rotated. Besides this aide he has a native secretary; in 1955, Major R. C. Shaw, a long-time MATS pilot who was seldom surprised by anything that could hap-

pen to either himself or his job, had in his employ a Thai young lady of a fam-ily which in earlier times would have thought itself unbearably shamed by having in its ranks a female office worker. She is an excellent secretary.

The plane arrives around 11:00 A.M. at Don Muang Airport, Bangkok. The major has already made arrangements for housing any traveling MATS officers and other priority passengers at the Princess Hotel in the city, about fifteen miles from the airport, and quickly gets busy arranging for the discharge and dispersal of cargo and for transportation. (Service people on leave make their own hotel arrangements and for them MATS has no other responsibility.)

An able and trustworthy Siamese who has managed the business of hauling both cargo and passengers for MATS for several years consults with the major and then directs passengers into a bus, and freight on its destined way. His dependability and resources make up to a large extent for the sort of frustrations that occur on any line when weather and unexpected delays make it necessary to deal with late arrivals and shipments that need special handling. In this practical pattern the Embassy flights are dispatched every week, and the Bangkok specials from Hickam are hurried along on their turn-around.

Apart from these rituals there is the hawklike supervision of travel papers, incoming and outgoing mail pouches. (He is also equipped with a good deal of extracurricular advice about the country's character—restaurants, jungle trips, and those spots which

provide the best settings for taking pictures.) In spite of occasional long waits for planes that are weather-bound, neither the administrator's nor the transient's life is dull. There is always good curry and the kaleidoscopic life of the Pacific southeast.

In contrast to the city's flowery noise and disorder, Don Muang Airport is modern in every practical way. It just seems a little odd to Westerners to see women as well as men laborers, toting gravel ballast in shallow wicker baskets, unhurriedly working on the extension of the airfield. Dutch, French, British, Australian, Indian, Indonesian, Scandinavian and Thailand airlines share the airport with the MATS planes which make the overnight halt.

MATS representatives in these stopover stations have no immediate superior to rely on for corroboration—a most unusual situation for a military man to find himself in—and no on-the-spot back-up facilities, and so must always be ready to improvise, cajole and drive, while he bears in mind the sensibilities of many, but most of all, the uninterrupted schedules along his part of the line.

PEDI-TAXI

BANGKO

INDIA

The art of flying an airline efficiently these days has been so refined that nothing is left undone to protect not only the passengers, but the surrounding world which is affected by the plane's approach. Accordingly, in order to safeguard against bringing harmful insect life from one country to another in the east, a plane is always sprayed with insecticide before landing. The Embassy flights from Thailand to India are so sprayed. But when the craft comes down at Calcutta for refueling, an Indian official comes in with spray gun and, before anyone disembarks, the interior, which is already reeking with fumes, is disinfected again.

This is part of the pattern of regulations set up by India to govern the procedures of foreign craft—including the military planes that pass through by agreement. The regulations at such a short stopover as Calcutta are time-consuming, especially since there is a certain amount of ritual in simply setting a big plane down and getting it off again. Another is that before alighting to stretch their legs all passengers must produce papers and fill out questionnaires as to where they have been for the last eighteen days, in order to make sure that none has unwittingly passed through some epidemic-infected area. Preliminaries completed, Calcutta becomes a matter of a fine curry lunch served by—to Western eyes—sultry-eyed waiters in scarlet turbans and sashes. The MATS resident representative, who is here largely in an in-case-of capacity, chaperones ship, crews and travelers.

The passage northwestward across India is an ascent into the realm of the great cold Himalayan range, which travels on the northern horizon, rising imperiously to the ice spire of Everest. Below, Benares, Jodhpur and Cawnpore drift flatly by and the pilot pampers the sight-seeing passengers with a quick sweep downward across Agra and the ivory-colored marble dome and slim minarets of the Taj Mahal, a stirring sight in the slanting sunlight. The secretaries say, "Ooo!" The flight engineer strolls through to say he likes Hollywood better. And the State Department men aboard take a quick look and go back to their briefcases. The pilot begins to review his maps and radio charts for the landing at New Delhi just ahead.

The arrangement between Indian and American officials as to the status of U.S. flights across the country is understood by themselves, but not very clearly by anyone else, except that almost everyone knows that no foreign military installations are allowed in India. But New Delhi is a great place for VIP's on big international missions, for protocol, weighty embassy pouches and incoming and outgoing air travelers on Far and Middle East business, and the representative here has a lot of rules to be complied with and duties to perform with a minimum of friction. The Embassy flight halts overnight, which gives the people aboard a look-in on this new-old world capital, and the crew a night's sleep.

Part of the crew spend the night on the plane as guards. Meanwhile landing and customs duties have been attended to. The sun has long since set and the evening is a little chilly. As the bus rolls toward the city through the dark of the Indian night, huddled erratic shapes are picked out by the car's lights—small knots of animals patiently prodded aside by lank, turbaned figures and wide-eyed children, obscure dwellings and big-wheeled lumbering vehicles. Everything tilts this way and that because the road is bad. The flight engineer suggests that Indian turbans ought to be wired like an electric blanket and lit up on these lampless roads at night.

New Delhi is an Oriental city designed by Victorian English architects infected by passions for many schools including Moorish. The robust Maidens Hotel, the stopping place most favored by MATS passengers, has a fine red plush and plump, pompous British look about it still, though its British owners have been replaced by Indians and the service has the splash and dignity brought by the Indian to almost everything he does. On a shopping tour the navigator—the ex-Our Gang child actor—pulls out the aircraft "dead reckoner" he always carries in his pocket and, to the admiration of his confused friends, computes the value of native rupees in American coinage in swiftly arrived-at mathematics.

PAKISTAN

There is a good deal of mail for the morning flight out of New Delhi and at Karachi, Pakistan. The flight has picked up, among others, a U.S. government courier and an embassy secretary returning to duty in Saudi Arabia after a conference in India. At Karachi an American Air Force sergeant who has been injured in an accident is brought out to the field by a British ambulance. This field—Manipur—was once the home station of RAF Squadrons who flew many important missions from here during the war. Now, handsome armed Pakistani military police patrol it with black suspicious eyes which crinkle pleasantly when the American military behave correctly.

The pilot of the Embassy ship which strums out over the Arabian Sea and the Gulf of Oman, Lieutenant Robert Klimetz, U.S.N., sits dreamily at his controls; he has seen these hot blue waters, the converging sands and black hills so many, many times. Every inch of land and sea between Hawaii and Saudi Arabia is as familiar to him as his own home town of Escanaba, Michigan—an intimacy that developed while he was running the acceptance tests of all the Super G Constellations, including this one, used by the two MATS Navy Squadrons as, one by one, the ships were delivered to the Air Force by the manufacturers.

koracui, pakistan

SAUDI ARABIA

The plane is bringing to the Dhahran post a movie film showing "Decameron Nights," but Lieutenant Klimetz hopes the passengers have no alcohol, knives, guns, girlie maga-

zines or figures of worship in their baggage, because if they have
there will be trouble with the Saudi Arabian authorities.

Dhahran is a focal junction in the Middle East. The Embassy
flights and Navy pre-eminence end here; Dhahran airfield's distinction ties in with wholly different matters. It is the place where
MATS' Pacific and Atlantic Divisions meet. The complex relationships of small and large countries, of aims and responsibilities among
civil and military authority are here tenuous, though the position
of the U.S. military in this part of the Arab world is of unquestioned
importance.

The dry, shimmering heat of the airstrip, as the plane from
Karachi lands, beats up from the concrete and down from the sky,
and customs men in flowing robes and a new kind of headdress
come to poke investigating fingers through the baggage.

MOSQUE ON AIR BASE - DHARAN - SAUDI ARABIA

A simplified run-through of the station's history is this: Dhahran is nowadays one of a sizable chain of large and small African and Mediterranean U.S. bases, brought to its present status by previous agreement between the U.S. State Department and the late King Abdul Aziz Ibn Saud, the majestic and towering absolute ruler of Saudi Arabia.

In 1933 Ibn Saud conceded the right, by a formal understanding with the Arabian American Oil Company (ARAMCO), to begin an exploratory search for oil. On finding the world's largest petroleum deposits, ARAMCO gradually built a modern city to house its employees, and between '33 and the present, the extent of the company's contract rights has expanded to cover an area of four hundred thousand square miles. The company now employs eight thousand U.S. citizens besides large numbers of the native population. It also helped the Arabian government build a railroad from the Persian Gulf seaport of Damman to Dhahran, where its holdings centered, and thence to Riyadh, the capital city—where before, only camel caravan routes existed. It also helped to locate and drill water wells, an absolute necessity in that parched, remote territory.

Early in World War II the present airfield was built, five miles from the ARAMCO community, primarily as a refueling station on that long, troublesome stretch between the Atlantic bases, Africa and the Far East. It is strategically so well located for flying the route to India that in recent years, after being expanded, the airstrip has become a regular stop for TWA, KLM, Middle East Airlines, and unscheduled runs, besides being the eastern terminus of the Royal Saudi Arabian line and ARAMCO's own supply line.

King Ibn Saud, who died in 1953, was not unaware of its value and

DHAHRAN

the vital protection it gave to his immense oil revenues from ARAMCO; and his son, the present King Saud, has continued his father's policies. The present king is undoubtedly a more modern-minded man than his father, whose character seemed at times almost to belong to Biblical eras in spite of his astute acceptance of the changing conditions of his own stormy day. But it is still too early to say how deeply current trends in political and economic thinking go in the younger man's mind. Traditional Moslem reserve screens him from appearing to have accepted outright the westernism that in many ways is slowly and inevitably penetrating the old desert he rules, and makes it doubly difficult to read his thoughts.

Running a military airline through countries not only torn by intense nationalistic fever but sometimes seeded by violent overt Communist hostility, and/or sub-rosa intrigue, requires a high degree of diplomatic surveillance—more than commercial international carriers have to put into parallel operations. The fact alone that MATS military uniforms and plane markings tend to offend the pride of nationals who are sensitive about their own military standing among independent countries is one of the most severe handicaps; American officers can move about in some of the Middle East countries only in civvies. American officers and men of Jewish faith are not permitted to enter some of these Moslem states.

The respect shown by the Americans resident in the host country of Saudi Arabia to individual Arabs is in point of fact real and actuated. Every effort has been made by the directing staffs to teach the permanent residents of the base to understand Arab customs and feelings. Brochures are distributed covering the Moslem religion and its beliefs, its prejudices and taboos; the country's history and all that Arabs have contributed to the world; the language, which those who are to be in Arabia for any length of time are urged to learn—at least enough for politeness' sake; and those innumerable small things that help people to live together agreeably.

In personal relations Americans are warned against addressing any Arab of any station in life in other than polite tones; since the Arab is habitually soft-voiced in ordinary conversation, a harsh utterance is thought to be intentionally insulting. Again, an inflex-

ible Arab rule is never to pass anything with
the left hand, which is considered a violation
of courtesy. Also, if one is invited into an Arab
house where there are no chairs, one never sits
with the soles of the feet pointed toward a
Moslem. Then, if offered tea or coffee, accept
one cup or three, but never two.

DHAHRAN
SAUDI ARABIA

No alcohol is allowed, even in the ARAM-
CO town, much less on the military post. Many
American magazines are banned. Some of the edicts and forms of
courtesy are comprehensible and some are not. The lease of the
base is a transitory one given by King Saud, and the base personnel
are therefore considered guests of the country and expected to ob-
serve the niceties of such a relationship.

Inasmuch as the Saudi Arabians shut themselves away from the
non-Moslem world for centuries, and only recently have been exposed to American ways on a large scale, it is remarkable that they
accept as well as they do the easygoing give-and-take of our
customs.

Many Arabians work closely with both the military and oil-
station personnel, and officers and men of the Saudi Army, under the
guidance of the Military Assistance Advisory Group (MAAG), take
courses in handling modern weapons from both the U.S. Army at
Taif and the Air Force at a station in Jidda. This work is an
excellent eliminator of cursory misunderstanding.

A great deal of the good feeling that exists is because of the
work of the officers who have a high degree of training, wisdom,
tact and finesse; Brigadier Generals O. L. Grover, Wentworth Goss
and George Schlatter are outstanding examples of the polished
officer at his best.

Quite a lot of uneasiness has been created in the past in these
sensitive Asian areas by the occasional visits of congressmen seeking
to inform themselves of conditions, who, although they are sometimes in no way equipped to understand either the specific problems dealt with by MATS' work there or the people they are examining, have not hesitated to offer tactless criticisms of both the
country and MATS' service. There is a time and a place for such

appraisal; the place is not a podium in the middle of a situation that is already difficult to handle wisely; nor the time one to be decided by any one man's convenience.

Saudi Arabia has two capitals: Mecca, the center of Islamic sovereignty to which only Moslems are admitted; and the old secular city of Riyadh where King Saud receives foreign diplomats and runs the practical side of the government. One of the difficulties foreigners have to deal with is that in Dhahran there are five different ways of computing time. One is Greenwich (for the military, Zebra) time; the next is local sun time; third, the Arab way of noting the hour by figuring it from the sunset call to worship which is Arab midnight; and fourth and fifth, the time the sun sets over a given place such as the king's palace at Riyadh *or* over another of his palaces on the far side of the city, both of which times will differ from the moment the sun sets over the airfield. The last is most important when an American has an appointment with the king or his counselors. (There is no such thing as an invitation to drop in for a cup of coffee at five o'clock. When *is* five o'clock?)

All these things can be learned, however, and in the close cooperation between the ruling and official Arabs and the U.S. State Department, American military and ARAMCO officialdom, imposing dinner parties play a big part. Some of the King's old Arab-style state dinners take on an opulence that for Western guests is tinged with a strong flavor of the *Arabian Nights.*

The Arab love of color as a foil to the brown-gray of his environment sets the palace scene in a blaze of red and gold. Down the middle of the room stretch long tables loaded with rich food, of which whole carcasses of lamb and mutton, pastries and fruit form a large part. At a central point beside the table sits the king, surrounded in medieval style by his crimson-robed king's guards, left hands on their swords and eyes *never for a moment* off the person of their ruler. His service is carried out by his own retainers. Other retainers stride up and down the tops of the tables, helping guests to food on the points of jeweled dirks. Since the Arabs do not remove their headdresses when dining, the American officers also keep on their uniform hats. The camaraderie which grew up between Arab leaders and the U.S. military in the past has been more formalized since the new king's accession, but the feeling is still moderately easy and companionable.

In contrast to the regal splendors of these Arabian ceremonies, MATS work goes along at the usual routine pace. Weather reports for the pilots here are supplemented by observations gathered along the course of the oil pipelines that run in a straight line over the sands from the pumping stations at Dhahran, across Jordan and Lebanon, to the Lebanese seaport of Sidon on the Mediterranean.

Occasionally there are reasons for MATS to use its planes for extracurricular missions, which are a tangible expression of the American good will that is essential to sound American-Arab relations.

The great "Hadji Baba" airlift of pilgrims to Mecca is the best known of these missions and the reason that it is the best known is because it was given oceans of world-wide publicity, which caused some few Moslems to shrug it off as propaganda. The fact was that the airlift was intrinsically a sound expression of the courteous American attitude toward their Moslem hosts in the Middle East— of respect for the deep needs of others, which is the basis of good international relations.

What happened was that a great gathering of Moslems, on their way as pilgrims to Mecca in Saudi Arabia from the Islamic countries between Turkey and the East Indies, had got as far as Beirut, Lebanon, and found themselves stranded. They had bought airplane tickets all the way to Jidda, the airstrip nearest the ancient city—which every Mohammedan * so aspires to visit that he makes tremendous sacrifices in order to do so—and the original arrangement had been for Middle East and other local airlines to fly the pilgrims from Beirut on the last 819-mile lap of their journey. But it was suddenly discovered that those airlines did not have available craft and thus many hundreds of pilgrims, their fares paid, were left helplessly stranded. The clamor that went up soon reached the ears of Harold Minor, the American Ambassador there, through Prime Minister Saab Salam, who was also president of one of the local airlines.

---

* Some Moslems, especially those in Lebanon, do not like to be called Mohammedans, Mohammed being considered but one of several revered Islamic figures.

Knowing the devout reasons behind the desire to reach Mecca, Mr. Minor got in touch with the MATS authorities at Dhahran and quickly received permission from Washington to handle the last lap of the airlift themselves.

Advance figures of the size of the lift were originally estimated at fifteen hundred passengers, but when Brigadier General Wentworth Goss arrived in Beirut to set the action in motion he found the number heavily increased. After sizing up the situation and the importance of going through with the job successfully, he called in seven C-54's from Wheelus Air Base, Tripoli, and five from Rhein-Main, Germany. At the end of the operation fourteen craft were in the air, making twenty flights every twenty-four hours. There was a complement of 129 airmen and eighty MATS officers. Commercial airline personnel on hand in Beirut supervised loading the planes and organized some kind of physical order.

The name "Hadji Baba," given the lift by publicity men, was unpopular with the crews actually flying the planes, who thought it too much on the sanctimonious side, and they called it "Mission Flying Carpet" or "Operation Magic Carpet." * The first C-54 transport took off on August 24 with more than fifty passengers, and similar loads were airborne toward Jidda steadily for five days until every pilgrim had reached his goal. Each trip was a rainbow of brilliant costumes, a cacophony of the dialects from many different nations, but predominantly Turkish. In all, 3,763 (out of the 250 million Moslems in the world) made the five-hour journey.

As the last flight of the airlift went off, tragedy seemed inevitable when engine trouble made it clear to the passengers that the ship was going to put back for Beirut. Lamentations rocked them and a sense of urgency rocked the crew. At Beirut another plane was hastily found to replace the defective one and again the pilgrims swirled off. The clouds parted, the Red Sea skimmed below, Jidda loomed and was achieved.

One of the passengers, who until that time had been expressing his hatred for non-Moslems loudly and unceasingly, prostrated himself to kiss the pilot's boots.

---

* The title "Hadji" is given a Moslem who has been to Mecca.

Aside from this day's delay there was no accident of any sort.

The venture was not accomplished quite as smoothly for the crews, who were snatched from routine work and ordered to scurry away before provisions were made for their overnight accommodations in Beirut. They found themselves in strange hotels with no money and adrift from the military procedures that cover irregular demands within Air Force jurisdiction.

However, vaulting daringly over red tape, somebody managed to get checks to the men within three days and the crew's shaky economic standing was stabilized.

Prime Minister Salam of Lebanon saw the service as a sincerely friendly gesture. The amount of the fares paid by the pilgrims for passage from Beirut to Jidda, about $228,000, was pressed on General Goss to repay the cost of the airlift and for a time there was some confusion as to what could be done about it. The final settlement was that MATS accepted the money and turned it back to Lebanon to erect a very badly needed transport center in Beirut. The fund was spent wisely in cooperation with municipal associates under a Moslem committee, on a 13,500- square-meter terminal for buses and taxies, with restaurants and shops providing an income to be turned over to charitable purposes.

In the present tumult of feelings in that part of the world the Moslem pilgrims may remember the real emotions of that experience. But with a thousand years of prejudice against Christian motives behind them, they also may not.

As in every airfield where MATS functions, the technical services—maintenance, communications, weather—carry on their work more or less behind the scenes. But here at Dhahran, with its relative isolation, the 59th Air Rescue outfit (under the over-all control of the 7th Air Rescue Wing, headquartered in North Africa) must range far afield. Because of the distances between Dhahran and its nearest sister organizations—Clark Field in the Philippines and the Libyan base on the far side of Egypt—this ARS protects an area five times the size of the United States. It trains over and carries out active missions in the vast surrounding deserts, in the rugged, scarred old mountains and on the sun-blasted waters of the Red Sea and the Persian Gulf.

The principal part of training cannot be left wholly to active missions. It goes on, day by day, in practice flights aimed at preparation for emergencies and polishing techniques. Those teams who are not on alert put in forty hours a month of intense workout and all take turns in manning the alerts. To sharpen the eyes of scanners one training trick is for a crew to drop a yellow barrel into the almost equally blinding yellow of the desert, or the sun-slivered sea, for another crew to find. Paramedics make frequent practice jumps in unlikely terrain to keep up their well-known fitness.

When a real call comes in, all facets of the proposed rescue are studied promptly but very thoroughly, and the mission commander must make his decisions swiftly as to the number of planes, men and proper equipment.

One day in May of 1955 the 59th received a report from the No. 5 Navy Communications Unit at Dhahran that two cargo vessels of unknown registry had collided in the Persian Gulf and that one of the ships was in flames . . . other conditions still uncertain.

This was at eight o'clock in the morning. The report to the Navy was neither clear nor precise about whether or what kind of help was needed or wanted; surface ships in the vicinity of the collision were said to be responding. But in accordance with standing rules, as soon as the Navy's message was received by the 59th, the squadron commander ordered one SA-16 on the flight line and a second to stand by. The 59th's radio operator began to listen for more detailed news.

At first it was known only that the disaster had occurred about two hundred miles off the Bahrein Lightship—Bahrein being an island in the Persian Gulf a short distance off the coast of Saudi Arabia, where there were British oil installations and an RAF base. Flashes of piecemeal information were being picked up by various radio operators in the area, and a little later the ARAMCO station relayed the intelligence that one of the ships in the collision was a Dutch freighter called the *Tabian*.

Forty minutes after that a message came in saying that the Bahrein station identified the second ship as an Italian tanker called *Argea Prima;* that she was burning fiercely, that her men had abandoned her and had been picked up by the Dutch ship's lifeboats.

It was not until ten o'clock that the alert crews of the 59th got word that the *Tabian's* captain wanted one man, who had been seriously burned, evacuated by air to a hospital.

A surgeon at the Dhahran Station Hospital, Dr. Thomas F. Connolly, had been warned that he might be needed and, with an aeromedic, was ready with the crew when the call to start off came. During the waiting time the two SA-16 captains had been briefed on weather and sea conditions for that day.

By this time communications between all the radio stations on land and at Bahrein, as well as on the nearby British Flagship *Valcour*—which was uncertain as to what would be needed from her —were humming on various wave lengths, and when the two SA-16's shot off they navigated with the guidance of radio beams from those sources which directed them to the "target ship" in the Gulf. The surgeon and his assistant flew with the commander of the mission, Captain Jack C. Miller, who was to make a sea landing if he could manage one, while Captain James A. Parker, Sr., flew the second Albatross to act as air cover.

The *Tabian* was located, Captain Miller brought the SA-16 down on the water without trouble, and the well-drilled system of transferring the victim from ship to plane was carried through. Dr. Connolly and the aeromedic began treatment in the air. The patient was dangerously burned and in shock, but before he could possibly have reached a hospital by any other means he was given the benefit of antisepsis and curative drugs, without which he could not have lived. The 59th's official concern ended when the patient was safely turned over to the excellent ARAMCO Hospital.

All the rescue crews are realists; they head into any kind of trouble with no more or less flummery than each one would put into anything else he did. And, like all professionals, they have a savage contempt for foolhardy, unnecessarily dangerous and inept flying, especially if one flyer imperils the safety of others by taking chances. Bad luck or accidents are something else again.

In the fall of 1954 the 59th was asked by the anxious Iranian (Persian) Air Force to help search for the red-trimmed Beach Bonanza, single-engined plane flown by Prince Ali Reza Pahlevi, brother of the Shah of Iran, which had disappeared overnight among the lofty Elburz Mountains that border the Caspian Sea.

The prince enjoyed flying his own plane and was accustomed to pilot his friends around the country on trips for which he seldom filed formal flight plans, so that the airports scattered around upper Iran, accustomed to seeing him often, had not kept any particular track of his last flight.

Tehran, the capital, is on the far northern rim of Iran, just below the arc of the Elburz Mountains, whose two arms circle up around the Caspian Sea to meet Soviet territory on both upper boundaries. Between Tehran and the Caspian the wall of fourteen- to fifteen-thousand-foot mountains and their rough foothills creates extremely hazardous flying conditions. To avoid the rugged crests a south-bound plane must fly through one of the fairly high passes which nightfall makes dangerously hard to find—especially in late October when thunderstorms and snows are frequent and the days are short—and there are virtually no facilities for night flying.

Prince Ali Pahlevi had had no experience as an instrument pilot or in dealing with bad weather conditions.

It was known that, on October 27, he had taken off with some passengers from one of the fields on the edge of the Caspian intending to head for Tehran. He did not arrive there that evening and the Shah and the government became alarmed.

The next day the ARS Commander at Dhahran was asked to help look for the missing plane. It was four o'clock in the afternoon when the request came in and, because of the 650-mile flight to Tehran across the Persian Gulf and the whole of Iran, studded with mountains and formidable peaks shrouded then by stormy weather, the search operation which was immediately called into action could not be sent off until early the next morning. Two SA-16's were loaded that evening, the crews were briefed and were airborne at dawn, with Major Louis Griffing as mission commander. They arrived at Tehran at 9:00 A.M.

The Iranian Air Force had already sent out planes to search, but it had not as yet learned which mountain pass the prince had attempted to use. Immediately upon arriving at Tehran, Major Griffing met General R. A. McClure, who was Chief of the U.S. Military Assistance Advisory Group (MAAG), then in Iran; Colonel E. W.

Richardson, Chief of the Air Section of MAAG; the U.S. Air Attaché, Colonel Hempton; and Colonel Kadame of the Iranian Air Force, who was directing the Iranian Army efforts.

Thenceforth Colonel Kadame worked actively with Griffing and the other American officers. Headquarters and a MATS mobile radio unit were set up. In a search of this kind many incidental things must be taken care of, including plane refueling, maintenance, as well as attendance on radio systems, all of which have to be arranged to fit conditions existing in the place where the search makes its headquarters. In a case involving a royal prince there are extra considerations of protocol and strong public feeling.

There was almost no information as to where to begin the search. Storms and dark overcast made it impossible that afternoon to send the SA-16's over the cloud-hidden mountains where there were no suitable landing facilities. Instead, Colonel Kadame and a group of Iranian officers went off by road during the night to contact military and local authorities and interview anyone who might conceivably have seen or heard the plane's passing.

They brought back a few vague clues and soon random accounts began to come in slowly. Most of the reports described the sound of a plane engine heard over some village in the mountain dark; one villager had seen small red and green lights reflecting brilliantly on thick clouds high overhead; a man in Sari had heard the motor of a plane in the sky; another in Shahi, many miles away, had heard it; another near Gurgan . . .

It was gradually established that the prince had left an airfield at Gunbad-i-kawus, landed for a very short time at a farm fifteen miles to the north and had left the farm about four-thirty in the afternoon for the capital.

The Elburz region of rugged slopes (the birthplace of the caliph of the *Arabian Nights*) with its deep valleys and foothills has been populated since the beginning of historic time. But it is remote, in most places primitive and with almost no modern communications system, and was at this time covered by newly fallen snow. The planes scattered leaflets over the suspected area, offering a reward for information. Although there seemed to be little chance that the prince could have survived, hope could not be abandoned.

Iranian light planes carefully scanned the deep, glittering snow-banks in the lower gullies, and the SA-16's flew one carefully laid-out sortie after another, bringing the flight plan closer in as reports indicating the course the prince had taken began to assemble around one particular area. On any long sortie special care had to be taken by the pilots not to penetrate the Soviet border. Renewed storms interrupted flying, but Iranian Army ground parties went on.

Over the thickly forested foothills two small Iranian planes—an L-20 and a T-6—ranged more freely at low levels than the bigger ships dared venture, but the shadowed gorges and slopes covered with new snow kept their secrets. Arrangements were made to fly paratroops in for a drop, but the terrain in the more likely places seemed to make any such attempt of doubtful value and the scheme was abandoned by common consent.

On the night of November 1-2 a farmer near the little village of Yush went out hunting and, scrambling through the snowy brush, found the lost plane badly shattered on a forested mountainside.

Colonel Kadame received the news that morning and informed the Americans of the discovery. Although the MATS officers offered to help bring out the bodies of the prince and the three passengers who had been with him, the Iranian officers preferred to rely on their own Army forces to complete the last services. So, after a hundred hours of extraordinarily difficult flying, the 59th crews returned to their home base.

Another instance of MATS' help to its Near East hosts took place in the early spring of 1954. The Tigris River in Iraq overflowed its banks above and below Baghdad, flooding hordes of people out of their homes. There were heavy rains and thunderstorms and the floods began to spread to the great reaches of Biblical lands. The Tigris is one of the two large Mesopotamian rivers which have made this incredibly old seat of civilization fertile and habitable long after desert engulfed much of the surrounding country, but its spring floods have more than once wiped out the work of those who lived beside it.

Baghdad is about six hundred miles northwest of Dhahran.

On April first, the Honorable Burton Perry, American Ambassador to Iraq, called the 2nd Division Commander at Dhahran,

Brigadier General Grover, and asked for the use of two helicopters to give help to the hundreds of people who were isolated among the flood waters—to make air surveys of the distressed terrain and drop food, tents and means of rescue. The Iraqi Air Force owned no 'copters and were unable to make landings at the worst spots in the planes they had.

There are certain difficulties in using helicopters for any purpose entailing very long flights, as the whirly-birds have a small fuel-carrying capacity. So when the two H-19's started off from the 59th ARS base for Baghdad before dawn on the morning of the second, they were in the care of three big planes which were to carry extra gas and maintenance crews. The H-19's started very early in order to make the first part of the flight across familiar territory in the darkness of early morning, approaching the bad weather conditions in Iraq in daylight. Two SA-16's and a C-47 followed, intending to make a rendezvous with the 'copters at two pre-arranged points along the way for refueling, which they did. Major Shockley, squadron commander, was the appointed commander of the rescue plane group and flew as copilot in one of the SA-16 Albatrosses.

General Grover took off from Dhahran before the SA-16's in order to get to Baghdad and supervise the over-all operations of his own men from there. But when his plane reached the region of the Iraqi capital he found conditions too stormy to land. He then flew back to Dhahran and told the H-19's by radio to go to Basra, out of the flooded zone, and wait there till morning.

On the third, General Grover got into the Baghdad airfield and met Iraqi and American officials in conference; Colonel Bull, U.S. Air Attaché to Iraq, was given over-all authority to coordinate MATS' work with the Iraqi Army's and plans for beginning food drops began at once. On the fourth, the H-19's went out with forty- to fifty-pound food packages and in eleven sorties that day delivered 8450 pounds.

On the fourth, Brigadier General Aboul Razak Hammoudi of the Iraqi Army took over responsibility for the Iraqi part of the operation and from that point on, worked tirelessly and forcefully in an effort not only to coordinate the work of both parties in the rescue mission, but also to spur his own town magistrates and other local officials along the Tigris flood areas into getting surface salvage methods into gear.

The storms continued and the waters spread sixty and more miles beyond Baghdad. The possibility of epidemics became a threat and, even for those who had received food drops, as the days went by there still remained the need for more supplies and rescue from the danger of drowning. The 'copters kept busy, reaching people sequestered in small isolated high spots; because of their short range they had to keep hopping back for fresh fuel supplies even though they carried extra gas in five-gallon tins.

After several days of this the tired MATS crews came down with a bout of diarrhea, but in unfailing high spirits they hung up a sign reading, "YOU CALL, WE HAUL, YOU ALL," and went off with another lot of fifty-pound drop packages.

General Hammoudi had by now shaken up the work of minor Iraqi officials in the riverside villages and was using his own army manpower to great advantage. When a cloudburst threatened to take out the dikes around northern Baghdad, he kept the soldiers piling up sandbags against them all night. For a day the 'copters were grounded, but the planes—both the SA-16's and Iraqi craft—continued watching and reporting conditions from the air and making occasional drops. The work continued through the twelfth. Two doctors and two nurses were carried to the danger zone at Al Kut and landed. One of the H-19's responded to a plea to come to the rescue of a woman on an island who was said to be dying, but when it twirled down she turned out to be more afraid of the strange machines than she was of death. The crown prince was flown to Amir Rabia Palace for a conference and the 'copter's performance so delighted him that he inquired with enthusiasm into every detail of its makeup. All in all, the mission accomplished more, if anything, than it had set out to do.

General Hammoudi understood that the ARS ships were needed for other missions and the work was wound up between the thirteenth and fifteenth, ending in banquets and feelings of warm mutual friendliness. A great deal of the historic old earth was under water but some of the country's antiquities were shown to the crews

on a special tour, beginning at the Baghdad Museum. The pilots
then discovered that they had been flying over both the site of the
Garden of Eden, which the Iraqi believed was near a town called
N'amaniya, and the ancient city of Babylon. And the fliers also
found that they had been using one of Iraq's oldest and choicest
ruins, the Arch of Ctesiphon, as a check point on the return to
Baghdad from the "target" areas.

LIBYA

Between Dhahran and McGuire AFB, in New Jersey, there is
a string of MATS African and European installations, many of
which were organized principally to support NATO. Each of these
MATS outfits has some specialty, developed because of the characteristics of its location. Wheelus MATS in Libya performs as an
adjunct to an unusually big Air Force gunnery training program
carried on there because the country's open spaces offer more
extraordinary opportunities for such work than are to be found
around most other posts.

Libya is a largish country almost due south of Italy and Sicily,
made up to a great extent—465,362 square miles—of what is called
the Libya Sahara, a broad, nearly uninhabited desert plateau. Off
the coast, by virtue of the contours of the Mediterranean, there is
also an enormous expanse of comparatively open sea. This space is
created by the Gulf of Sidra, which dips shallowly into the central
third of the Libyan shoreline and converges on the southwestern

part of the Mediterranean
where the coastline of Tunisia, Libya's left-hand neighbor, takes an abrupt upward
turn toward Europe. Since
this almost right-angled
corner of the sea and the
gulf waters is somewhat off
the main shipping lanes, it
is possible for the military
to reserve a restricted section of it for sea training.

Egypt is Libya's right-hand neighbor; she shares Egypt's entire western desert border. But Libya's population is mainly Berber with only an Arab admixture and, besides this differentiation, her lack of resources has recently kept her apart from the Arab world that began, twenty-odd years ago, to revolve around the possession of oil. Set between Tunisia and Algeria and the rapidly changing Arab oil countries of Saudi Arabia and the Levant, Libya has been dominated in recent times by Italy—in 1911, Italy "freed" Libya from the Turks and, after 1933, under Mussolini's reconstruction, administered it according to his version of European principles.

Wheelus AB consists of Navy, Army and Air Force units, serviced by MATS and occasionally used by SAC. The big lively base is about five miles from Tripoli, the Libyan capital, in a belt of fertile green farmland and small towns and villages that fringe the sea. This rich belt contains something like seventy percent of the population; for two or three generations an Italian element has made up five percent of that population, but since the last war their number

LIBYA

has been rapidly diminishing. Here is where most of the Italian impact was felt. From 1911 on, the farmland was largely taken up by Italians who brought in improved European agricultural methods, although some part of the agriculture and pastoral economy was of a desert type, olives, citrus fruit and grains being cultivated in addition to dates; camels and goats were raised. The Italians built a railroad along the coast, laid out good roads through the populated regions and introduced electrification.

Today—and since Mussolini's time—Tripoli looks like a Europeanized capital built by twentieth-century Moorish architects of great imagination and talent. It is a vast, dense mass of glittering, sun-lashed white blocks and domes, from whose hidden depths delicate minarets point aspir-

ing fingers upward here and there. The eyes of the buildings
are small, regularly spaced dark rectangles and now and then
a beautifully set indigo disc; the fretted Moorish gallery is missing, but occasionally a traditional curved wall breaks the cubic
solidity. Against the blinding whiteness of the flat walls the sun
casts lovely shadowed designs through the palms and olives set
in courtyards and open spaces from which the clean, well-kept
streets diverge. In this, the king's palace is a prototype of severe
Occidentalized Moorish beauty. There are many first-class restaurants and business buildings. And within this strangely Latinized
conglomerate stands the immensely ancient walled inner town
which is out of bounds to U.S. military personnel. There seems
little evidence, except in the walled city, of nomadic Berber influ-
ence, for Tripoli creates an illusion of modernity; the Berber tradition takes hold immediately at its outskirts.

With a climate much like southern California, summers that
may bring temperature readings up to 118 degrees, and the habit
of gentle lethargy that hovers over so many of the desert tracts of
northern Africa, Libya has an atmosphere of genuine, indigenous,

emotional serenity that is less felt
at other points along the coast.
The roads are lined with eucalyp-
tus trees whose foliage sighs in
the sea winds, above high red-
dish compound walls topped
with cactus to keep out intruders.
Date palms and old black olive
trees, against the prevailing brilliant blue and golden rustiness,
give the landscape design and
depth of color contrast.

There are medieval water
wells everywhere outside the
towns, the high skeleton frame-
work against the sky supporting
the skin bucket that a meager
steer drops and raises by tread-

TRIPOLI

NEAR TRIPOLI
LIBYA

ing his monotonous way up and down a trough cut into the sand. A small boy urges the steer at a leisurely pace and the filled bucket empties into the sluiceway that eventually drains the hard-won water into a reservoir.

Since the Wheelus community consumes a tremendous amount of staple foods, it takes advantage of Libyan production to buy milk and eggs from local farmers. In order to keep production at a desirable level of sanitation, quality and quantity, the U.S. has helped provide the farmers with up-to-date dairy machinery and methods—which is more satisfying than importing everything.

Around the modern military machine thread the Berbers in long, full, white woolen robes—which are their form of protection against the blistering sun—the camel trains and desert life, much as it has flowed through this comparatively little-known nation for centuries. In the great days of Rome the country was Latinized for the first time and stately ruined Roman monuments and amphitheaters still stand wherever those marble-minded early conquerors settled. With the various incursions of foreigners and the flux of North African nomadic life through the centuries, the genealogical strain has become just faintly confused, but the Berber stamp is still handsomely dominant, with its tinge of medieval romance and other-worldliness pre-eminent in spite of spurting jets and clattering electronic guns.

The eleven-hour flight to Wheelus from Dhahran is made nonstop because there is no airstrip diplomatically usable in the breadth of Egypt.

The trip is mainly taken up in traversing the tremendous low sandy plateau that stretches from eastern Saudi Arabia to the Tunisian boundary of Libya. Not far from Dhahran a plane passes over rough desert rimmed on the southwest by twisted and tortured blackish mountains pocketed by sandy drift, then reaches the Sahara, incised by the straight blue line of the Suez Canal reaching southward into the Red Sea. More desert, the beautiful delta and the blue-green curling highway of the Nile. Between the Nile delta and Tripoli, on the undulating tawny dunes it is still possible to trace, from the air, the swirling tank tracks left by the battles that were fought over El Alamein, Tobruk and Bengasi.

Wheelus' MATS has a very heavy transport-flying schedule, because of its big training programs and the large numbers of personnel that are constantly in migration between the U.S. and various other African and European bases.

Although the Embassy runs end at Dhahran, the take-over by the Atlantic Division moving westward pivots at Wheelus to extend transport service northward to Germany, where it fans out over Europe. There are also occasional unscheduled MATS transport flights from Libya to Italy, Greece, Turkey and the new U.S. bases in Spain. It is to NATO's interest—and SAC's—that this traffic flow freely when and where needed at any given time.

In addition to the long-range flight schedules to and from the base, there is the Wheelus training program, which requires special airlift for trainees and weighty equipment. Because of the benign climate as well as the open spaces, Libya is a particularly favorable country for flying, and the Air Force, Army and Navy bring down to Wheelus from other stations a continuous succession of rotating groups for courses in air gunnery, missile launching and other specialized arts. Libya's inland desert which stabs far down into the interior alongside Egypt to meet the Sudan and French Equatorial Africa, is one of the least inhabited, most desolate large spaces

ROMAN RUINS AT SABRATA, LIBYA.

on earth, with its wind-driven red sands, an absence of water except for a few widely spaced oases and almost complete lack of cultivation. Here experimental arms, gadgets, and firing methods can be tested while the airmen and other ratings, brought down from the chillier North, sop up the sun.

With all this rush of business the base is habitually congested to the point of giving at the seams, and even off-base housing is hard to come by. Officers' and Service Clubs are always jammed. The food is good and an effort has been made to cheer up the men's off-duty hours and offset their sense of isolation by giving them familiar kinds of entertainment.

A little unexpectedly, perhaps, the orchestra at the Officers' Club is led by one of Rommel's Tank Corps soldiers. He is an attractive, blond, youngish German named Werner Schiller. He liked this part of North Africa when he was here with the tanks and when the war was over he simply came back and found a more agreeable outlet for his musical talent and conviviality than his earlier visit presented.

There are the usual weather, communications and rescue sections, but though Wheelus has its share of dramatic rescue missions, its most unique job is the training of paramedics.

The paramedic is a relatively new concept of medical attendant —a superior sort of doctor's third hand and ministering male angel to those who fall in war or disaster—coming straight down from heaven, trailing the bright wings and ribbons of a parachute behind him, the latest in first-aid equipment at his command and a head full of healing knowledge. Although doctors and surgeons also parachute into disaster scenes often enough, it is obviously impossible for any base to maintain enough doctors to attend to many victims at once, and the paramedic is the assistant who must be capable of making a rescue drop where there is no doctor. He must prepare a victim suffering from any sort of wound for evacuation to a hospital and use the time getting there by air to attend to the patient's needs by administering the best of interim medical remedies. Since his work may mean plunging into such places as the heavily forested, wild, rough mountains of Formosa or the freezing Arctic Seas without bashing up either himself or his equipment, and accepting the extreme dangers into which he is thrust, it takes a fairly unusual type of soldier to fill the job. It also takes stiff training to prepare him for it.

The student groups at Wheelus are put through their stunts over and over and over again, until their responses are so automatic that in case of real peril they are prepared to give the smooth and faultless performance that might mean survival for both themselves and the wounded. Sparked and guided by a few seasoned sergeants and surgeons, the Wheelus trainees are given a course that is conducted with the utmost realism both over the Mediterranean and in the desert.

The sun that beats down on the Libyan sands is fierce but the winds are often cold. The sand is red and as fine as that in an hourglass. Outcropping rocks are studded about like ossified tortoises. Foxes lurk behind the rocks and almost invisible shrubs. A training sortie follows this line:

Two men who are to pose as victims of disaster and an examining surgeon from the hospital take off from Wheelus in a helicopter, whir out into the wilderness and come to earth. The surgeon places the "victims" prone, where they have presumably fallen in agony. He pins notes on their chests explaining the affliction of each: "Broken hip, fractured ankle, suspected concussion"; the other, "Injuries to chest; internal bleeding, patient in shock." He then stands by. While this group waits, the cold wind blows the red sand over them with gruesome realism. They shiver but the tone of af-

Bob Tambrell

fliction and derring-do is slightly marred by a puppy brought along by one of the men, which is alternately driven to hasty retreats from the unreal arena and engaged in puzzled but enthusiastic lunges of participation.

Very soon an SA-16 appears overhead, spots its target and makes a trial run, dropping a small red chute to test the wind's direction and force. On the next circle round, at a little

MATS' Paramedics are trained to go to the aid of the stricken, anywhere or anytime.

less than a thousand feet, parachutes begin to spill down from the great open sky. There is a cerise-and-white striped one with a paramedic dangling from its lines and under another canopy swings a second medic. The men drift until the chutes are fully open and then begin to guide them by deft pulls on the shroud lines. They land easily, quickly collapse the chutes and race to their patients.

The SA-16 continues to circle overhead, dropping medical supplies by a white chute, and blankets by a white one with brilliant cerise streamers to ensure quick identification.

Shortly after the supplies come down a seasoned sergeant comes drifting down, to check on the two novices, disengaging himself from his parachute on landing as though he were getting off a bus. He is lean, learned in his own department and strongly tanned by the Libyan sun.

The students have already got to work. The victim "in shock" is quickly covered with blankets and given "plasma" and "antidotes." While the surgeon and sergeant watch critically with folded arms, the other man is bandaged and fitted with a splint preparatory to evacuation. In a matter of minutes first aid has been given, folding stretchers have been assembled and the victims are carefully eased into the helicopter for transfer to the hospital.

This, and equally exact replicas of what the paramedics will have to perform seriously later on in drops over the sea, are drilled into the students until they are prepared to perform without hesitation the incredible feats so many MATSmen before them have performed from Adak to Afghanistan.

Colonel Horace Adlai Stevenson, a relative of the leading advocate of the desirability of a Democratic administration in the U.S., commanded the 7th Air Rescue Group at Wheelus and supervised the rescue work of the 56th ARS at Sidi Slimane, the 57th at Lages in the Azores, the 58th at Wheelus and the 59th at Dhahran.

He entered the operational work of air rescue at Lages Field in August of 1947. Before that he had gone through a rigorous course, mastering the basic principles of the kind of flying on which rescue work is founded as well as the organizational methods used to govern that branch of the service. He entered the Air Corps in 1941 and was commissioned in '42. During his term at Lages from '48 to '51, his squadron maintained a zero accident record. He himself flies all types of craft used in the job, from helicopters, for which he expresses a notable fondness, to four-engined transports, and has won the Air Medal for experimental flying in thunderstorms.

During the nine years he has spent in air rescue he has personally taken part in many outstanding missions—among them, the successful interception of a disabled Pan American airliner lost over the seas around the Azores; the search for one of the great Globemasters when it was lost in the North Atlantic, in which he served as mission commander. His present job as Inspector General of the 17th Air Force keeps him in the same area where he supervised MATS rescue work but he is headed for a course at the Air War College at Maxwell AFB in Alabama.

The 7th operates rescue missions that cover, in addition to the area protected by the Dhahran contingent, a sizable expanse that extends across the whole land mass of Tunisia, Algeria and the Moroccos. In this western hump of northern Africa there are other NATO and SAC bases which do not have some of the standard MATS provisions.

The interception of an Air Force plane which found itself in trouble with several men aboard on July 29, 1955, was a typical any-day ARS rescue. A C-47 carrying fifteen regular military personnel, one American civilian and three Turkish Army officers from Athens to Libya developed engine trouble while still some distance out at sea and had to call the 58th ARS Squadron at Wheelus for assistance.

The Wheelus (Tripoli) Field, Base Operations Control advised its 58th's duty officer that the C-47's pilot believed he would have to ditch. At that time—six-thirty in the evening—another C-47, No. 5290, was already airborne on its way from Wheelus to an auxiliary airstrip at El Adem, and was asked by the Tripoli Approach Control to watch out for the distressed craft. No. 5290 promptly altered course, veering from its own flight plan toward the crippled plane's reported position. No. 5290's radioman had already heard the other C-47 reporting its position at the time the SOS was sent, giving its altitude then as one thousand feet, and saying that the pilot was trying to reach the auxiliary strip at Misurata, Libya, but was steadily losing height. At 7:18 No. 5290 spotted the craft flying low above the water, still many miles from land.

No. 5290 relayed this information to the SA-16 search plane, which had taken off at 6:53, helped to give bearings for interception and continued this service (on what is called an ARA-8 homing adapter) until the SA-16 reached the scene.

After contriving to level off at fifty feet above the sea, the pilot of the disabled C-47 had managed to cover a skittish 125 miles, but when his second engine backfired and began to lose oil pressure he was forced to make a sea-ditching. Eight minutes later the ARS SA-16 swung down on the water beside him. With a smooth sea, the crew and passengers in the C-47 were able to leave the sinking plane and paddle to the rescue craft in their own rubber rafts.

More than twenty minutes were then spent searching for two bags of highly classified mail the plane had been carrying, which were found floating and intact.

With the additional nineteen men on board, the SA-16 was overweight, out of balance and there were neither enough seats nor safety belts, so the commander taxied the big amphibian across the intervening twenty-five miles of sea to Misurata. He called by radio for all kinds of vehicles in the normally unlit harbor to show up with any kind of illumination that could be turned on, and with the help of their lights brought the big craft safely into the dark port, where the men were all rowed ashore. Next morning the SA-16 flew home. By such unheroic milk runs the ARS men spoil many a potential drama.

Surface shipping and air traffic in the Mediterranean area covered by the 58th ARS at Tripoli is heavy and varied, including U.S. military and Naval craft, RAF planes from Malta and Tunisia, civil airlines and every conceivable type of commercial and pleasure boat as well, from the red-sailed native felucca to giant cruise ships. The 58th, under its parent, the 7th's Group, does not do all the rescue work alone—the RAF has a station on Malta—but it goes out whenever nothing but its great seabirds, with their extraordinary ingenuity in landing and taking off even in heavy seas, are all that stand between shipwrecked men and death.

With the sea whipped up in angry turmoil, a British Dakota en route to Bengasi was forced to ditch at 1:40 on the afternoon of July 27, 1952. The first word was that the plane was in trouble because of engine failure; twenty minutes after the call came in an SA-16 was airborne and heading out on a search pattern. The second word was from a British European Airways Viking craft saying that it had spotted survivors being tossed about in two rafts, had lost sight of them, but was circling the general area until U.S. rescue ships got there. Homing on the Viking's radio to pinpoint its target, the Albatross reached the spot at four-thirty. A half hour before, another SA-16 had left Wheelus for the scene with two medical attendants aboard. Malta Rescue Control Center had also sent out two Lancasters for cover, and surface ships as well were steaming toward the rafts.

Captain Kendrick U. Reeves commanded the first Albatross to arrive. From the air he had noticed that the rubber boats, partly deflated, were surging in the high waves with people clinging to the sides and swimming nearby; there had been at least thirty people on the Dakota, too many for a couple of eight- or ten-man rafts. When Reeves learned that no other amphibious planes were due to come in, and a British liner, the S.S. *Asturias*, was still leagues away he asked for and received the crew's agreement to try for a sea-landing in spite of the unusually high and turbulent cross swells. It was agreed among them that once landed it would not be possible to take off again. Under these threatening conditions the sea-landing was carried out.

Setting the ship down was a rough and anxious business, but she squatted at last and the pilot taxied toward the crowded rubber lifeboats. Fifty feet from the first one he saw a man swimming toward them with a line attached to the rafts. Another rope was tossed down to him and the cockle shells pulled up within reach of the crewmen. The swimmer was the Dakota's copilot.

Despite the promptness of the action up to that time, several days of unmitigated trouble passed before the sadder, wiser, and far less regal SA-16 got home.

There proved to be thirty-two passengers from the Dakota, who, with its own crew, made a total of thirty-eight now in the Albatross,

which is cramped for space with a dozen aboard. Most of the survivors were suffering from shock, bruises and acute seasickness.
When it was found that there were too few blankets to cover all the
ill people, the crew contributed jackets and parts of their flying
clothes. Seasickness, because of the rocking of the plane which no
amount of jockeying could steady, increased among the victims and
spread to the rescue crew.

The survivors were at the point of exhaustion. About a third of
them were women—one pregnant—many were elderly, and two were
children. The exposure, the battering and the swallowed salt water
had made them, when they were hauled through the hatches into
the rescue plane, too stupefied to reply to questions or do more than
slump wherever they were put down.

The Dakota's raft accessory kits had been lost when both cap-
sized in the waves and the rafts had immediately begun to leak because of damage. The survival gear dropped to them from a Lan-
caster could not be opened in the surging seas. The two Dakota
pilots had spent most of the waiting period swimming from one
raft to the other, reinflating them as well as possible with the single
pump that had been preserved.

Shortly after five o'clock the SA-16's radioman got word that a
British Naval flotilla was on its way to the scene. A destroyer screen
was part of a fleet heading for Egypt because of growing political
trouble there. At seven o'clock Captain Reeves saw the ships approaching. When he shouted to his passengers that their troubles
were about to come to an end, only one man so much as lifted his
head.

But the approach of a destroyer's whaleboat brought more
trouble as well as relief. The howl of the gale and crashing waves
drowned out the warning cries of the amphibian's crew and in spite
of frantic efforts, the left wing, ailerons and hull were severely
damaged in the whaleboat's attempt to come close enough to take
off the Dakota's people. However, during a lull, they were all transferred to the destroyer in the rescue plane's rubber boat towed by
the ship's whaleboat, in four trips—the last in darkness, about nine
o'clock.

When the liner *Asturias* appeared a little later, the destroyer received radio orders to transfer the survivors again in order to go on about its business, and with the rescued in safe hands the 59th's mission was officially complete.

Two British frigates and the second SA-16 from Wheelus now came into the picture. The newly arrived second Albatross was warned not to try to come down to help its sister craft, as the sea was too rough for a landing, and Captain Reeves began an effort to taxi his damaged plane toward Bengasi, the nearest seaport. The frigates and his companion plane remained on duty for protection.

Henceforth the crippled SA-16 suffered as only a craft of almost incalculable endurance could without sinking. To taxi against the wall of water beaten against the propellers by the gale proved impossible and an effort at a tow by the frigate failed when the line parted after many tries. Every man of the plane's crew, including Reeves, was desperately seasick; one man vomited blood. Just before midnight the SA-16 commander asked permission of the frigate to bring his crew aboard, since they were obviously not going to be able that night either to drive the plane into port under its own power or make a towline hold. Their six-man raft had not been returned by the destroyer when it left and the plane's smaller four-man one was used to convey the crew to the frigate's whaleboat. The fliers received every kindness, medical attention and relief in the comfortable quarters of the British frigate, but shortly after they came aboard her the ship received orders to turn back to her original course. At five the next morning, however, a new message directed her to shepherd the damaged SA-16 and crew directly into Bengasi.

For the next two days the desperately seasick airmen fought the crashing waves and the plane's now serious unseaworthiness, aided first by one of the two frigates and when that was ordered to leave, by the second.

They had set off on the twenty-seventh of July; it was three days later, at nine-thirty at night, after a long, hazardous surface journey, still in tow, that the Albatross and her crew came safely into the care of the Bengasi port authorities.

There was no "without incident" comment on that report.

12

GERMANY

In ORDER TO AVOID DAMAGING TIME
lags and interruptions, MATS round-the-world system has been
given a built-in flexibility enabling it to bypass most kinds of un-
avoidable trouble.

Political fireworks may make it necessary to overfly such trouble
spots as Egypt but the line has the competency to do it. In time, a
change of political climate in Iceland might demand a rerouting
of all North Atlantic traffic, avoiding landings on what has been in
the past a crucial midocean halt; a reappraisal by MATS of alternate
operational routes will be planned, if that should happen, while
the U.S. State Department explores the delicate considerations that
are involved.

There are the normal shifts of emphasis that can be anticipated
in the line's system and there are the big unexpected things that
happen. Constant realignment and adjustments stem from Pentagon
policy and General Joseph Smith's administrative rulings.

Recently a strike of airport towermen in France completely disrupted all airline schedules in northwestern Europe—including Air
Force programs. Ordinarily MATS flies regular transport, with supplies and needed men, in and out of France, which is the heart of
NATO; but it would have been both unauthorized and diplomatically senseless to continue its schedules during a labor strike. In
such a case alternate plans call for briefing crews and fueling planes
to overpass the immobilized airfields and the matériel for the NATO
bases was trundled into France by truck from the nearest air-freight
terminal.

The freight base nearest to Paris is at Rhein-Main, Germany, which is a long, but not impractical haul. While the French control towers remained struck, the clutter of extra craft at Rhein-Main taxed the base's facilities, to say nothing of the dispatching personnel's patience and ingenuity, but within organized limits since arrangements are shaped for that kind of thing.

It is obvious that any air operation can be snarled up at one time or another; weather alone can sometimes do a pretty good job of defeating efficiency. But MATS European facilities have been set up to carry on NATO business under very nearly any known conditions and a few imagined ones, and the air base at Rhein-Main is a bulwark in that plan. Between the German habit of doing things promptly and well, and NATO actualities, this place hums.

The German U.S. bases are forthrightly military defense air fields equipped for instant and deadly action: the redoubtable first line. Fighters, bombers and pilotless Martin Matador missiles stand in eternal readiness to reply to attack. The maintenance chores on such bases require a large mélange of specialized service people.

More than eighteen thousand servicemen and their families pass through the Rhein-Main airport gates every month. The base is the liveliest MATS traffic center in Europe. To accommodate the

RHEIN-MAIN - GERMANY

horde of servicemen and officers, it contains a sprawling collection of mossy green buildings extending out around the military airstrip and adjoining the Frankfurt commercial air terminal. The Post Exchange resembles a department store in any small American town; and there are a moving-picture theater, a well-stocked library, excellent housing areas and the usual service clubs and et ceteras—all on a bigger than usual scale.

Because of rotation there is of course a good deal of turnover and twenty-four hours a day, men and families form a human jam in the airport where traffic officers scrutinize orders and passports, direct transients to money-exchange windows or lost sheep to their destinations. The ferment resulting from this congestion, despite the best efforts of men who are doing their darnedest to control it, shows up in messages thumbtacked to the terminal bulletin board, like these:

"Mrs. E——— R———— Sit tight . . . I'm here in the terminal. Joe."

Scribbled beneath it:

"So am I. Bess."

MATS temporary passengers are put up in nearby Frankfurt commercial hotels and there is a bus service for them between base and town. German civilians are employed in such jobs as driving the buses, some official cars and other non-sensitive work—handling baggage, clerking and, if women, serving at the many snack bars.

Inevitably many of the Germans around the camp see the expenditure of money and the evidence of American comforts as a temptation to look for some of those opportunities themselves. The big C-118 transports taking off for America every day look an awful lot like flying carpets. A German chauffeur of an official limousine, handed a pack of American cigarettes, says wistfully in his recently acquired English, "More than anything I want to go to the United

"DEPENDENT"
RHEIN-MAIN
GERMANY

States when there is opening in the quota lists." The good cigarettes, the big transports, the PX's—for better or worse—are more
than their ostensible actualities; they are symbols people are very
much aware of, in the world outside America.

Airmen living in Germany call it the Land of the Folding Nickel.
The U.S. Government issues its own money or scrip for military
use, as it does on many foreign bases. The paper currency looks a
good deal like coupons, but instead of stopping at one-dollar values,
it continues on down to represent fifty-, twenty-five-, ten- and *five*-
cent pieces. Ceaselessly exchanged in snack bars and PX's, they
grow frazzled early in life, and this dilapidation, together with the
counterfeiting business that goes on, means that new scrip has to be
issued periodically with a change in color and design.

As Dhahran is the turn-around point for the Embassy runs, so
Rhein-Main is one end of the elite Atlantic schedules. These flights
also carry high-level personnel and special missions and are therefore got up in dressier design—in fact, almost equal to the better
commercial airline standards, with hot meals, two expert flight attendants, more comfortable seats—known to the G.I. variously as
the "hot dog" or "blue plate" specials. They carry VIP's and those
lucky ducks whose government business in the European zone
makes their rapid transport from one place to another especially important. Since the ordered practice is not to send MATS planes out
with empty seats, the unfilled available space is allotted to men with
priority reasons for swift travel recognized by the military—an electronics expert on a special project, a boy given compassionate leave
at the request of the Red Cross to reach the bedside of a dying parent. When the final list is made up it may include weary "stand-by"
men who have been haunting the dispatching counter for days, able
at last to sigh gratefully and snatch up kit bags for the flight back
home.

The flight controller at Rhein-Main handles an almost unlimited
number of things at one time. Even though Air Force fighters and
bombers are homed on other airstrips, the Rhein-Main landing field
looks like the switchyard of a great railroad center. Taxiing freight
planes, just landed, are directed to the proper unloading zone; regular flights are eased to the dispersing or collecting gates; and the

"blue plates" or "hot dogs," coming in with military, State Department or impressive foreign personages, are led with proper deference to the express right of way, for these craft are the "Twentieth Centuries" of the air world. And because the space in front of the passenger terminal is chronically cramped, the ships are unloaded with a minimum of delay and promptly taxied away to the overhaul docks where maintenance work goes on around the clock.

At any moment, a "blue-plate special" may be standing spotted on the ramp, freshly cleaned and ready for its outgoing load. A "put-put"—a portable power unit—stands beside it, plugged into an outlet in the plane to provide light and heat or air conditioning, as well as to turn over the engines preparatory to the start, without drawing on the plane's own precious batteries. While this is happening, inside the terminal building loud-speakers announce the flight's departure, the line of passengers forms for a last inspection of orders certifying each individual's right to make the flight and the issuance of boarding cards. Rechecking his line-up list, Major Cowin, director of traffic, discovers that one of the passengers, a colonel, has not shown up, though his baggage is on hand. He telephones the Officers' Club and any likely place where the colonel may have been waylaid, but he is not found and as soon as the briefed crew has run through the take-off ritual the plane goes off without him, on scheduled time. His seat has been hastily released by the traffic deskman to the next name on the priority list.

Alternate routes from Europe to the U.S. depend on the turn of weather vagaries over the Atlantic, of which the grisliest are the circular sweeping storms that haunt certain northern sections. If the meteorological chart shows a "low" between England and Greenland with westbound winds on the northern arc—a prediction that means a tail wind pushing the plane comfortably forward over most of its course—flight plans for planes from Europe call for stops at Prestwick or Burtonwood with possible refueling at Iceland or Greenland en route. Once across the ocean, a refueling halt at Gander or Goose Bay, Labrador, may be necessary before the set-down at McGuire. The islands can sometimes be overflown and with really strong tail winds the entire course from Scotland to McGuire can often be made nonstop. The joker is that if the McGuire

terminal is shut in by fog or storms the passengers may end up almost anywhere on the eastern seaboard of the United States.

With the northern air lanes out because of threatening atmospheric conditions, the flights turn southward, taking in Orly, in
France, if the field there is open, the Azores or the Bermuda base
when necessary, and McGuire. Maintenance and accommodations
to make the passengers comfortable are kept up in all these stopover
points at all times.

Weather shifts often cause enough last-minute changes in schedule to double up pressure on the traffic boys. The energetic officer
in charge of getting off the "blue plates," is apt to suffer most when
late changes occur. "Just had to hustle a double supply of hot meals
aboard those planes. None available in Iceland," he explains, breath-
ing hard. Just previously, two "blue plates" have taken off simultaneously on the northern course, one of them having been suddenly
diverted to that run because of a reported gale threat over the
Azores.

There is no extra pay for overtime in military circles—a condition which is met in Rhein-Main with the expression, "So what?" or
"*Macht nichts*," in Bangkok with "*Mai phen arai*," in the Azores,
"*Não faz*," and elsewhere perhaps by an equally commendable
philosophical shrug—all meaning the same thing. In Rhein-Main
overtime work on the field is habit-forming. Eight hundred passengers a day pile into or out of eighteen incoming and outgoing
flights, keeping all the services on the field in unchanging high gear.
It makes for tension even among immunized airmen.

AIR PHOTOGRAPHIC AND CHARTING SERVICE

The picture at Rhein-Main presents one side of MATS' job in
Germany. At the U.S. air base in Wiesbaden, an hour's drive away,
a totally different MATS enterprise is busy with one of that military organization's more novel and fascinating essential jobs.

The crowd of specialists here is the 1363rd Photographic Flight
Unit, who, under Lieutenant Colonel Robert Elliott, carry on a be-
wilderingly varied lot of services for the Air Force in general. They
are installed in a building near one that is occupied by the Com-

mander in Chief of the Air Forces in Europe—commonly known as USAFE.

Thanks in large part to this ubiquitous unit,* wherever an official military camera shutter clicks—on a news event, the test of a new weapon, a delicate surgical operation or aerial mapping—a MATS cameraman is flicking the release lever. Although directed from the base headquarters at Orlando AFB in Florida, much of the 1363rd's work is governed by day-to-day Air Force events in other countries. Several teams of photography experts are on duty constantly, ready to answer all calls. In order to prevent border delays and red tape *snafus,* the men are provided with special passports kept scrupulously visaed and up to date. This unusual privilege was obtained only after long negotiation between the U.S. State Department and European governments, by Mrs. Ruth Shipley, formerly of the U.S. Passport Division at this end. The sensitivity of all the countries concerned toward the camera as a weapon was overcome everywhere this side of the Iron Curtain except in Switzerland. The photographic teams are, needless to say, heavily screened for security, and of unblemished character. In their steel lockers are stowed well-tended equipment suitable for any kind of photography and clothing running the gamut from tropical to arctic.

On one of their normal days, the standby team was called to run out and photograph an airplane crash in Dhahran, and an hour and five minutes later they carried the tools of their trade aboard a plane on the Wiesbaden flight line and the job proceeded.

A doleful sense of being left behind is felt by the technicians who wait at home to develop films made by these rovers who range out over Scandinavia, Iceland, England and the Mediterranean. But they dutifully process fifty thousand feet of film every month in the finely equipped laboratories. When it is cut and prepared for release it is distributed for study to the department which has asked for it.

Beyond such work the technicians who remain at headquarters have plenty of fascinating problems calling for imagination and ingenuity. One of them was this:

_____

* There is a Hollywood unit, the 1352nd Motion Picture Squadron; other units are at Yokota, Japan, and Elmendorf, Alaska, and Pepperell, Newfoundland.

Air armaments experts, who were unable themselves to find an explanation for the odd behavior of some machine-gun and air-cannon ammunition at the split second it struck the target, asked the 1363rd to find some way to take motion-picture films of the crucial moment of the projectile's contact with solid matter, in order to figure out what happened to it. The photo-technicians assembled some of their own materials and some bought from a German optical firm and produced a contraption they thought would work. They placed the camera close to the target, encased in a thick concrete container with a quartz window, having attached remote-controls to the camera mechanism. The concrete box took a terrible beating when the exploding shell ripped up everything around the target, but the camera inside had ground primly on, producing the exact filmed record the armaments experts wanted.

Intrigued by the possibilities of this concrete-walled contrivance, the boys then shot films of exploding napalm—a jellied gasoline that produces astronomic temperatures—from which the camera, after performing its duty, also came out unscathed.

Over the last few years the organization has developed a complete photographic aerial map of Europe, surveying some parts of the continent that had been inadequately photographed before, covering a total of 17½ million square miles. It includes Scandinavia, Great Britain, Germany, France and the Mediterranean area. The finished product—thousands upon thousands of overlapping prints—was shipped to the Aeronautical Chart Center at St. Louis, where every sort of information needed by pilots is incorporated in maps of extraordinary accuracy. The range of this bureau's service, which is now prepared to offer charts of most of the earth's surface except that pre-empted by Russia and some of her satellites, is shown by the five million maps a month which the Center sends out. And because the goal is to be absolutely and correctly up to date, each map bears a note: "Military users of this chart will mark hereon corrections and additions which come to their attention, and mail direct to USAF Aeronautical Chart Center, St. Louis 18, Missouri."

What with all the boundary changes brought about by our constant political readjustments, the emergence of "prohibited areas" of "air corridors" where there were none before, and the shifting and alteration of radio beacons and frequencies, the St. Louis office has its hands full keeping up its obligation to provide pilots all over the earth with the daily "Notams" * or chits that inform them of what's going on—data of vital importance to the safe approach to innumerable airports everywhere.

One time the Wiesbaden people produced a film called "No Sweat." It was a little horror on safety flying, depicting every imaginable mistake any crew could make in the air, and was warmly welcomed by every training officer on every base where it appeared. Motion pictures are filmed of parachute drops, of difficult river crossings by combat teams, of arctic survival exercises, of air evacuation of wounded procedures; cut and supplied with scripts, they are an integral part of training methods. When three of the most eminent of military surgeons performed a delicate brain operation lasting sixteen and a half hours, every tense moment was photographed in colored moving film.

Staff Sergeant Meyers of the 1363rd introduced a note of excitement into the regular routine when he became the first American to bail out of a Vampire jet plane safely, on an assignment to photograph a flight of Vampires from one of the planes, a stunt that took place in England. There was a crash, several of the RAF fliers were killed and Sergeant Meyer's craft was entangled in the melee.

This photographic branch of the Air Force is the most junior of MATS groups, transferred to MATS on April 16, 1952, The headquarters at Orlando is its hub, Wiesbaden is one of its most active working arms, and the branch in Hollywood keeps a sharp eye on the newest movie techniques.

GREAT BRITAIN

The flight of five to six hundred miles that, plus the divisional barrier of the English Channel, separates the buzzing American bases at Wiesbaden and Frankfurt from the equally important MATS facilities in the British Isles is usually made at the British end through a typical cover of billowing cumuli that screens the lush

---

* Notices to airmen.

greenness below. Prestwick, on the southwest border of Scotland, though it often suffers from spates of high wind, for some reason is ordinarily more open than the air bases that dot southern England. Because of its good weather it long ago became a British overseas airport and, with the last decades' evolution of air travel, has become an alternate touchdown point for European transatlantic air traffic.

MATS' two main British installations are at Prestwick and at Burtonwood, near Liverpool in England. Both bases have specialties: Burtonwood, its Globemaster traffic and an active weather squadron; Prestwick, reception of the great body of European and overseas transport and the jet-ferries from America.

Burtonwood and Prestwick are to a large extent the axis of NATO supply distribution.

Because of its situation as a transatlantic terminal, Prestwick is the dispersal field for the countless (to the lay mind) numbers of eternally shifting officers and rotating servicemen, and their train of small families, who make the NATO system work.

The 7551st Personnel Processing Squadron at Prestwick attends to all details of billeting; briefing the transients on their behavior and personal appearance during a stay in the British Isles, as well as arranging their transportation by bus, train or air to their next assignment.

The MATS installations at Prestwick, despite their importance, are small and compact, set on a sloping hillside overlooking the runways. On the opposite side of the field the commercial airline terminal waiting rooms and snug little airport hotel are always

DEPENDANTS EN ROUTE
BURTONWOOD, ENG

crowded. While some billeting of the permanent MATS staff is done on the post, most of the men with families live in the town of Prestwick proper and the neighboring villages of Ayr and Troon. This naturally makes for a closer affiliation with the Scottish people around the base, since the American children go to the local schools and their parents not only attend P.T.A. meetings with the Scottish parents, but find themselves far more deeply involved in community life than is usual for the military. Integration with local Scottish life is amiable, in fact, and the Americans benefit from the pleasant degree of hominess and the interesting background. They come to picnic on historic sites, to glow with borrowed pride in Robbie Burns' cottage within the town and in the tradition-laden Bridge of Brigadoon.

There are a couple of unbenevolent factors in Scottish country life in the winter; one is the cold damp, especially for U.S. southerners, and the other is the awesome price of gas. Almost the first act

SCOTLAND

of a new family is to rush out and buy electric heaters to step up
the degree of warmth considered adequate by the Scotch. And for
those who brought their own cars, the second act is to rue the day
they forgot how thirsty those U.S. Fords and Buicks are. "Petrol,"
at best, costs three times what it does in the States, and there are
no fuel stocks in the PX at this military base such as German installations provide.

A visiting congressman once fancied he was discovering damn-
ing evidence of high living here in the Air Force and exploded
caustically, "What kind of a base is this anyhow? I just saw an airman second class and his family drive up to the PX in a Rolls Royce
. . . with a chauffeur." It was true that he had; many of the taxis
in Prestwick are ancient Rollses, and the airman was doing his
week's shopping in one, because there was no other transportation.

The arresting feature of MATS life at Prestwick is the arrival
of one of the formations of jets from America which are called the
High Flights.

Although overseas flying is largely taken for granted everywhere nowadays, and at Prestwick must be one of the most familiar
of commonplaces, the High Flights hark back to an earlier, more
dashing, flying era. For it can never be commonplace for one man
alone in a plane to fly the ocean, even though he flies in formation
with others of his kind. When the planes are jets, following a course
of eight hundred miles over fog-banked arctic seas with a safety
margin of a half-hour's supply of gas to find their goal, they evoke
emotions that routine schedules have almost eliminated. Long before such a High Flight is due, Prestwick begins to prepare for it
and the entire atmosphere is charged with concern until the bat-
winged ships come peeling out of the stratosphere, streaking the

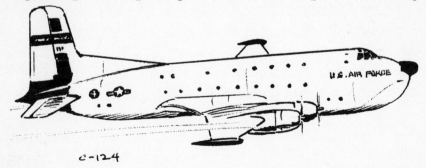

C-124

sky with the lacework of their triumphant comet tails.

The flights are a throw-back to the Air Transport Command's teething days, to the time in May, 1941, when President Roosevelt directed General Hap Arnold to "speed up the process of getting these planes to England."

That early ferry business dribbled off with the end of the war, but on April 4, 1949, when the North Atlantic Treaty Organization was signed by twelve nations, it was renewed in order to furnish jet fighters to our overseas forces as well as the European and Near Eastern countries allied with the U.S., and MATS was given responsibility for delivering them.

The Command's wartime experience in ferrying, coupled with possession of a string of completed bases, now permit a leap-frogging operation suited to the range limitations of jets.* And with MATS' usual careful routing and respect for weather, it has delivered thousands of combat aircraft to France, Italy, Greece, Turkey and Norway since the project first began. From Prestwick the planes are fanned out for delivery to MDAP (Military Defense Assistance Program), to America's Air Forces stationed on the Continent and England.

Leaving their headquarters at Kelly AFB in Texas, pilots of the 1708th Ferrying Wing detachment pick up at American factories the F-86 and F-100 Sabres, T-33 jet trainers, F-84's and some of the newest Century jet fighters. Leaving the U.S., they refuel and await safe weather predictions at Goose Bay, Labrador, at the Greenland bases and at Keflavík in Iceland. From Keflavík they set out on the last long overwater flight to Scotland.

On runways such as those at Prestwick, which are crowded with cargo carriers, civil airliners, MATS craft, and the multitudinous types of RAF operations, ground control is a serious business.

Contrary to the custom at most other MATS fields, the Prestwick airport tower is operated by civilians except when a High Flight from Iceland is due. Then, not only does an experienced MATS officer take up a position beside the civilian towerman, but all in-

---

* The range of jets varies according to the capacity of the fuel tanks each type carries, range being sacrificed to speed, which consumes fuel rapidly. Jet bombers are refueled in the air by tanker planes.

stallations on the base go on the alert and remain so until the last
of the incoming formation is safely on the ground.

The ferry jet flights come from Newfoundland oftenest in formations of about fifteen, flying in three units. At each quadrant of the
circle they are under the protection of long-range craft of one or
more air rescue squadrons, and the last fogbound lap to Prestwick
is covered under an umbrella of radio guidance. Taking off from
Keflavík at noon, they rise to thirty-five thousand feet at a speed of
something more than six hundred miles an hour. Long before this
the preparations for their safe crossing have begun. At dawn a
slower-moving but longer-range rescue ship has left to take up Station "Zulu" midway in case of a ditching in those cold remote seas,
and to give radio bearings to wanderers. Nearer Scotland another
aircraft hovers expectantly. At the tower the MATS officers listen to
the intercom chatter from the jets and presently the pitch of the
pilots' voices rises to a new exhilarated tone. They have sighted
the Hebrides. "Yeah, Leo, that's green grass down there. We're
going to make it . . . right on the nose."

The ground controller monitors their progress over northern
Scotland and presently they report from above Stornoway. Minutes
later the covey flashes past the tower and with a final triumphant
flourish the individual ships peel off and one by one are landed.

During the watch the towerman, one ear cocked to the High
Flights, has methodically brought
in and dispatched a BOAC and an
SAS airliner going overseas, and su-
pervised the landing of an RAF
Vampire jet.

The ferry pilots slide out of their
cockpits, their boots clumping comfortably on solid ground. They lose
no time getting to the fliers' ready
room, tossing their logbooks and
special code instructions into a receiving bin, and struggling out of
the thick constricting cocoon of
overwater gear—bulky survival

suits, Mae Wests and coveralls. They begin immediately to show a letdown from tension which is the inevitable aftermath of dependence on a lone engine and the half-hour margin of safety, and this letdown usually takes the form of genial baiting by the veterans of the "virgins" who have just come across for the first time.

The word "virgin" is inapt here, in the sense that it is usually associated with the word "youth"; most of the fliers' hairlines are receding and several of them are remarkably easy to spot as solid family men.

Captain Charles Bennette—a first High Flighter—has a family of five daughters at home; during the Second World War he brought down eleven enemy planes.

Lieutenant Leo Pagitt—a sixth-tripper—shrugs, "I'm probably the oldest first lieutenant in the whole Air Force." He was General Nathan Twining's crew chief very early in the Great War when Twining, before he became Chief of Staff, was doing his own flying. Pagitt flew the Hump with the ATC in the CBI days, and seventy-five missions in P-51's over Korea.

Captain Donald O'Connell also flew seventy-five missions in Korea, in the cockpit of an earlier edition of the same F-84 jet he has just piloted on his ninth High Flight.

Captain Carruthers has just made his fifth trip with the outfit.

There is an understanding that transfer to a less dangerous job may be sought after the tenth completed trip. 1st Lieutenant Bruce Broussard has just made his tenth but he says, "I'm keeping on. Faster jets with longer range are coming off the line already and pretty soon this ferrying will be a breeze."

On their arrival at Prestwick, a flight-control officer with a sheaf of orders before him tells each one where, next day, he is to deliver his plane for its final bourn—Norway, Italy, Turkey or one of the other NATO countries. The men groan and the officer adds soothingly, "Reports we get say it's going to sock in tomorrow." As he distributes the mail that has beaten them to the base he adds, "That's all. I imagine you fellows need a drink."

The Officers' Club where the fliers gather when they have transformed themselves into tidy officers again, is in Adamton

House, once a Scottish country seat. Set in wide, gracious grounds among ancient mossy trees a mile or so from the airport, it is a haven for the eight hundred transient officers who use it every month, a retreat from the gripping pressures of military life, from the cramp and flicker and chatter of cockpits, the sullen loneliness of arctic fog, the unnaturalness of coded speech. British television; darts; wide, glowing hearth fires; and, above all, ease are here, the salvation of many a nervous system wound too tight. The turreted rose-brick structure, with its spreading wings, old-world porte-cochere and wide mahogany staircases, was built by a Scottish coal baron as

ADAMTON HOUSE
OFFICER'S CLUB — PRESTWICK

a wedding gift to a daughter and could not have been better planned
to provide comfort to the throng of migrant officers in MATS'
eternally restless airline.

The High Flights are primarily eastward deliveries. But a certain number of planes which have reached obsolescence abroad are
also flown home by the ferry pilots to be used, after reconditioning,
for some kinds of training in the U.S. And in addition to protecting
these formations, the Air Rescue "duck butts" along the carefully
guarded arctic course watch over Canadian missions ferrying planes
to their own stations in Europe, in an operation called "Random,"
with the same radio navigational help and, when necessary, rescue
aid.

Because Prestwick is one of the main ports of air entry to the

British Isles and the scene of constant movement of aircraft—both military and civilian planes coming in from the 2500-mile Atlantic crossing or preparing for the jump-off—Air Rescue here assumes giant proportions. Its highly specialized job is, of course—as every MATS enterprise must be—support of the mass rotation of SAC bomber squadrons as they move between the continental United States and bases abroad, accompanied by the tremendous MATS airlift they require. Any such migration starts the air buzzing and immediately puts MATS Communication Service on extra alert. As the radios crackle with orders and progress reports, the Prestwick-based 67th Rescue Squadron curtails all social activities until the SAC mission has safely reached its goal.

Together with the 53rd ARS in Keflavík, and another at Manston Airbase on the Kentish coast of southeastern England—the 66th— the three squadrons of the 9th Group protect an area that covers Britain, the north Atlantic and the North Sea zones, including the western Norwegian shore. At that point, the 12th Air Rescue Group based in Germany steps in to provide coverage for the entire Euro-

PRESTWICK
SCOTLAND

pean scene. The bailiwick of the 6th Group consists of Canada, Greenland and large stretches of the arctic wastes.

The immense flocks of American airmen which these bases and the others scattered over Britain bring in to the countryside and cities are sometimes overwhelming to the British people as they find crowds of homesick Americans jostling into their favorite pubs and amusement places, buying up their favorite this and that, and walking out with their favorite girls. Foreign uniforms can never be welcome in a proud country with a history of such military accomplishment as England's. American military authorities are very sensitive about it and have made an intense effort through briefings and lectures to curb the turbulence that is built into young airmen. During the recent Suez crisis, when emotions were almost uncontrollably torn, the rein held by the higher authorities—together with the genuine sympathy of the soldiery themselves—seems to have been effective. There was not only no ruffling of feathers, but the British themselves seemed to feel the evident desire of the Americans stationed there to respect the painfulness of Britain's position by allowing no acts of their own to stir it up.

Parts of the British press have not always been reserved about ugly incidents involving American airmen that have occurred, but their petulance invariably evaporates after each air rescue that is publicized. "They are always rescuing somebody," one editor stated with mixed feelings, for it is hard to be grateful, even in fairness, to someone you resent—even mildly—having around.

The rescue missions carried out by the various American ARS groups at times have been conspicuous. The 66th from Manston alone completed sixty relief missions during 1954 which resulted in the saving of ninety-six lives and the British are nothing if not realistic about the importance of that sort of thing.

When floods ravaged the lower lands of Holland in 1953, cutting off towns and isolated farms, Lieutenant Richard Bragg of the 66th evacuated every man, woman and child from the hamlet of Nieuwe-Tonge by helicopter, transporting 110 of them to high ground, and then soared airily off across the English Channel for home.

Some of the rescue missions are more complex and doomed by

natural forces beyond the airman's complete control. There is a spot called Goodwin Sands in the North Dover Strait, a little way off the southeast English coast, which is called the Graveyard of Ships. It is a shallow shelf about ten miles long and there, during a roaring storm, the anchored lightship broke loose from its moorings. Mountainous seas driven by the gale rolled it on its side and the entire crew was either trapped below by crushed bulkheads or washed away.

Visibility was almost nil and squalls made flying dangerous but a helicopter from the 66th braved the winds and fog to circle the spume-drenched derelict looking for the crew, of which they could find no sign. That night, in the squadron briefing room, one of the officers, Captain Parkins, recalled that he had once visited a similar lightship and said that he believed he knew the layout well enough to identify places that might shelter survivors. He asked for permission to make a try next day and received it.

The wind was still howling over the shoals at daylight and the air was filled with spindrift when Parkins brought his H-19 slowly down to deck level and hovered precariously while he studied the wreck. Someone in the helicopter spotted an apparently lifeless figure huddled in the lee of one of the bulkheads but the noise of the rotors and the gale made it impossible to shout loudly enough to rouse him. A cable with a sling attached was dropped and dragged across his body and as it touched him he looked up. Later it was learned that he was temporarily blinded by the salt spray and thought there was a fog too thick for rescue, but he struggled into the sling and was hoisted aboard. He confirmed the suspicion that the crew was lost; those who had been trapped below had been under water too long to have survived. It turned out he was a scientist, Ronald Marton, visiting the ship to study marine life. The Royal National Lifeboat Institute of Britain rewarded Captain Parkins with a silver medal for gallantry—a most unusual recognition for an American. And the editor of the *London Evening Standard*, which had reported other rescues made by the U.S. airmen, mused gratefully in print of the ARS that "they are fundamentally incapable of minding their own business."

It cannot be overemphasized that the men of MATS, including

the ARS, are always minding their own business, and once in a long while their business is to give SAC a fortunately infrequent kind of support.

The record of successfully carried out SAC bomber flight movements is high. But on August 5, 1953, when a SAC formation was on its way from Goose Bay, Labrador, to Lakenheath, England, and still 660 miles from Prestwick, a fire broke out in one of the B-36's with twenty-three men aboard. The first report reached the 67th Rescue Control Center at Prestwick at three in the morning and by three-twelve every man on the burning craft had bailed out. The seas were high and the estimated position of the crash was a long way from land.

An immense sea search was put into motion swiftly, not only drawing heavily on the 67th's facilities but on rescue squadrons in Africa, Iceland and the Azores, as well as rescue teams of the British RAF. A total of twenty-nine planes took part in it and eleven surface vessels.

Even before word was received that the crew had bailed out, two B-29's with droppable boats took off from Prestwick for the disaster point with cigar-chewing Captain Wilfred Ridenour in command of one, and Captain Shirley Shaw of the other. Shaw's navigator, Lieutenant Duke, pinpointed the ditching site and the two craft reached it together. The oil slick was sighted some time before Ridenour's scanners detected the small rubber rafts of survivors bobbing around in the steep depths of the troughs. The first lifeboat was dropped at 11:56 in the forenoon and, circling above, the rescue crew watched the survivors paddle furiously to it and climb in. A minute later, the lifeboat's radio snapped, "Howd'ya start this damn boat engine?"

The second group of survivors was discovered an hour later and a lifeboat was dropped for them. Two British freighters now steamed up, moving slowly into the area, to take the crewmen aboard from the lifeboats and pick up two more airmen who were alive and two who had died. Air and surface search found no more survivors; of the crew of twenty-three, eleven were saved.

The weathermen at Burtonwood, who spend most of their time

in intimate contact with every feature of the atmosphere and the sea, thumbing their noses at those moody elements' eccentricities, have their chivalrous moments. Their range, which covers a weather track of over three thousand miles, carries them so far that they are constantly in touch with remote installations that are otherwise almost cut off from communication with mankind.

At the behest of the U.S. London Embassy, they often drop mail, messages and magazines onto the decks of British and American ships anchored on lonely ocean stations, or a Dutch ship keeping solitary vigil within the Arctic Circle. A 53rd weather plane from Burtonwood discovered an Icelandic trawler in distress just off its own course, and stood by, homing a rescue craft to the spot by radio signals.

One WB-29 of the weather group created its own excitement in pursuit of information about a brewing storm when, on the way home, its fuel was exhausted bucking blustery head winds. The eleven-man crew was forced to bail out—fortunately safely—into some benign English hills. The unit's accident record, however, is strangely low for craft which are so continuously in action and so continuously defy all ordinary civilian safety rules.

The 53rd Weather Squadron—commander, Lieutenant Colonel Richard O. Stowell—is the oldest reconnaissance squadron in active service; it has been in full operation now for twelve years. Ranging so far that on the westward swing their planes can give Newfoundland its own weather predictions for the ensuing eight hours, their findings are of such interest to the Royal Meteorological Society of Great Britain that the Society sends its own scientists to confer with Colonel Stowell and his officer experts.

There is very little about the sea and its surrounding phenomena that these men do not know and what they don't they are learning—including the contradiction of some hallowed old sayings. One pilot came in from a duty flight muttering, "No matter what they say, it happened." His plane had been hit by lightning in the air eight hours after another weather ship had been struck at exactly the same point. Neither had been damaged except for a hole where the bolt went in and out, but lightning *had* hit twice in the same spot.

Burtonwood MATS, whose tenancy is leased from the RAF Station it shares, has been the principal central headquarters for the transport planes' maintenance since the end of World War II. Planes worn down by the Berlin airlift were overhauled here. It also handles immense quantities of air freight and both regular and contract passenger traffic. Set a few miles from the rail connections of Liverpool, it feeds men and material out across all parts of Britain.

The station's cargo warehouse—a mile long and half a mile wide —is the largest in the world under one roof, which it needs to be to receive the shipments unloaded from the gaping interiors of the C-124 Globemasters that operate in and out on steady schedule.

Major Calvin Shapira was executive officer of the 1602 Support Squadron at Burtonwood, and though his work may have been routine, his thinking was not. He learned one day that a London hospital and medical authorities were searching desperately for a particular kind of oxygen-helium for a patient who was failing fast and that nothing of the kind was to be found. Wasting no time, he used the network of MATS Communications which covers Europe to discover that several bottles of the gas were being held at the Lages Field in the Azores. He arranged for a Globemaster to pick it up and the dying person was saved. This flexibility of movement in MATS, it should be remembered, this ability to use its facilities at any moment anywhere, unexpectedly, is a quality which only ceaseless experience and training in meeting emergencies effectively can give. Few other agencies of the government possess it. Today one man is saved; another day, other conditions, and it could be a city that needed desperately something that MATS could bring.

THE ATLANTIC ISLANDS

MATS' Atlantic island constituency is made up of bases whose geography gives them a sort of operational unity, although each is, like every other MATS installation, carefully planned as a distinctive link in the airways defense chain.

The stopover stations of Lages in the Azores, Kindley AFB in Bermuda, and Keflavík in Iceland are the only wholly MATS-administered fields on foreign soil; all of the other overseas MATS facilities are tenants on Air Force fields. Set up to be steppingstones

across the seas, the importance of the three island havens as refueling stations for transient SAC bombers with MATS back-up and
transocean passenger traffic is obvious. In a way they are the rest
points which even the longest-range aircraft crews need for practical purposes.

Lages (pronounced "Lodges") is on the Portuguese-owned island of Terceira. The second largest of nine semitropical islands in
the Azores group, Terceira has fifty thousand inhabitants and measures only twenty miles long by eleven wide. Besides MATS, Lages
Airfield is occupied by the Portuguese Air Force with an Air Rescue
Squadron which operates successfully and uniquely with the American ARS group.

LADGES
TOWER
AZORES

An air station on Santa Maria, another island of the Azores
archipelago, was used by the ATC in the latter half of the late World
War but in 1946 the base of operations was moved to the British
RAF field at Lages; since the RAF withdrew in September, 1951,
the field has been operated—under an agreement with the Portuguese government—solely by MATS. It is located at the northeast
tip of the island and the airport tower stands on a high rounded
bluff. On the bluff, MATS housing mingles gently with quaint native
cottages dominated by a weathered pink church—all of this over-

looking the long runway which begins at the shore line and is flanked by hangars and the Portuguese terminal buildings. Beyond the concrete airstrip a checkerboard of cultivated, walled, incredibly green fields stretches away to a low mountain ridge sparsely clad with old trees struggling to survive against besetting gales.

Azores weather is often tumultuous, though it is more a matter of high, ocean-borne cross-winds than of fog. The history of Terceira—where Columbus' and Vasco da Gama's ships took on water before sailing out into the great mysteries of the unmapped western waters—the native old-world culture, the vivid color of the tile-roofed houses and the serene harmony of the general atmosphere all tend to make the place warmly romantic. And the Washington authorities have augmented the harmony by appointing officials to the base who understand the native culture.

PORTUGUESE CHURCH
ON LAGES AIR FORCE BASE
AZORES

The main job here is, of course, refueling planes and feeding and sheltering overnight passengers. Maintenance of the big cargo and transport craft that alight from east and west is a lively enterprise. During the busiest times, when a backlog of craft has been stacked up by storms in Rhein-Main or McGuire and is released, two thousand passengers may pass through Lages in a single twenty-four hours. And since schedules bring most planes to the island, midway across the Atlantic, at night, the life of the place goes on uninterruptedly, and the terminal, restaurants and public rooms are never closed.

The Portuguese Air Force and MATS rescue services have identical equipment, aims and, it is said, skills, and they work well together on most of the rescues and intercepts. MATS' 57th ARS, under Lieutenant Colonel Gordon Stallings, and the Portuguese, under Operations Major José Rosa Rodriguez, protect approximately two and a half million square miles of sea and shore, from Dakar on the African coast, north to a line parallel with Great Britain, and west to mid-Atlantic. Both groups have traditional rescue aircraft, but MATS operates, in addition, a small fleet of surface crash boats

ANGRA
DO HEROÍSMO

based near the end of the runway, which respond to either tower control or directions sent down by rescue planes on missions where surface aid is called for.

The rescue planes are concerned with the safety of the ships that fly a veritable web of service schedules between America and European and African Air Force bases.

Among the craft flying long overwater trips in this web are the huge Globemasters with their vast investment not only in human lives but in equipment and cargoes. The threat of danger to one of these sounds an alert—even an indication of possible trouble ahead calls for a protective intercept.

One such Globemaster was on its way from Châteauroux, France, to Bermuda and, after leaving Lages, was eleven hundred miles from land when one of its four engines began to leak oil. With one engine out of commission, the aircraft commander, Captain Dwight Deming, asked for protective cover and five minutes after Lages heard the call—just before noon—a Portuguese AF SB-17 headed out for intercept. Meanwhile one of the Globemaster's other engines, now overloaded, had caught fire. Captain Deming had almost reached the equidistant point when the trouble started and he made the difficult decision to turn back. With two dead engines he could not maintain a safe altitude and he ordered the loadmaster to dump a heavy generator he was carrying as well as much of the rest of his 29,000-pound cargo. By the time this had been accomplished both the Portuguese and a MATS SB-17 had arrived alongside. With its hold emptied, the crippled plane gained height slowly and Deming managed to pull up to 11,500 feet. For three hours he flew toward Lages, marshaled on either side by the interceptors, the yellow lifeboats slung under their bellies gleaming reassuringly in the afternoon sun. As they neared land thick clouds forced the three pilots to fly on instruments.

Meanwhile four other Lages ARS craft had gone out for cover in case of a possible ditching—one, a Portuguese SB-17 flown by Major Rodriguez, who diverted his course from a weather flight he was making. At the home airfield, crash boats and fire equipment were lined up along the runway. With skill born of long experience, Captain Deming brought the damaged ship to a landing on two engines, and that was that. "Misery loves company," he told the SB-17 captains who had shepherded him home.

His loadmaster's reaction was more practical. "I certainly hated to hit the lever and watch that big generator go through the hatch. We could sure use it back on the farm," he groaned.

A dreadful, and unfortunately typical, sea disaster that brought out Lages help began when the boiler of the SS. *Darnell* blew up about 350 miles off the northeast tip of Spain one night. One of the crew was frightfully burned and several men badly hurt. The ship went out of control in heavily rolling seas and in the foggy midnight darkness the captain radioed a call for medical help for his men.

The SOS was picked up by the RAF at Prestwick and relayed to all stations within the area. A quick interrogation among the rescue bases revealed that Lages was closer to the probable position of the ship than those at Gibraltar, Prestwick or France, and even before any decision was made, the 57th ARS asked the Lages hospital to prepare watertight containers of medical supplies suitable for such a disaster; three identical packages, with directions for their use, were made up in the hope that at least one might land on the deck successfully. An alert crew commanded by Captain George H. Mason was given instructions for making drops under the extremely difficult sea conditions they would encounter.

An RAF plane had taken off as soon as the call came in but could not arrive on the scene for some hours. Meanwhile, seven hours later, the Lages craft found the *Darnell* and circled it at 150 feet, studying the best approach for the drop.

The ship was wallowing broadside to the swells, tremendous seas were washing over the decks, the sixty-knot wind created such frightful turbulence that the drop man could hardly stand, and visibility was intermittent.

For all the care taken by the crew of the SB-17, the first container missed the ship altogether, the second disappeared in a mountainous wave surging across it and when the third and final drop was attempted, it too was washed away. The crew was desolate but could do no more. They circled above the *Darnell* until the *Kilo*, an ocean-station vessel arrived, but unfortunately the ship had no doctor aboard. It was not until many hours later, after Captain

Mason had reached Lages again, that he learned the second bundle had been washed back to the deck on the wave that had snatched it, and had been retrieved by the *Darnell's* crew.

The mission, insofar as the 57th was concerned, had been successful. (Immediately after the SOS went out, all surface vessels in the vicinity were warned, and after the rescue plane had gone back to base, the *Kilo* was joined by the USNS *Pvt. William H. Thomas*. The Navy ship took over, put a doctor aboard the damaged *Darnell* and took off the injured.)

The readiness of Lages' and all MATS' rescue squadrons to respond immediately in full strength to any distress signal is a feature of the organization's combat readiness; every unit, in case of war, is prepared to pack up bodily and move *anywhere* with planes, staff and communications deployed for duty at a new base upon two hours' notice—a directive which is rigidly enforced as a prime MATS objective.

BERMUDA

Kindley Air Force Base in Bermuda, like Hickam in Honolulu, is considered by MATSmen as a duck-soup assignment, as well it might be with its heavenly climate and jeweled seas. Primarily it is a refueling stop on the middle Atlantic overwater island-hop and, aside from special weather reconnaissance and a vigilant rescue squadron, it is concerned with little beyond its obvious function as a safe haven, part way across the ocean between the mainland and the Azores.

Both MATS and commercial airlines use the field, the only one in Bermuda, occupying separate terminal buildings but the same runways. The field is on an artificial fill of sand dredged up from nearby Castle Harbor, the build-up extension having added one twentieth to the island's former land area. The rights to create the airport were obtained from Britain during the most perilous time of the second World War, in March 1941, under a ninety-nine-year rent-and-charge-free lease in a swap for destroyers. Named for Captain Field E. Kindley (who shot down twelve German planes in the first great war), it has been used as an American base, first by the U.S. Army and the ATC, and since 1948 by the Military Air Transport Service.

Up to a short time ago the installation was under the direction of Colonel George W. Peterson, a 1930 graduate of the U.S. Army Corps Flying School, a command pilot who has behind him thirteen hundred hours of flying time. Before the Kindley assignment he had seen service in Kwajalein and the Marshall Islands.

Under his regime at Kindley, MATS provided air escort for Queen Elizabeth and the Duke of Edinburgh when they passed through Bermuda by air; a B-29 was sent as protection for the couple's English airliner from mid-Atlantic to Montreal and down to the island of Jamaica. Colonel Peterson was also base host to President Roosevelt and Prime Minister Churchill when they met in Bermuda, at which time a discriminating goat, kept as a mascot by the resident Royal Welsh Fusiliers, lightened the tone of the solemn gathering by developing a passionate fondness for Mr. Churchill's cigars.

The 1604th Air Base Wing includes all the subdivisions that make the foreign bases self-sufficient and prepared to care for transient passengers and aircraft: Field Maintenance, Supply, a USAF hospital, AACS for communications, Air Police, besides Air Rescue and Weather Reconnaissance. The 29th ARS also has a crash-boat detachment that prides itself—although it looks suspiciously like a Navy unit—on being one hundred percent Air Force. Some embarrassment was experienced when an inspection tour by the base commander discovered a men's-room door on which was painted the legend, "HEAD," and the humiliating error was quickly corrected.

The 29th has a fine record of rescues of both civilians and military, running as high at times as thirty-seven missions in a six-months' period, in which the crash boats have played their useful part.

A search by Kindley B-29's that lasted for four days in December '55, located a small disabled fishing boat awash in heavy seas and murky weather. The Coast Guard cutter *Chambers* was called in, took off the two fishermen and, inshore, transferred them to a crash boat.

On Christmas Eve in 1955 a Bermuda weather plane exploded in midair when a propeller ran away. It was an unusual accident and nine of the sixteen-man crew managed to bail out, the others going into the water with the ship. The alert brought out ARS planes, the U.S. Coast Guard Cutter *Aurora,* and drew two other surface vessels to the scene; in all, the three surface vessels and twelve aircraft from Westover, Kindley and Miami joined in the difficult search and pickup. It was eleven o'clock Christmas morning before the nine survivors, scattered in heavy seas, could be rescued and the bodies of the other seven were found.

The 59th Weather Reconnaissance Squadron crews in Bermuda, working with the AF Hurricane liaison officer of the Hurricane Warning Center at Miami, Florida, are inevitably known as the "Hurricane Hunters." There is, meteorologists say, a difference between the behavior of the Caribbean-born storms of the southern Atlantic and the far Pacific typhoons, and it is the 59th crews' business to reveal to the afflicted eastern seaboard of the United States what the Caribbean brands' characteristics are—where the winds are coming from, where they are going, and all other data pertaining to their behavior of the moment. By this, these hardy weather lads have saved the coastal strip from much of the violent damage that followed the unexpected arrival of hurricanes before their work began. The methods followed by the Atlantic reconnaissance planes are the same as those of the Tokyo squadron—penetrating the storm's eye and reporting its progress and strength at regular intervals. On their plane's radar, these boys say, the storm looks like a blazing pinwheel, and when the eye is penetrated, all seems quiet, except for the sea below, which is whipped into a wild froth of utter confusion.

ICE LOCKED BAY AT THULE

THULE

The Greenland base at Thule is an Air Force defense project, to which MATS contributes heavy support. The number of MATS personnel stationed there permanently, however, is very small, and of a liaison type except for the special services such as ARS and Communications, which are under MATS jurisdiction.

The base itself is different from other stations where MATS operates in that it is not a spot *through* which their planes pass en route from one place to another along the line; it is the system's one and only dead end. Although this most northerly base is loosely circled by smaller arctic installations of one sort or another, the only course out of Thule for a MATS plane or man is back home again. Back home, for MATS, means McGuire AFB—or Dover, Delaware —for the northern outpost is sustained by material and staffs sent up from those two bases and the air traffic between them is Thule's umbilical cord.

Thule is also different in that the airport installations were not imposed on an ancient community; the structures now in existence *are* Thule. (Pronounced Thoola by Greenland Danes; Thool by some; *Too-lee* by instructed personnel. The arctic explorer Knud Rasmussen called that part of the world Thule, in the sense of the

literary *Ultima Thule,* meaning the uttermost ends of the earth.)
When the military post was begun, there was a small turf-hut
Eskimo village which had been founded by Knud Rasmussen in
1910, some distance off from the actual site, at the foot of flat-topped
Mount Dundas, but the Eskimos found that the sound of the jets
disturbed the game they hunted and moved up sixty-four miles
where they were resettled in houses on the edge of Smith Sound.
The original settlement was called Pitugfik, or "The Place Where
You Tie Up Your Dogs."

Thule is a purely military community built on permafrost set
against the western edge of the Greenland Icecap, about nine hundred miles from the North Pole and almost exactly equidistant, on
the great circle track, from Washington and Moscow. About three
thousand service people live there in flat-roofed buildings constructed to resist the cold and the terrible winds that whip the
gravel of the low hills with hurricane force. So violent are the winter
gales that the gravel bombardment and runaway fuel drums become hazards that keep everyone indoors who has no duty that requires going out. The few nurses who work in the excellent hospital
seldom wander from its protection.

Fuel and the heaviest cargo are brought up by ship only during

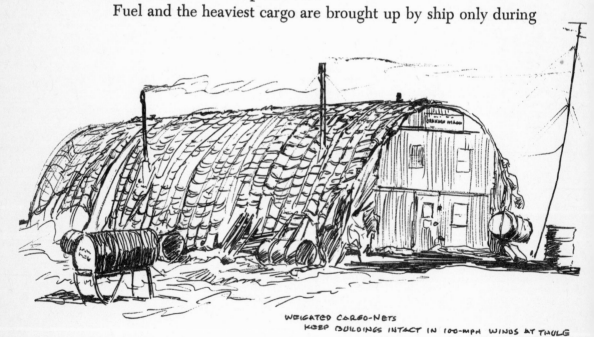

WEIGHTED CARGO-NETS
KEEP BUILDINGS INTACT IN 100-MPH WINDS AT THULE

AIRMAN
EN ROUTE
TO THULE.

the three open months of summer. For the rest of the year the place is frozen in solidly, its fine concrete runways and wide cold skies the only avenue to civilization. Because of the station's loneliness and the weather, which forbids the companionship of dependent wives and children of family men, a television station KOLD-TV has been set up and is on the air evenings and Sundays. An Armed Forces radio station also broadcasts news and music.

The fight for survival on the icecap, by plane crews unlucky enough to be trapped by disaster there, is taught by arctic experts brought in periodically. The scenery, although coldly beautiful, produces little of interest as, except for occasional seals and polar bears detected by crews on flights remote from the base, the only animals ever seen are foxes, brown in summer and white in winter, who scrounge around the food dumps, and a remarkably unattractive lone-wolf species of crow. Outside of a splatter of minute botanical specimens, only one plant—arctic cotton, a sort of outsize dandelion—appears in late spring. There are no trees. Though this is scarcely an assignment a New Mexican or Tennessean airman would select, given any choice, the men manage to make the tour a comparatively comfortable and sometimes agreeable experience; and while requests for extension of duty do not glut the Pentagon, they are not unknown. There is, for one thing, the comforting pile-up of savings during a year-long stay, which tends to modulate the ruggedness.

The United States, by agreement with the Danish government, received permission to build airfields in Greenland in 1941 when the Nazi threat was greatest. Airstrips were hacked out along the rough west coast at Narsarssuak (Bluie West 1) and Sondrestrom (Bluie West 8) to provide refueling stations on the bomber delivery route to Europe.

Work on the multimillion-dollar Thule base was not begun until March of 1951, and every year expansions are made during the summer months of twenty-four-hour daylight. Each spring about fifteen hundred workers are flown up on contract for the construction work that is done on buildings and runways, the contracting firms paying the government for their passage in MATS' own carriers or chartering air transportation on civilian nonscheduled lines.

The Thule Army and Air Force engineers paid little attention to ancient arctic building customs. All the new structures which replaced the tents used while the base was being constructed are of weatherproof insulated aluminum siding set on timbers laid on the permafrost, with doors like those of a butcher shop's refrigerating room. Heat is carried in from a central plant by fifteen-inch pipes laid aboveground, and fresh water brought from a lake five miles

away by truck is pumped into each building individually; waste is pumped out and carried off by other trucks. Because of the unbelievable dryness of the arctic air and the scarcity of water, fire is a constant hazard. Strangely enough, there is no great snow problem; in fact some of the New England states suffer from arctic difficulties far oftener than Thule does, simply because the extremely high winds sweep off from roads and runways the comparatively light, dry snow of this region as it falls. The icecap is believed to be ten thousand feet thick, eight hundred miles wide from east to west and twelve hundred from north to south. In view of this, it is a jolt to hear an officer storm into the lounge complaining like a suburban husband that the refrigerator is on the blink and there are no ice cubes for the drinks.

Thule is a strong installation in the U.S. defense program. The Air Force jet fighters stationed on the field are a permanent part of this defense system, and it is a vital long-range base for SAC flights which come up here for rotational cold-weather practice operations. Aerial tank craft accompany the SAC bombers, and many of MATS' flights between this place and McGuire or Dover are also for SAC support. Between 1951 and 1955 MATS made more than five thousand round-trip flights, a large number during early construction

N.C.O.s MESS
THULE, GREENLAND
MAY 7TH '5-

years; six hundred were made in 1956. Hangars for the jets are of
all-weather construction with doors that roll up effortlessly, so that
as they open, the jets, four of which are kept on instant alert, are
always ready to roll.

The 318th Squadron of the 64th Air Division of jet fighter-inter-
ceptors works closely with the 931st Aircraft Control and Warning
Squadron. And on the base, Thule's radar scanning equipment is
used to give early warning of the approach of any questionable
craft. These warning posts are manned by the 549th Antiaircraft
Artillery Battalion of the Army, whose job is ground defense. Radar
and radio beacons for the navigational aid of pilots are maintained
by MATS' Communications.

A singularity of flying over this part of the earth is that, with the
north magnetic pole exerting its pull considerably to the southwest
of Thule, ordinary methods of compass navigation do not work.
Instead, a system called Polar Grid Navigation is employed—a process which the curious reader may ask any polar flier he knows to
explain.

The helicopter plays its unique role up here almost as well, apparently, as anywhere, its delicacy of maneuvering serving both

vital and odd jobs. Some Thule Air Force men who were told
to paint the exterior of a huge radar dome built on top of a hill got
themselves dangled at the end of a rope let down by a hovering
"chopper" and did the job easily.

"Choppers," with the cooperation of other craft, came to the
rescue of a Norwegian vessel, the *Jopeter*. Carrying supplies to the
east coast of Greenland, the ship was caught by a shift of wind and
jammed in an ice pack. It was September and the weather was
frightful, with no visibility for days and sleety rain and bitter cold.
The *Jopeter* was wedged beyond the reach of surface help, though
a number of vessels diverted—one from the Shetland Islands—and
took great risks themselves trying to get to the endangered vessel
and her list of thirty-three crew members and passengers.

Under the control of the 55th ARS of Thule, rescue craft came
from that field, from Goose Bay and Iceland, a Navy Neptune
Patrol aircraft from Thule, some of them being refueled during the
thirteen-day mission by SAC tanker planes. Supplies and emergency clothing were dropped by parachute immediately but the
extraordinarily bad weather made the usual air-rescue methods un-
workable; the runways on the few rough auxiliary fields within
reach of the wreck were so glazed as to be dangerous to heavy
craft. Nevertheless C-124's carried dismantled helicopters from
Goose Bay and Thule to two barely usable runways on the coast,
at Nord, 325 miles above the ship's position, and at Mestervig, to
the south of it. At Mestervig the airmen managed to get one of the
H-19's in flying condition on the icy gravel and existed meanwhile
as well as they could with the sole protection of sleeping bags and
K-rations.

The *Jopeter's* captain reported his ship in danger of being
cracked up by the ice and no other ship could manage to work its
way through the loose outer floes to get near enough to take off the
marooned men. During the worst of the weather the captain managed to move a few miles but the ship then lost her screw and was
completely helpless. When the 'copter was put into flying condition
it took off twenty-six of the men and landed them aboard the motor-
ship *Totten* lying outside the ice pack, flying six sorties to do so. By
this time another surface ship, the *Kista Dan* from the Shetlands,

had worked her way in through the ice and, though the crews at Mestervig stood by for another three days unable to fly through the murk, the *Kista Dan* at length got within walking distance of the sinking *Jopeter*. Rescue groups brought out the rest of the stranded men on foot across the solid ice and, while one man was attacked by a polar bear, he managed to escape, and the only casualties among all who had taken part in the work were frozen hands and toes.

In the early, wartime days when the Greenland bases were just being laid out by such men as Bernt Balchen and Benjamin Giles, heroic rescues of air crews lost among the crevasse traps of the ice-cap were pushed ahead with tremendous hardships for all involved. This was before the days of Air Rescue Squadrons and much of the best of modern communications and aircraft equipment. Present-day rescues on the cap are not picnics but they are infinitely better geared for fast precision search and pickup.

Besides keeping all the northern bases—Goose Bay, BW-1, BW-8, and Thule—supplied daily with fresh provisions, mail and a thousand and one needed items, MATS services cover remote weather stations beyond Thule, the migrant High Flights and, using ski-equipped C-47's, support parties working on scientific projects and at distant radar sites scattered across the icecap.

13

McGUIRE AIR FORCE BASE, THE U.S. TER-
minal for most of MATS' transatlantic traffic, has not been left to
the last few pages of this record because it stands at the end of any
descending scale of importance: on the contrary, it is a colossal
establishment, where the line's activities reach staggering proportions. Standing between New York and Philadelphia at Wrights-
town, New Jersey, its location on broad flatlands makes it a highly
valuable terminal station for out- and inbound traffic of the Atlantic
Division. More than sixty scheduled flights a week go through Mc-
Guire to and from the north and middle Atlantic routes and Thule.
A sister station on the seaboard is the heavy cargo base at Dover,
Delaware, also of the Atlantic Division, through which pass great
quantities of priority matériel used by NATO and SAC in Europe
and the various island bases.

The ocean-spanning statistics piled up by these two terminals
are towering: over ten thousand transatlantic crossings were made
in 1956, airlifting roughly four hundred thousand passengers and
patients and eighty-eight thousand tons of cargo. McGuire's role is
dominant, the size of its operations imposing. Figures dealing with
the single operation of the Hungarian airlift—"Operation Safe
Haven"—suggest the scale of work done, since that mission was carried out without seriously altering the field's regular transport
schedules. Coming directly on the heels of another unexpected
heavy operation, the Hungarian airlift was a good example of
MATS' ability to meet emergency in stride.

In mid-November, 1956, 1,306 Indian and Colombian U.N.
troops with 110 tons of equipment were picked up from their home
stations and flown to the staging base at Naples, Italy, for transport
by Swiss airplanes to the trouble spots in the Middle East. Two

MATS Navy Super G Constellations drawn from Hawaii, six Globe-masters from Dover and twenty-four C-121's from Charleston AFB flew out to India or down to Colombia, and back to Naples with their charges.

The Hungarian airlift began operation on December eleventh, under Brigadier General George B. Dany as mission commander, using four-engined McGuire-based C-118's, Liftmasters and DC-6's of the commercial lines. In 110 flights MATS brought 6,409 refugees from Munich to McGuire, and contract carriers another 3,291, in 46 flights—a total of 9,700 up to January 3, 1957, though this was not the end.

These were both dramatic and meaningful episodes and should have knitted together any peoples who were susceptible to such mutual good will.

In the short halt in India, while the Americans were gathering up their tough Indian passengers—mostly war-trained troops from the rough northern border provinces, impressive in cockaded red berets—they were beautifully entertained by Indian officers and treated to visits to the Taj Mahal and the peculiar fascinations of snake charmers manipulating hooded cobras.

The appeal of the Hungarians—the many small bereft children, the tragic implications of possessions that could be contained in a handkerchief, the difficulty of communication between those who were giving and receiving help, when communication was so important, the insistent, overwhelming motif of homelessness hammered into the consciousness day and night—created drama in the transports and at McGuire that has seldom been transcended. It brought reporters and cameramen in droves and through this, too, MATS' schedules were planned and carried out with unflurried precision. A substantial part of all MATS overseas airlift, as noted previously, is made by both scheduled and nonscheduled commercial lines—contract carriers—and in an urgent project such as the rapid transfer of refugees, such contract help would always be sought and be invaluable. General Smith notes that throughout "Operation Safe Haven" "the day-to-day mission of transporting military personnel of the Army, Navy and Air Force, plus patients, mail, dependents and priority cargo still was accomplished."

From the first day the number of flights gathered momentum rapidly, reaching a daily total of five hundred refugees brought overseas in a day, topped on December twenty-fourth by a count of 984 men, women and children flown here in sixteen aircraft.

The top man of the Atlantic Division at McGuire is Major General Emery S. Wetzel, whose preoccupations deal not only with routine and any irregular demands, but with the unceasing intrusions of the future. Just now that means the prospect of substituting faster jet transport planes for those in use up to the present, plus the conversion of crews to their new flight techniques. (MATS is, in fact, everywhere in an interim stage between piston-driven, jet-prop and pure jet types.) There is, besides these problems, the grind of maintenance, which is a major concern of all big airlines. In the ordinary course of things, MATS trains twenty-seven thousand new maintenance men yearly to keep up with the ravages of rotation. One measure that has recently been taken to cut down on time lost in maintenance delay, based on commercial airline methods, has proved extremely successful. That is, instead of taking planes out of service for complete periodic overhaul by static calendar calculation, such depot overhaul is made according to the number of hours each individual craft has been flown. The new method means more planes in use at any given time because of the cut in time lost in maintenance stacking. Although routine maintenance will be carried on by MATS' own men, it is also planned to extend the practice, already in use in some bases, of having extensive overhaul done by civilian contractors, in most cases using government-owned hangars and facilities.

Some criticism has been aimed at MATS for its more costly practices, among them the custom of airlifting spare engines, which it has been said can just as well be shipped by slower surface methods. But MATS has found by experience that balancing the average of five days required to airlift an engine from Air Force warehouse to overseas "using unit," against the forty-five days' average eaten up by sea transport, showed that the airlift cut down the large inventory lying idle, either in a ship's hold or in stock, and therefore saved vast sums of capital investment in engines required. The same charge has been applied to moving personnel. The most expensive of the transport jobs, airlift has proved that air travel is the most practical in the end because it cuts down on the nonproductive time of men in transit. It is also in accordance with MATS' obligation to be prepared for quick, heavy transport traffic in the eventuality of a sudden outbreak of war.

McGuire's various services are occupied with duties evolving from the many thorny issues of today in Europe and Asia, and there are few weeks when some sort of world tension doesn't bring repercussions in its program. Its busy field is partly shared with an Air Force jet-defense outfit.

The air-freight terminal at Dover AFB is one of the line's youngest but it has burgeoned with the shipping abroad of defense matériel to keep up with the growing strength of the overseas bases it serves. It is a bustling out-of-scale sort of place, where the man-dwarfing C-124's are ranked in eye-filling lines near the storage warehouses, awaiting cargoes for bases almost anywhere on earth or for a follow-up to some new SAC foray. Also, very recently the two-thousandth High Flight jet took off for its ferry trip to Europe from Dover. Two C-124 flight simulators and a jet simulator are installed here and in use twenty-four hours a day—not just because they cost $560,000 each to buy; all qualified C-124 crews are required to take one turn a month in these monsters and a week's special refresher course once a year. The jet simulator is used to train Allied trainees from abroad as well as U.S. Air Force and Navy crews.

At Charleston AFB, in South Carolina, the 1608th Air Transport Wing has been newly equipped with Super G Constellations for trips that are made on schedule and for more specialized purposes than most regular routine flights, to Dhahran as the terminal to a cross-African route, to the Caribbean and Rio de Janeiro, Brazil.

A recently added venture for the Charleston crews is the run to the reopened base on little Ascension Island between South America and Africa. This arrangement was made to place indispensable electronic equipment and experts at the convenience of the officers who control the guided-missile range that arrows out five thousand miles from Patrick AFB in Florida into the middle South Atlantic. Charleston sends several planes monthly to this dour, unloved outpost.

MATS' actual transport business within the continental U.S. is very light compared to its transocean and intertheater activities. For one thing, to avoid competition with commercial airlines, the only scheduled *passenger* run made by MATS across the country is between Washington National Airport and Travis AFB in California biweekly, designed to provide a link between the Atlantic and Pacific Divisions.

There is, however, an extensive aeromedical airlift from each ocean terminal by litter-equipped Convair C-131's over a national network of routes linking four hundred hospitals, to speed patients to locations nearest their homes.

Quite apart from these two activities, there is an "on-order" fleet of planes set aside for Presidential use, as well as for other local and long-distance flights made by officials of the government—senators and the like—and on Defense Department demands. This organization, the 1254th Air Transport Group, based in Washington, where it is familiarly known as SAM—for Special Air Missions—had the admirable good fortune, by the end of 1956, to have flown for fifty-eight months without an accident.

Atlantic Coast installations besides McGuire are at Dover and Charleston.

The key base for MATS global operations is at its headquarters at Andrews AFB, a dozen miles below Washington, D.C. Andrews maintains close liaison with the SAC planners in Omaha, Nebraska, and particularly with the Pentagon, since all policy directives and all priority requests for MATS airlifting come to it from the heads of the Defense Department.

The parkway between Washington and Andrews hums with official cars. This MATS nerve center is a relentlessly shorn-looking establishment in which the graciousness of the newly built Officers' Club is almost intrusive. Unlike many other government sites the field has almost no pleasantly distinguishing aesthetic features; the prevailing impression is of a place briskly busy, and of hurrying officers and machines of one sort or another. Beyond the light gray headquarters office building—MATS' Little Pentagon—are the long, hot, flat airstrips. Marching here and there with an intent air are officers and airmen, often balding but with remarkably youthful physiques. Cars circle the roundabout roadways from checkpoint to checkpoint on business errands and planes stand waiting to go off, circle overhead or buzz away into the flat horizon. (If you ride in one of the airmen's cars you may well find a child's toy on the seat; no more the World War II devil-may-care flying man.)

The home of General Joseph Smith, Commander in Chief of MATS, is just inside the perimeter of the base in lovely wooded grounds that have preserved the slightly rolling character of old Maryland landscapes. All around this area red brick houses and new apartments are going up in an effort to keep pace with the growing military population.

In the ordinary course of things Andrews presents a scene where Things Are Going On. But in the event of one of the massive intercontinental SAC missions, a mounting stir begins; first in offices and communications rooms, with no visible external results. Security on all levels governs every word said and measure taken. Planning officers lay out an over-all scheme and piece by piece the responsibility for carrying out each separate factor of the plan is extended through the intricacy of all MATS departments. Communications is perhaps busiest; weather, complete landing preparations, both at home and on foreign soil, housekeeping management, supplies, spare parts and complete coverage of all necessities for planes and crews en route are arranged for meticulously and to the last detail. The plan involves clearing the air for the big jets' arrival at a given time at all touch-down points. Exact specifications for everything required are first laid out and then provided on a time scale. Despite the vastness of such an undertaking, the blueprints are adhered to with almost unbelievable fidelity.

Supplies and support personnel are dispatched on schedule by air transport to every point, both continental and abroad, and the SAC mission goes off. The responsibility in Andrews headquarters office does not end until the last SAC jet is at its foreign base, its crew debriefed. This accomplished, the MATS craft and crews who have taken part are dispersed to their regular locations and jobs. Another such plan brings SAC home. A single SAC flight will entail the use of countless men and planes and tons upon tons of freight. And the miracle of one of these phenomena is that the tremendous movement of men and material is run with such clockwork lack of fuss that the average citizen of this country is not aware that it is going on.

The matter of international policy with which these flights are concerned is set by directives from the Defense Department; talk and actions by MATS personnel inevitably reveal the single-minded attention that is paid throughout the organization to keeping military performance just that—military performance, controlled by its directives from Washington. This cool attention is focused on what is called D-day and on a steady unswerving improvement and constant adjustment of resources to keep flexibility and strength at the highest level.

In addition to the bases already noted, the airline has working units or operational tie-ins with several other U.S. bases and fields. There are the arctic bases at Goose Bay and on Greenland. And MATS weather reconnaissance planes are not always confined to exact stations; some of them work with such government organizations as the Severe Weather Warning Center, now headquartered in Kansas City—recently in studying the behavior of what they call the midwest's "tornado alley." Kelly AFB near San Antonio, Texas, is an Air Matériel Command base, and therefore of special interest to the line; MATS maintains Continental Division Headquarters there, with a transport wing, ferrying wing, and turbo-jet test squadron.

At Palm Beach AFB, crews are trained both on simulators and in actual flight, specifically for transport duty. Four thousand students successfully went through training in airline-type aircraft in '56. Orlando AFB, housing the Air Photographic and Charting Service headquarters, also provides basic training in survival, paradrop and the kindred contingencies the Air Rescue Service encounters in a variety of climates over sea and land. This training is given to the Army, Navy and Coast Guard, as well as to visiting students from friendly countries.

The system's aeromedical evacuation group headquarters is at Brooks AFB, Texas. A Continental Division transport group is at Brookley AFB, Alabama, and a MATS Naval Transport Squadron at Moffett Naval Air Station, California. A support squadron works hand-in-hand with the Air Force Command at Elmendorf AFB, Alaska. And MATS is a tenant on McChord AFB, in the state of Washington, the jump-off point for Alaska and the Aleutians, which is a more significant link in the defense system than its diffidence in making current news suggests.

There isn't an officer in the upper ranks of the military who doesn't realize what some of these services take out of young men and the strain they are often under. In order to lift morale where it is most apt to sag, MATS leaps at a chance to take performers who are not only willing but determined to give what they've got to entertain men stationed in lonely spots. Bob Hope has made a brilliant, unselfish career of traipsing to Greenland and Alaska or Iceland since he first won the world's heart during one of the bad war years, by congratulating a hospital-bound soldier on his good fortune in having powdered eggs instead of the kind civilians back home were forced to use—the old-fashioned kind that had to be broken from shells. His wry humor has made nonsense of monsoons and glaciers, 125-degree temperatures and twenty-four-hour-long nights.

An excellent production of *South Pacific*, composed of talented servicemen and -women, was sponsored by the Honolulu Community Theater and sent on an eleven-thousand-mile tour of the Pacific Islands from Midway to the Philippines; a MATS Navy R6D from California flew the performers around and a C-124 took scenery and lights.

These are only a few of the people who have gone to the outposts with touches of familiar life and the kind of fun that clicks with servicemen.

THE PRESIDENT'S PLANE

The most famous MATS Continental unit is probably the small group of expert airmen who fly the Presidential planes.

With the responsibility of piloting one of the most important persons in the world, it is quite understandable that this particular operation is surrounded by a tight wall of security. The crew itself, as well as any mechanic who works on the planes, those who prepare the food served on them, those who guard them as they pause on terra firma, are all checked and double-checked to insure against *any* sort of mishap.

Colonel William G. Draper, USAF, Presidential Air Force aide and chief pilot for Mr. Eisenhower, is a trim, brown-haired, youngish officer who is fully aware of the gravity of his responsibility. And he is surrounded by a loyal plane crew of fifteen other equally reliable Air Force men. Under Colonel Draper is Major William Thomas, pilot, and Major Vincent Puglisi, navigator. These officers are also on call for special authorized trips to fly other government officials. A group of master sergeants fill the posts of radio and radar operator, flight engineer and flight steward. And, to guard the President as well as the plane at all stops, eight guards are carried along on all long-distance and international flights.

The Lockheed Super Constellation the *Columbine,* known throughout the airways as "US-No. 1," is equipped with the latest flight instruments and air navigational aids. Cruising at better than 335 m.p.h., it can fly nonstop thirty-five hundred miles.

The President of the United States by tradition seldom moves outside its continental borders. But there is always the possibility that he may find it necessary—as he did when he flew to Geneva for the "summit meeting"—and the plane and crew are ready at all times to make such a flight.

Presidential flights are never made on the spur of the moment but are prepared for by detailed planning. The first hint of an impending Presidential international trip comes to Colonel Draper through the State Department. The colonel receives a brief outline of the President's plans—the time he wishes to arrive at his destination, the length of his stay—and forwards his own flight suggestions.

At a meeting at the White House a timetable is then discussed with Presidential advisers, the Secret Service, State Department men and the Press Secretary.

The colonel supplies a list of alternative airports along the route that may be used in case of emergency. This is given the Secret Service so that their own men on the spot can be alerted and ready to guard the President at any of the alternate airports, should a landing be made.

The two flight stewards are told the number of meals to be served aloft, as well as advised of other things that are needed for the comfort of the guests and the crew. The source of all food, either supplied by an Air Force station or ordered for the return journey, is checked.

Pressmen detailed to accompany the President use a commercial airline; their flight must be coordinated so that they arrive at the President's destination ahead of him in order to record his landing.

The Secret Service guards are responsible for the President's every moment wherever he appears.

Colonel Draper explains, "If our route is a strange one—an airport we haven't been in before—we do a 'dry run' a day or two before the Presidential flight, so that I can be perfectly familiar with the approaches, airways procedures and radio facilities. And," he adds, "I usually shoot a landing or two at the destination, as well as at the alternate airports."

When the official cavalcade rolls through the MATS terminal gate at the Washington Airport before the take-off of a trip, Draper meets the President and his party, escorts them aboard, moves quickly to his own entrance up forward and awaits the light signaling the closing of the rear door.

One of Draper's departure habits—contrary to general usage—is to start all four engines of the *Columbine* at once, which he can safely do because his flight engineer has made trial run-ups shortly before the President's arrival. Within seven minutes after the passengers are seated the plane is airborne.

A radio telephone and the latest radio teletypewriter are carried so that the President is never at any time out of touch with his office in Washington.

The forward third of the ship with seats for twelve—for either off-duty crew or guards—is separated by an all-electric kitchen from another compartment accommodating sixteen. For overnight travel these seats are convertible into comfortable berths.

Most of the rear third of the *Columbine*, in soft tones of green and gold, is fitted as a lounge with easy chairs and a pair of power-adjustable divans facing a broad table that can be used for Presidential conferences or a rubber of bridge. Directly behind the lounge is Mr. Eisenhower's private stateroom.

Unlike a distinguished contemporary, Sir Winston Churchill, who enjoyed taking over the controls on long flights, Mr. Eisenhower settles for an occasional visit to the pilots' compartment.

The *Columbine* and other Presidential craft are sometimes used to fly special guests of the government here and there, gaining for their crews a few out-of-the-way experiences. All were a little surprised when King Saud, on his way to Madrid, came aboard with a group of guards armed to the teeth with elaborate daggers and .45's, which the watchful Arabs were persuaded with great difficulty to put into suitcases as unnecessary. The trip was a pleasant one except for the fact that the flight took them through patches of rough weather. When the pilot went back to express his regrets, he was reassured by the nonchalant reply, "Oh, camel riders are used to turbulence."

The stable of Presidential planes also includes a smaller version of the *Columbine* which can land in less space when minor airports are to be visited, a light twin-engined Aero Commander for such short trips as the thirty-minute flight to Gettysburg, and two helicopters.

In all, MATS' airline covers 115,000 miles, its Atlantic, Pacific and Continental Divisions operating through thirty-eight countries. It employs more than 107,000 military and civilian personnel—the Air Force contributing 104,000 and the U.S. Navy, 3700.

Transports have averaged an ocean crossing every forty-eight minutes since 1948.

Every hour of every day throughout 1956 MATS flew about one hundred passengers and patients and twenty tons of cargo overseas for the Defense Department.

In the same year MATS' world-wide weather planes rolled up more than 69,000 hours—9,713,000 miles—in over 3800 missions.

The Pacific Division's overseas flights in 1956 topped ten thousand.

The all-time flight total (June, '48 to December, '56) is 108,271 transocean crossings.

While the company's bookkeeping shows the achievements of each of its three divisions separately, the story of MATS' real scope is told better by the yearly reports of the different service branches. For instance, Airways and Air Communications handled forty-two million point-to-point messages in 1956. Its Flight Control units monitored more than twelve million aircraft landings and take-offs. And its Ground Control Approach members are credited with 246 "saves"—that is, bringing aircraft in safely which, but for ground control, would have met disaster and loss of human life—the function that underwent its greatest single test in the Berlin airlift.

MATS' Air Rescue Services around the world flew nearly 27,000 hours of search and intercept, gave direct help to 28,000 people and by conservative estimate saved the lives of 790. It also made the best safety flying record in its history.

Accidents in 1956 over the entire line were reduced by eighteen percent to an all-time low of five per 100,000 hours of flying time. As recognition of safe-flying perfection, the 3rd Air Rescue Group of Nagoya, Japan, in spite of its hazardous duty, won a safety award for 9,126 accident-free flying hours for the first six months of '56. The 1611th Air Transport Wing of McGuire rivaled it with 61,741 accident-free hours over the same period.

No group has failed to make some radical improvement in method and equipment as a result of modern research and study.

Any appraisal of what the Military Air Transport is and does that is based entirely on statistics is grossly inadequate. While the figures make it possible to visualize the tenacious vigilance and extensive military knowledge and logic the governing officers have used to bring the system's complex operations to their present peak, it is less easy to comprehend the selfless, superb devotion given by the rank and file in most areas. The ritualistic grousing that is endemic in young servicemen is heard as often in MATS as in any other military group but seems to have very little to do with the personnel's real attitude toward what they are doing. Few peacetime enterprises have ever brought out so much concentration on seeing jobs through as has MATS, from top to bottom echelons.

The spectacular feats of the weathermen and rescue crews highlight the picture; the summit of accomplishments of other members of the line's less conspicuous branches, together with the steady excellence of performance throughout all ranks, deserve the public's commendation.

This is not a system run by wholly arbitrary military rules; every effort is made to allow for the normal development and interests of the young people involved, insofar as such interests do not conflict with service. In fact, to a large number of MATS' enlistees the term of service brings unexpected advantages. The embarrassment of slow re-enlistment reflects not the system's shortcomings but heavy external pressures, some of which are candidly material; no army today can pay what private industry can easily afford to offer the most competent technicians.

But it is a tenet of our national tradition that once a young man has given a prescribed number of years to the protection of his country he has done his share, and a remarkable thing about MATS is that while its personnel are devoting that period of their lives to military service, they do much more than their share.

To say that overseas service is educational is not as apt as it seems superficially. It ought to be, but no one absorbs from wide experience much more than he wants, or has the capacity to use. The ability to gain advantages from foreign contacts was a potential in the lad before he ever donned a uniform. On the other hand, one can see that this great dispersal of young Americans around the world has brought and will continue to achieve a general broadening of a generation's outloook.

Technical training of the younger generation, the saving of hundreds of civilian lives, improvement in communications and the advantages civilians get from weather reporting—all these benefits are willy-nilly by-products of a great military airline. The main thing is that what MATS sets out to do, with intelligence and devotion to a fine concept, it is doing usefully. How much all this is going to affect the course of history, history itself will have to tell.

INDEX

INTERNATIONAL ROUTES OF THE UNITED